BEYOND MULTINATIONALISM

Indo-Dutch Studies on Development Alternatives-2

Indo-Dutch Studies on Development Alternatives

The present study is the second volume in a series of studies sponsored under the *Indo-Dutch Programme on Alternatives in Development* (IDPAD). This programme grew out of intensifying contacts and cooperation in the seventies between Indian and Dutch social scientists willing to share each other's industrial experiences in development research. Led by a common concern about the need to critically assess existing structures and policies from the point of view of meeting the basic needs of large masses of people and to conceive alternatives that heighten the capabilities of the latter to serve as creative agents in the evolving world economy and society, a workplan of joint research was agreed on in 1980 forming the first phase of IDPAD (1981–83).

Since its inception, the programme is being jointly implemented by the Indian Council of Social Science Research (ICSSR), New Delhi, and the Institute of Social Science Research in Developing Countries (IMWOO), The Hague, and financed to a major extent by a grant from the Dutch government and a generous contribution from the Indian government. Following the second phase (1984–88), which is based on the same principles, a third phase has been prepared (1989–93) by the Joint Committee of IDPAD under the co-chairmanship of Professor S. Chakravarty, Delhi School of Economics, and Professor J. Breman, University of Amsterdam.

This series includes only those research results obtained under IDPAD which are considered essentially qualified for wider dissemination. However, the views expressed and facts stated therein are, of course, those of the authors.

1. H.H. de Haan, *Alternatives in Industrial Development: Sugar-cane Processing in India* (1988)

BEYOND MULTINATIONALISM

Management Policy and Bargaining Relationships in International Companies

Jairus Banaji   Rohini Hensman

INDO-DUTCH STUDIES ON DEVELOPMENT ALTERNATIVES-2

Sage Publications
New Delhi/Newbury Park/London

. . . for the people who labour,
so that the future may flower.'

Victor Jara

First published in 1990 by

Sage Publications India Pvt Ltd
M 32 Greater Kailash Market I
New Delhi 110048

Sage Publications Inc
2111 West Hillcrest Drive
Newbury Park, California 91320

Sage Publications Ltd
28 Banner Street
London EC1Y 8QE

Published by Tejeshwar Singh for Sage Publications India Pvt Ltd, phototypeset by Aurelec Data Processing Systems, Pondicherry, and printed at Chaman Offset Printers.

Library of Congress Cataloging-in-Publication Data   23.75

Banaji, Jairus, 1947–
    Beyond multinationalism: management policy and bargaining relationships in international companies / Jairus Banaji, Rohini Hensman.
        p.   cm.—(Indo-Dutch studies on development alternatives: 2)
    Includes bibliographical references.
    1. Collective bargaining—International business enterprises—India—Bombay. 2. International business enterprises—India—Bombay—Personnel management.   I. Hensman, Rohini, 1948–   II. Series.

HD6815.B6B36   1990   331.25—dc20   89–49711

ISBN 81–7036–182–6 (India)
        0–8039–9637–3 (U.S.)

62398

CONTENTS

9.1 Centralising Crucial Decisions
9.2 Possible Responses

LIST OF TABLES AND FIGURES

FIGURES

PREFACE

Already by the fifties Bombay was a city suffused with the glow of industry, a city that seemed to drive itself on the sheer sense of its modernity, the obscure consciousness of an industrial mission which, like Hegel's Idea, was the basis of its reality. A decade or two later and Lang's *Metropolis* could have been about Bombay! Certainly by the early fifties, Bombay could claim to have the biggest concentration of foreign investments anywhere in India— with Firestone, Glaxo, Metal Box, May & Baker, the foreign oil refineries and a host of other early investors. In some extraordinary way, even a child growing up in the euphoric expansion of those years could have sensed the power of a new kind of evolution, appropriated a landscape whose features, completely familiar, flaunted the operation of gigantic foreign businesses, become progressively aware of a city dominated by work routines determined, ultimately, in the head offices of the large private companies. Those offices formed an enclave tucked away at the far end of the city, to one side of the docks. They are still there, of course (at Ballard Estate), but over thirty years have passed and new enclaves have emerged, closer to the heart of the city, and in that period whole industrial areas have come into being which were only faintly adumbrated in the prognostic liberalism of the fifties. Much of this revolution is the work of a bureaucracy which consciously set out to 'industrialise' a country whose sole experience of manufacturing, or at least main form of manufacturing, till then had been the sweatshops of the textile industry. But much of it was the work of foreign companies, who became 'direct investors' when their trading connections were jeopardised by tariff barriers, and brought into India a set of attitudes and practices self-consciously distinct from the plantation mentality of British businesses.

Of course, no child or even adolescent could have fathomed precisely what revolution all this brought with it—even today it is difficult enough to document the process since what was involved, fundamentally, was the emergence of a new social group whose attitudes and ways of reasoning, in principle profoundly revolutionary, were still massively conditioned by and mixed up with cultural backgrounds of an altogether different type. This book is not about the deeper and more fascinating problem of the kind of working class which has emerged in India behind the factory gates of the new manufacturing sectors, but about something less subtle and perhaps more obvious—the conditions of employment which the foreign companies have engendered and how far these diverge from or are moulded by *local* patterns; the 'external' world of the new working class in India and how far that world is still shaped by purely parochial (management) traditions.

Since conditions can never be described in some purely 'objective' way, the descriptions contained in this book start from the experience of the unions and presuppose both *their* perceptions and their general order of priorities. Businesses are naturally interested, primarily, in costs and profitability, and for them cooperation with a workforce matters only in so far as it can be shown to contribute in some discernible way to reducing one or increasing the other. How workers experience their jobs, or how secure employees feel about those jobs, are of only incidental importance to the people who own and manage companies. Not so for unions, however, since they are the organic expression of the hopes, fears, ideas and aspirations of employees themselves.

The immediate origin of this book is work done in Bombay with the Union Research Group (URG) over a period of some eight years from the late seventies to the middle eighties. Much of this work—indeed the bulk of it—brought the group into contact with workers and unions in multinational companies. Its own perspectives were unique for India—against the 'political' common sense that international investment was simply a form of bondage to world capitalism, that international firms were simply out to exploit cheap labour and dominate national markets and should therefore be limited or even entirely removed, to us it seemed evident that only through the flow of capital into the more advanced types of manufacturing could workforces emerge with the potential for a new type of social relations and a new, more purely 'industrial' rationality. It was striking that the employees of multinational plants displayed none of the *swadeshi* sentimentalism about foreign exploiters, and yet their own styles of unionism and methods of struggle could show undiminished militancy. A paradox? Only if we accept the premises which have dominated international discussion of multinationals and labour. So without the URG and its perspectives this book could not have been conceived, let alone written.

Our greatest debt is to the individuals who contributed collectively to creating and defining its peculiar 'style': Arun Subramaniam and Ammu Abraham pulled us out of the wilderness, and made the unions central to our activity and understanding. Sujata Gothoskar co-drafted and executed a marvellously detailed study of the work pressures on women in the Bombay pharmaceutical industry. The results are used here with only the usual anonymous acknowledgement of the *Bulletin*. Ravi Shevade and Sujeet Bhatt innovated a method of comparing average classifications across establishments. Much of the chapter on grading draws directly on the results secured by this brilliant invention. Ram Puniyani made the group focus on the lethal safety conditions prevailing in most plants; Jagdish Parikh repeatedly drew attention to the companies' drive for flexibility and their ways of securing this both externally and internally. Raju Damle felt it was essential for unions to have a coherent strategy on new technology. These and the many other contributions are acknowledged here only in the most summary form—to indicate in the most general terms that the vision and the types of analysis presupposed in this book were pioneered by their individual and shared ideas.

In Holland, Job Dijkman and Hugo Levie of the Industriebond/ FNV were immensely helpful in launching a bewildered outsider on a perilous enquiry. Their colleague, Rob Tophoven, responded generously, giving up his time and sharing his invaluable experience to explain the intricacies of job evaluation and to set Dutch employers into a badly needed context. Paul Elshof allowed himself to be taped on repeated occasions and produced a fascinating picture of how Unilever employees were setting about tackling one of the world's largest multinationals. Those sunny Amsterdam mornings in the SOMO office will always be remembered! Steven van Slageren and Ria Hermanussen opened the superb Philips archive at SOBE's office in Eindhoven and, together with Andries de Wit, made crucial contributions to a truer understanding of what the company is and what it has meant for ordinary employees. SOBE is perhaps a unique example of how the research generated around a large company can be secured and organised in the most practical and systematic fashion. In return, we hope that this book reflects at least part of the picture they communicated.

Frans van Doormalen, Ruud Vreeman and Jelle Visser were responsible for some of our most stimulating interviews; G. Jansen of Corporate Personnel and Industrial Relations, Philips International bv and his colleague Dr. J.C. Ruter for a frank and immensely useful discussion of their company—to all of them we are of course profoundly grateful!

Pieter van Stuijvenberg made it possible to undertake the research in Holland, extending IDPAD's resources and providing constant encouragement when the task seemed too formidable. His role was altogether supportive and indispensable. Huub Coppens handled the headaches of a manuscript too unwieldy for publication, with admirable patience. Ruth Waterman and the indefatigable Peter made life bearable with their characteristic warmth, their infinitely stimulating company and the abundant helpings of muesli. To Nelleke den Braven one of us is grateful for the possibility of shifting to Amsterdam to start work. Truut van Kleef and Pierre and Sally Rousset were exceedingly generous with their hospitality, and Elsa and Wim gave incisive pictures of the companies they were familiar with.

In Britain, the Don Thomson Memorial Trust made it possible for one of us to extend the enquiry to companies in the UK, and Mel Doyle gave us unstinted access to the WEA's archives.

Among the many unions who cooperated actively with their time, experience, ideas and information—in Holland the most important were the committees at ICI, Shell and Unilever, all of whom consented to group interviews at short notice and came up with fascinating accounts. The exceptional activity of the unions at ICI Holland bv should really be an inspiration to trade unionists everywhere! In Bombay, our greatest debt is to the several unions we work with, for they have been an inestimable source of encouragement to us—in particular, to Bennet D'Costa, Franklyn D'Souza and B.P. Ghuge of the Hindustan Lever Employees' Union, who above all gave us some idea of what a militant union movement might look like, to V. Ramnathan for acute observations about his management's policies, to R.R. Mishra who has led the Philips Workers' Union through its most difficult period, to G.R. Khanolkar (Dyes and Chemicals Workers' Union), K.S. Bangera (Siemens Workers' Union), A.W. Noronha (Hoechst Employees'

Union), V.A. Nayampalli and Kamala Karkal (Pfizer Employees'
Union), S. Raghavan (All-India Voltas and Volkart Employees'
Federation) and M.S. Sawant (Larsen and Toubro). This enquiry
is dedicated to them and the unions they have led, and to militant
trade unions throughout the Third World.

July 1989   Jairus Banaji
                                               Rohini Hensman

1

MULTINATIONALISM AND THE DECLINE OF EMPLOYMENT

1.1 RETHINKING MULTINATIONALISM

Since the early seventies, international firms operating in India have had to contend with government controls on the level of foreign holdings in their Indian subsidiaries. The reactions of these firms to the operation of the Foreign Exchange Regulation Act (FERA), 1973, which first introduced these controls and which embodies them today, reflect interesting differences in corporate strategy within the group of foreign companies operating in India. Philips complied, diluting its equity to 40 per cent in 1979 and changing its name. Hindustan Lever held out against reduction of equity, pleading 'high technology' and finally reducing its export obligations under FERA by a major reorganisation of its business structure transferring a share of 'non-priority' activities to Lipton. For IBM and Coca Cola insistence on 100 per cent shareholding would mean the abandonment of business interests in India. However, most FERA companies were more flexible, accepting dilution in the interests of further expansion.[1]

More significant than these contrasts, however, has been the rapidly changing balance of power which the operation and impact of FERA allowed for, as Indian business groups began a huge invasion of foreign-controlled firms, buying up shares or whole companies and taking over their managements. Of course, management control over corporate activities is not something we can quantify; there is no precise mathematical limit beyond which it declines or increases substantially. If the parent company chooses to retain control, it could certainly do so with 40 per cent, indeed 'even with 20 per cent,' said one manager of a large foreign subsidiary. In other words, the ability of Indian business groups to buy up shares in firms like Ceat, which is now a Goenka company, or Firestone, which is run by the Modis, or MSD (Merck Sharpe & Dohme) which the Tatas have taken over (and renamed), has largely been a reflection of the unwillingness of parent concerns to continue with their operations in India. This happened in the seventies and it is continuing today.

These underlying shifts in the balance of foreign/local control are the first reason why we need to make a drastic revision in some of the assumptions which dominate thinking about foreign companies in countries like India. In particular, the assumption that foreign subsidiaries are all-powerful, that they dominate the most important areas of manufacturing or that they are constantly striving to establish production facilities does not hold in terms of the actual experience in India. There have always been tight restrictions on the operations of these firms, major areas of manufacturing and industry have been closed to any possible penetration by them and much of their involvement has in any case always been through joint ventures where actual control usually resides with their Indian counterparts.

The second assumption which has traditionally dominated the discussion of foreign investments is that by virtue of their supposedly all-powerful nature, foreign companies are in general able to enforce much tighter control on their workforces, foreign managements pose massive resistance to the organisation of the labour force by unions, and so on. But this assumption collapses for a number of reasons. In the first place, it is not at all obvious that management characteristics in foreign-controlled companies constitute a specific or peculiar 'style' of management, something clearly and obviously distinguishable from the way professional managers run Indian concerns. Even in the fifties and early sixties, when it was the usual practice for international firms to staff top management functions in local subsidiaries with foreign managers,[2] there were sharp differences in the way these managers reacted to attempts to unionise—strong resistance in plants like Herdillia or Wyman-Gordon, conscious encouragement against the resistance of local managers in firms like Atlas Copco, welfare schemes typifying Swiss neo-paternalism in Ciba-Geigy, acceptance of settlements and bilateralism as crucial company values in Hoechst (but with stable internal unions). Today, after almost two decades of the Indianisation of management personnel, the notion of a unified labour relations style peculiar to the sector of foreign companies is even more dubious. What finally rules out the credibility of any such idea is the extremely rapid turnover and replacement rates among personnel managers, the incredibly high mobility of this group, and the fact that a lot of managers in both types of firms come from the same management training institutes.

Secondly, where elements of a style peculiar to these firms are traceable in some way, they reflect if anything a much greater willingness to deal with unions and to engage in collective bargaining. Certainly the workers who work for international firms in their local subsidiaries have the strong feeling that they personally are much better off working for these companies than for Indian employers. Sometimes this evaluation even operates within the same company, in the sense that the union prefers to deal with a foreign manager, bypassing all those levels of the plant hierarchy which are staffed purely by Indian managers (Siemens, Boehringer-Knoll). This conflicts directly with the widespread assumption that foreign firms are not wanted in the country, that the workers are hostile to them, that they deal with the labour force in a tough, uniformly ruthless fashion, etc. Of course, there is considerable hostility and continuing xenophobia about the presence and operation of these firms; but much of this opposition comes from the middle classes who have no direct dealings with foreign companies or from those sections of Indian business which feel threatened by large or foreign competitors, or finally from groups of academics who feel that any nation's interests are damaged by foreign investments. These attitudes and ideas are certainly not found among the workers employed in foreign plants.

This book is about employee relations in two international companies which operate partly or wholly from the Netherlands and have had considerable manufacturing investments in India—Unilever and Philips. (Among international firms which have operations in Bombay, these are also the *biggest* multinationals in India, see Appendix 1.) It is a systematic comparative study of transnational differences in the structure and level of earnings, grading practices, leave, working hours and labour use, conditions of work, management attitudes and rates of conflict. The point of these comparisons is that the book is, more fundamentally, concerned with the significance of international investments for the type of labour movements and industrial relations in the industrialised Third World.

Firstly, it attempts to develop a different set of premises from those which have traditionally governed the debate about multinationals. We do *not* argue that multinationals are bad, that they damage or hold back the economic development of host countries, etc. In fact, a crucial premise is that the modern world economy necessarily takes the form of mobile international firms which integrate production facilities across national boundaries and whose presence is an inexorable part of the growth of social labour as *world* labour. If international firms are historically inevitable expressions of a unified international economy, then opposition to the expansion and evolution of such firms is a hopeless utopia. Secondly, the book *also* attempts to outline an alternative basis for a critique of the way such firms operate—one which is both more practical, in the sense that it accepts the need for such investment, and closer to the interests of the people working in such companies.

The argument is as follows: Since international management controls decisions which determine employment and job security levels, company finance and plant design, it might be supposed that the international level exerts equally strong control over local labour relations. However, this is far from true. For example, one writer recently observed,

> A major problem in trade union relations with management in the foreign affiliates of the multinational corporations lies in the decision-making authority. A number of such companies assert that all decisions relating to manufacturing, finance, capital investment and marketing of products rest wholly with the parent organisation. *The field of labour relations, however, is excepted.* Management in the subsidiary, according to stated company policy, is responsible for industrial relations, especially collective bargaining (Bendiner [1987], p. 25, emphasis ours).

Decentralisation of labour relations appears to be justified by parent respect for local custom and regard for the autonomy of local management. But the practical experience of several cases brought before the OECD Committee on International Investment and Multinational Enterprises does not support this.

In March 1977, the Trade Union Advisory Committee of the OECD introduced the case of Philips' failure to inform the unions and cooperate with them on plant closures in West Germany. In the course of rationalising its international plant structure, Philips had closed down six subsidiary plants in Germany in 1976. One of these was the subsidiary for the manufacture of condensers at Herborn, with around 300 workers and described as profit making. The works council and the metal-workers' union, IG Metall, tried to get the situation re-examined, arguing that there were no grounds for closure in terms of efficiency or competitiveness, and that there were no other job opportunities in the region. However, management at the headquarters (in Eindhoven) simply refused to reconsider its decision, and the plant was eventually closed. The German Works Constitution Act requires that the works council be regularly informed of any plans which might affect employee job security. Yet it is evident that in this case a multinational did *not* comply with the locally prevalent legal requirements.

Early in March 1980, management at Philips' Finnish subsidiary, Oy Philips Ab, made an announcement to local employees that production at the Helsinki plant would be scaled down gradually and terminated entirely by 31 May 1981. The Finnish Act on Cooperation in Enterprises is quite explicit in requiring employers to negotiate with workers *before* any decisions on closure, etc., have been made in an effort to provide employees with background information including financial information on the underlying causes and to allow employees sufficient time after receiving the information to prepare among themselves for negotiation. In this case, however, workers' representatives were neither given the relevant information nor consulted about the closure; Philips had failed to comply with local legislation once again.

A whole series of meetings between the local management, works council, unions and government preceded Ford's closure of their Amsterdam plant in the early eighties. The works council and unions presented no less than seven alternative plans for the use of their plant. The intervention was ineffectual because local managers, far from having the authority to take any decision on this, admitted that even their request to see Ford Motor Company's long-term plans had been refused. The closure of the Firestone plant at Pretteln, Switzerland, in 1978 also seems to have come as a surprise to local managers. The latter had not only issued a public statement to employees and the press that activities of the subsidiary were 'more or less normalised,' but had actually advertised in the local papers for recruitment of new staff just a few months before the closure![3]

These examples show that respect for the 'national' setting and regard for local management cannot be the main considerations behind multinational policy on labour in subsidiaries. On the contrary, unions complained that they were negotiating with managers who were neither well informed nor authorised to make decisions on the subject under negotiation, and that local legal requirements were contravened. On other occasions, however, unions have complained when companies *did* make use of local statutes and practices—for example, when Shell Oil Company collaborated with South African apartheid laws to deny recognition to black trade unions, or when General Motors, Krupp, Fiat, Volkswagen and others used the Brazilian government's stance against labour to avoid signing agreements with unions representing their employees (Bendiner [1987], pp. 17–18). Both sides— companies as well as unions—seem to lack any consistent principle, but this is not so. Unions are consistent in defending the interests of their members when they complain about the evasion of protective legislation as well as the use of repressive laws. Likewise, multinationals are being consistent when they evade some laws which curtail their freedom but use others which extend it in relation to their workforces.

Multinational strategy has two major advantages. One is that it effectively insulates the management levels where the major decisions are made from bargaining pressures. The other advantage is that it enables the companies to utilise poor employment conditions and lack of union rights in some parts of the world by appealing to the principle of not interfering with local practices. Both disadvantage employees who on the one hand find themselves decimated by decisions over which they have no control, and on the other hand are divided from one another by huge disparities in the conditions of employment.

1.2 RESTRUCTURING AND EMPLOYMENT

From the early seventies corporate reorganisation and industrial restructuring emerged as employers' major responses to the massively increased levels of competition which most large firms faced throughout the sixties and seventies. Both Philips and Unilever rapidly internationalised management decision-making, shifting the crucial management decisions to product coordinations responsible for whole groups of countries. The function of these coordinations was to restructure and rationalise production facilities for the particular product group on an international basis through a variety of measures, almost all of which entailed job losses. Restructuring involved streamlining their operations by selling off peripheral activities (e.g., transport, petrochemicals and cocoa products for Unilever) and re-deploying capital through extensive acquisitions in their traditional industries (among many examples are Unilever's acquisition of Brooke Bond, Liptons and Shedd's Food Products, and Philips' takeovers of NKF, Magna Vox, Signetics, Grundig, etc.). The purpose of increasing product specialisation in this way was to reduce competition by buying up potential rivals as well as by concentrating investments in rationalising a smaller range of products. The sale of plants would mean loss of jobs since operations which are sold are 'mostly . . . bought by rivals who proceed to close down some sections as they then have surplus capacity and one less competitor' (TICL, 'Unilever'). Plants which are bought are subjected to a similar process with the same results.

Both companies have rationalised by relocating activities from some plants to others in a drive to centralise production in large modern units while the older or smaller operations are discarded. In the large units, productivity is further increased by automation; both centralisation and automation involve massive investments. But both Philips and Unilever have faced market stagnation and considerable competitive pressure within Europe; and increased productivity combined with a stagnant market can only result in job losses, as a Unilever manager explained in relation to detergents: 'We are reducing our numbers because every family in Holland has a washing machine and no one is washing twice a day if it's possible to wash once, so there's not much more growth. We are just producing for the market in Benelux: that means in detergents we will go down every year' (interview). Philips' management used a similar argument when they announced the closure of their Halifax plant for washing machines and tumble driers: over-capacity in the Large Domestic Equipment industry in

Europe meant a stagnating market and increasing competition; survival depended on concentrating production in large plants with economies of scale, i.e., getting the same production from a smaller workforce in fewer plants. In video, the result of this policy was that in the early eighties TV glass production was stopped at Eindhoven and Winschoten, while the tube plants at Monza, Simonstone and Stadskanaal and the Lowestoft TV plant were closed down; the whole of video production and assembly was massively concentrated in a few large sites, and here jobs were destroyed through automation (for example, Aachen in West Germany). Unilever spent £48 million to concentrate Birds Eye Walls activities in the UK in seven regional depots with the closure of several factories and loss of 1,500 jobs. Another example: the company closed down a factory at Sheffield and started a fully-automated, computer-controlled pea factory at Worksop, estimated to cost £14 million, run by just twenty-four workers per shift and capable of handling 30 per cent of the English supply of peas.[4]

Table 1.1 and Figures 1a, 1b and 1c are a dramatic illustration of the impact of restructuring on employment levels. In Philips, the destruction of jobs gathers momentum from 1974. If one measures the movement of the company's domestic employment from its peak in 1971, Philips appears to have abolished some 28,000 jobs in fourteen years at an average rate of 2,000 jobs a year. Internationally, the Philips labour force has been contracting by *c.* 3 per cent per year through most of this period, with the biggest reductions concentrated in Elcoma and Audio. In Unilever, the reduction in worldwide employment is even faster, falling from 385,000 in 1978 to 306,000 in 1983. It is important to note that the decline in employment levels cannot be explained by relocation of production or capital to areas outside Europe. Diane Elson correctly argues, 'The new international division of labour represents not a simple process of job transfer but a complex process of restructuring of accumulation in manufacturing industry, which is decomposing old forms of work and labour organisation both within and between countries in the capitalist international economy' (Elson [1986], p. 9). Annual reports show continuing high levels of domestic investments, but these are investments in restructuring and automation, which result in the loss of jobs.

The extensive rationalisations and reorganisations of the seventies and early eighties required a radical change in management

Figure 1a

Job Losses and Employment Expansion: Philips — Size of Labour Force in India (1962-84)

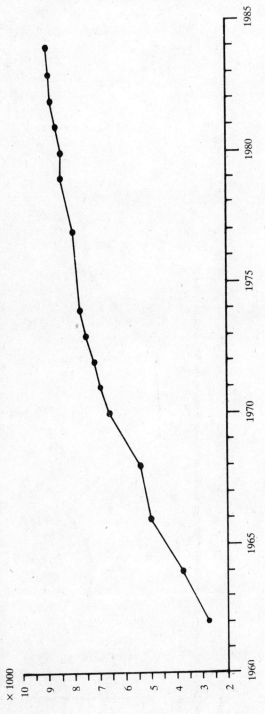

Figure 1b

Job Losses and Employment Expansion: Philips — Size of Labour Force in the Netherlands (1964-85)

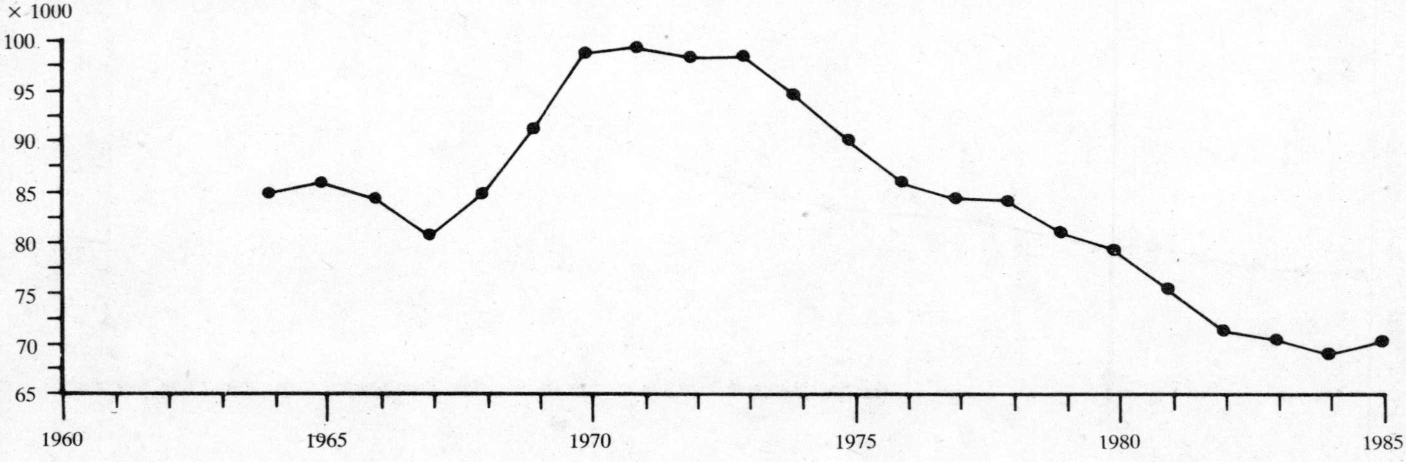

Figure 1c

Job Losses and Employment Expansion: Unilever — Size of Labour Force in the EEC (1975-84)

× 1000

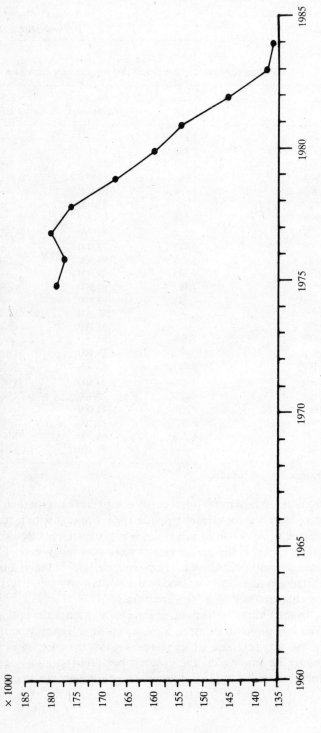

TABLE 1.1
Philips and Unilever: Job Losses and Employment Expansion

Year	Philips India	Philips Netherland	Unilever EEC
1960	2,137	—	—
1962	2,759	—	—
1964	3,714	85,000	—
1965	—	87,000	—
1966	5,052	84,000	—
1967	—	82,000	—
1968	5,446	85,000	—
1969	—	93,000	—
1970	6,587	98,000	—
1971	6,929	99,000	—
1972	7,193	97,000	—
1973	7,495	97,000	—
1974	7,728	95,000	—
1975	—	91,100	178,000
1976	—	87,500	177,000
1977	7,989	84,900	180,000
1978	—	84,100	176,000
1979	8,451	82,400	167,000
1980	8,409	79,500	159,000
1981	8,655	76,300	154,000
1982	8,850	73,000	145,000
1983	8,867	71,200	137,000
1984	8,975	68,300	136,000
1985	—	71,100	—

Source: Annual Reports.

thinking on how much job security companies can give their employees. That big companies provide their workers with a reassuring degree of job security is a claim few managements would want to make today. If the earlier claims were very much part of the new management orthodoxy of 'employee welfare' in the first phases of expansion after the war, today the thinking on job security could be characterised as a 'new' realism.

In the Philips agreement, several clauses leave the options open. The key passages occur in a clause entitled 'Employment,' where in the very sentence which states that it is the company's policy to assure its employees 'the greatest possible continuity of employment,' it is also stated, 'although no guarantees can be given in this respect' (Philips, cl. 6.1, p. 11). Paragraph 3 of this clause states that

> The employer shall during the period of this agreement refrain from forced redundancies in the case of employees who are in the company's service at the time of the signing of this agreement or who shall enter the company's service during the term of this agreement, unless special circumstances make this necessary.

In this eventuality, management first has to discuss the issue with the works council and unions before any concrete steps are taken. As to what constitute 'special circumstances,' there are, for obvious reasons, no guidelines in the agreement itself. Paragraph 7 of the same clause states, 'Despite the striving for continuity of employment, job losses may prove to be unavoidable' (Philips, cl. 6.7, p. 12). And, indirectly, clause 7 contains a reference to the sort of circumstances under which this could be true:

> In case the employer is contemplating a decision involving: (*a*) investments which result in a major contraction, expansion or change of jobs in a part of the factory, (*b*) closure and/or radical changes in employment levels of the whole factory or a part thereof, (*c*) a merger . . ., in taking his decision he shall take account of its social consequences (cl. 7.2, pp. 12–13).

In discussions with management, it was Unilever which expressed the new realism on job security in the most direct form.

> Let me give you an example [said a manager]. When I was the first Works Personnel Officer in a company in the meat group in Holland and I was discussing job changes in the department with one of the workers who was sixty years old and he wasn't prepared to accept those changes, I said to him, 'Yes, but do you really think that you can stick on to the same job you have at the moment till you're sixty-five?' And he said, 'Surely! I have been with Unilever for forty years. For me, it's like an insurance, nothing will change in my job.' And then I said, 'But it's not even certain that you will still be in Unilever in the next five years.' It was terrible for the man that I could actually say such things.

Another example: the management wanted to dismiss 350 people over a period of two years in the frozen foods plant, but the company finally reduced the number to 120 redundancies after discussions with the union. This was not an employment loss absorbed through gradual wastage or early retirement: 'Was it voluntary?' 'Oh no, forced!' (interview).

The Unilever agreement contains an even longer clause on employment than the corresponding one in Philips, but the formulations are similar—for example, 'Unilever shall not resort to forced redundancies . . . unless special circumstances make this necessary'. However, it contains provisions not found in the Philips settlement. In case the company finally decides it has to go for forced redundancies, it shall 'do so not earlier than six months after the works council has given its advice or had the chance to give its advice, and not until it has had fresh discussions with the unions' (Unilever, cl. 2.1, p. 5). In the agreement for the Shell refinery, the 'employment policy' clause likewise assumes that the company might have to 'resort to measures which could lead to forced redundancies,' and the most it allows is an obligation on the company to discuss the issue with the unions 'at the earliest possible stage' (Shell, cl. 23.4, p. 60).

In short, job security levels are now consciously defined in ways that allow large companies in the Netherlands to continue with the reduction in employment levels that set in around 1970. For companies like Philips this has meant 'a drastic change from the image of a company you are born in and die in. The 1980 reorganisations in Elcoma were the first time Philips publicly announced they might fire people. It was really a shock to employees.'[5]

The main difference in India has been an expanding market, which resulted in a steady increase of employment in Philips India (see Table 1.1 and Figure 1) as well as Hindustan Lever. However, the overall expansion of employment conceals two other related processes: on the one hand, as the Philips Workers' Mahaunion pointed out in a pamphlet dated 16 April 1984, while the number of *management* staff rose steadily between 1980 and 1983, the number of *workers* in the bargainable category scarcely rose at all, and in fact *declined* by 68 between 1982 and 1983. On the other hand, in India the same process of rationalisation is at work in the industrial establishments of these companies. When the declining employment figures for Hindustan Lever's Sewree factory (see

Table 1.2) were taken up with the management by the union, the management responded by pointing to the expansion of employment throughout India. But the opening or acquisition of new establishments failed to convince the union that the consistent decline in the size of the Sewree establishment was no cause for concern.

TABLE 1.2
Employment Decline at Hindustan Lever's Sewree Factory 1977–86
(No. in bargainable categories)

1977	3,326
1978	3,467
1979	3,534
1980	3,411
1981	3,279
1982	3,181
1983	3,092
1984	2,989
1985	3,002
1986	2,995

Source: Data supplied by Hindustan Lever Employees' Union.

As in Europe, a major cause of job losses in multinational firms in Bombay has been automation. Table 1.3 illustrates how automation of packing lines in pharmaceutical companies achieved significant reductions in staff strength even while production rose rapidly. Employment levels have also been affected by management's policy of decentralising production through subcontracting. In Philips, this has been the company's policy since 1954, and according to the union's estimate, something in the order of 60 per cent of production has been subcontracted; in the Philips India Annual Report for 1980, the company claimed to be providing work for over 34,000 people in 750 units throughout the country in addition to the 8,409 employees directly employed by them. In Hindustan Lever, as in Philips, subcontracting has been related to job losses. So far, however, restructuring in these areas of manufacturing has not resulted in forced redundancies. In striking contrast to the Dutch settlements for Philips and Unilever, the settlements concluded for the Bombay plants of these firms contain no reference to redundancies, partly because most of the job losses in these sectors of manufacturing are absorbed through natural wastage

TABLE 1.3
Productivity Increases on Pharmaceutical Packing Lines in Bombay

Plant	Product Line	Year	Line Strength	Production/ Shift
Glaxo Worli	Ostocalcium	1965	20	19,000
	syrup	1983	17	45,000
Pfizer Turbhe	Corex	1975	25	15–20,000
	syrup	1983	13	42,000
E.Merck Taloja	Polybion	1976	17	45,000
	ampoules	1983	11	70,000
Hoechst Mulund	Festal	1978	15	43,000
	tablets	1983	6	120,000
Johnson Mulund	Dacterin	1978	10	6,000
	ointment	1983	9	19,000
Parke-Davis	Benadryl	1980	18	25–28,000
	syrup	1983	13	35–40,000

Source: Union Research Group, *Bulletin* no. 3, 1983, pp. 8–19.

and voluntary retirement schemes, and because schemes of the latter type are not regarded as a subject for discussion with the union. In fact, retrenchment is explicitly ruled out in many agreements in the form of a 'No Retrenchment' clause; for example, the Hindustan Lever agreement states that 'as a result of modernisation or mechanisation there will be no retrenchment' (p. 2).

More recently, domestic plants of Philips have begun subcontracting production to smaller units: decentralisation of labour relations does not prevent an international company from introducing into one country management strategies which have proved effective in another. Rather, multinationalism is a type of management strategy which undermines the negotiating position of the unions which multinationals deal with at the local level because it restricts the scope of bargaining to the *results* of policies taken at levels where no bargaining is likely to occur; it is one out of a number of possible strategies to retain management control over the *policy decisions themselves*. This strategy has had a drastic effect on employment levels in Holland, whereas in their Bombay establishments managements have pushed through workforce reduction more gradually. In both places it has become clear that unions cannot halt the job losses without reconstructing their negotiating position vis-a-vis the companies and thus challenging the management's monopoly over these levels of decision-making.

2

MAIN DIFFERENCES IN
THE BARGAINING SYSTEM

Collective bargaining in the individual establishments of international companies reflects the influence of practices which define
bargaining systems *nationally*. In this chapter, the analysis proceeds
from these national or general determinations. To help establish
differences in the way bargaining occurs across national settings, it
takes up three major dimensions of the bargaining system—control
over bargaining, the level of bargaining, and the time taken to
reach agreements.

2.1 CONTROL OVER BARGAINING

2.1.1 Dutch centralisation

The absence of formal bargaining rights at the plant level is probably the most striking characteristic of Dutch labour relations in a
comparative setting. With the possible exception of France, most
countries of Europe which had some form of national or industry-
wide bargaining in the immediate post-war years, were destined to
witness a considerable devolution of bargaining in the boom years
of the fifties and early sixties. In the Netherlands too a comparable
process is discernible but in a drastically modified form which
continued to emphasise precisely those features of the bargaining
system which were declining in importance in other countries,
notably in Britain and Italy.[6] For Britain, a recent survey concluded
that whereas in the public sector it was rare for collective bargaining
to take place at all at the establishment level over rates of pay, 'in
the private sector, by contrast, plant bargaining was much more

common. The majority of establishments in the manufacturing sector that recognised trade unions engaged in plant bargaining, and in engineering, metal working and vehicle manufacture the large majority did so' (Daniel and Millward [1983], p. 184). Although this would not have been true of the British economy as a whole in view of the different forms of pay determination characteristic of different sectors, it does show that in one crucial sector there was considerable decentralisation of bargaining activity around 1980.

The only really detailed survey of workplace relations in Dutch manufacturing establishments was a study conducted by G.E. van Vliet into the actual functioning of *bedrijvenwerk* in six major plants in the mid-seventies. Although van Vliet for some reason chose to translate the term *bedrijvenwerk* as 'plant unionism,' his study establishes the clear lack of any system of this sort in Dutch industry. Apart from works councils (*ondernemingsraad* or OR), which were not conceived as representative institutions but as 'internal organs of consultation and advice' (their definition in clause 32 of the Philips agreement), the only plant-level structure which has anything to do with trade unionism is the 'plant union group' called the *bedrijfsledengroep* (BLG), but this only refers to that section of the labour force which actually belongs to a union. The BLG is the union membership of a factory or other establishment and, since the extent of union organisation fluctuates sharply between workplaces, the actual weight and importance of the BLG are variable quantities. By the late seventies, 87 per cent of all plants with a workforce of 500 plus were reported to have a BLG, and 64 per cent of middle-sized establishments with 201–500 employees, so it would be safe to assume that such committees would be a feature of most big factories today.

On the other hand, the BLG or, strictly speaking, tne active committee formed by the BLG, has no formal bargaining rights. As van Vliet says, 'The peculiarity of the Dutch form of industrial bargaining within firms is that the unpaid union representatives, as such, do not negotiate with management'; and he adds, 'Employers opposed the creation within the firm of a second negotiating body alongside the works council' (van Vliet [1979], p. 566). In Dutch bargaining it is the paid officials who handle formal negotiations with management. Since control over paid officials by the unpaid activists or lay members of the union is almost negligible, 'it follows that (in the Netherlands) pay bargaining is an area almost completely removed from the influence of the union membership' (Leijnse [1977], p. 156).

When Leijnse wrote this in the seventies, in a concise and brilliant assessment of what centralisation has meant for bargaining in Holland, he could say, 'Sometimes people from the union committee in the plant are involved in negotiations in some way, but they have no official status there' (p. 146). Today it is probably the usual practice for some people from the committee to accompany the union official in negotiations. For example, by the end of the seventies it was the declared policy of the Industriebond/FNV to make sure that the negotiating committee consisted of one or more paid officials of the union plus one or more local activists. This would mean that 'the BLG can then enable one or more of its members to participate in plant negotiations,' (Industriebond/FNV [1979], p. 61). In 1980, 250 of the 574 local committees affiliated to the Industriebond (some 44 per cent) had a negotiating team of this type. But BLG members cannot conclude agreements with the company on their own initiative or in any form which is independent of the paid officials.

It was in the early sixties that the main metal workers' union, the ANMB, formulated the ambitious programme of introducing union structures at the plant level and encouraging a deeper focus on workplace issues. In all companies where the union had members, it decided to have a local plant representative (*bedrijfscontactman*), and in the bigger establishments a factory-level committee (*bedrijfscontactcommissie*) to assist this person. These forms were destined to become the origin of the union committees which expanded rapidly in the early seventies, especially in the larger firms.

It is interesting that in the studies which the metal unions sponsored to encourage this restructuring, there were at least two occasions when proposals were made for a negotiating position at the plant level. Union publications in the sixties spoke of the need to 'have agreements (*afspraken*) in individual undertakings on the basis of, and as a way of working out, the more general guidelines in the main contract' (cited in Buitelaar and Vreeman [1985], p. 140). In other words, the national agreements would function purely as framework agreements, establishing guidelines and minimum terms, and it would be the responsibility of the local factory-level committees to flesh out these terms by concluding settlements for their own plants. But this was something Dutch employers were not inclined to accept either in that or in any later period.

> The initial position of the employers' association for the metals industry, the FME, was rather sympathetic towards the union's problems. Its board even issued a declaration indicating that it would have no objection if member firms agreed to furnish certain facilities to help the unions carry out their plans . . . . But when in early 1965 the ANMB began in earnest to ask individual companies for facilities, including freedom of movement in the plant for the new plant representative, union use of bulletin boards, office space, and an opportunity for contacts during working hours between the union's district office and the plant representative, most managements turned the union down flat (Windmuller [1969], p. 431).

It seems that the unions were not prepared to exert any more pressure to win these rights. On the contrary, they

> made apparently far-reaching concessions. They declared that they had no intention of interfering with any management rights, that they were not about to undermine the works councils, that their plant representatives would seek no direct role in handling grievances nor would they try to act as a link between unions and works councils, and that they could be trusted to forestall any development in the direction of a British-type shop steward system (p. 432).

But this didn't satisfy the employers. 'Most of them were not prepared to recognise the legitimacy of any kind of union activity in their plants' (p. 432).

In terms of facilities like time off, notice boards, office space and contact with the official during working hours, companies have modified their stand considerably since that period. For example, in the Unilever agreement there is a whole clause with some thirteen paragraphs entitled 'Facilities for the unions,' while other clauses include the right of employees who are union members to attend union meetings, training sessions or meetings with the management (it might be more accurate to say, include permission to do so, since all this is at management's discretion).

But there is no doubt that some employers, notably Philips, who would have been instrumental in determining overall employer responses in the sixties, are still basically opposed to a union presence on the shop floor. This is a major reason why the Philips group as a whole, i.e., all Philips establishments in the Netherlands, have an exceptionally low average density (rate of union organisation) and at least in the core region of Philips activity (the area around Eindhoven), there are very few active or functioning BLGs today.

Van Vliet accounts for the failure of plant bargaining in terms of the *strategy* the Dutch unions were committed to—the fact that they had already opted for a certain sort of bargaining structure and were not interested in plant agreements—and the internal resistance posed chiefly by some district officials. But this general explanation underestimates the role of employer opposition and of opposition from within the works councils. It is quite true that Dutch unionism has committed itself in a decisive way to a bargaining structure which involves centralised negotiations, either for multi-plant establishments or for whole industries or sectors, but this strategy was at least partly shaped by employer opposition.

> Employers insisted over and over again that unions were outsiders . . . . What owners did in their own plants—their relations with employees, their personnel policy, their shop rules, or anything else—was no outsider's business . . . . For unions to assert an interest in intra-plant affairs constituted an attempted interference with property rights, an undermining of employer authority, and a threat to efficient production (Windmuller [1969], pp. 401–12).[7]

Opposition to *bedrijvenwerk* from within the works councils was also significant. Although the works councils were originally established as organs of cooperation and were often dominated by the higher personnel, the unions played an active role in them in all phases. But this did not prevent these organisations from being one source of opposition to union work at the plant level. According to Visser:

> for the whole of the 60s some unions, especially the metal workers, experimented with plant-level organisation. But senior

members of the union were sitting in the works councils and they didn't like younger members coming as shop stewards and controlling them, so there was competition between the existing works council members and the newcomers who often represented the manual, low-skilled groups, whereas senior members were often people from the technical departments, who had accumulated some rights, who held office . . . (interview).

However, this was not the case everywhere and there were plants like the NKF factory at Delft where there was closer integration between these structures.

Insofar as local committee members have no independent negotiating status and can reach settlements only through the intervention of district officials or 'concern negotiators,' there is no resemblance between them and shop stewards in British factories or union office bearers in Bombay companies. According to Jelle Visser:

There is no bargaining at plant level, as there is in Britain, where the shop stewards encroached on these functions and came to be seen as the union in the plant. In Holland this has always remained the job of the union official, there have even been situations where senior union members at plant level have tried to bargain and have been suspended from union membership (interview).

Van Vliet concluded his study with a roughly similar assessment: 'The union did not give enough support to the unpaid union representatives within the firm . . . . The most important support that plant unionism might have expected from the union, but did not receive, was a strengthening of their negotiating position.' And he concludes by saying that the policy of the Dutch unions 'is still strongly centrally oriented' [1979, p. 569].

In the Netherlands, negotiations are the job of paid officials of the unions who may be responsible for the company as a whole (and deal with it as 'concern negotiators') or for all or some company negotiations within the area, as the district officials are. In Unilever, each of the local plant-level union committees nominates one delegate and the delegates from different plants meet six to eight times a year. They formulate the demands and the FNV concern negotiator for Unilever forwards the letter. From the FNV the actual negotiation is conducted by four persons: the chairman of the combine committee for Unilever (CKK or 'Central Contact Committee,' a body elected by the BLGs for three years), the secretary, one of the delegates, and the concern negotiator. Negotiations take place in Rotterdam where the company has its headquarters. A manager who was interviewed about the bargaining arrangements clarified that not all sessions would be formal meetings. Informal meetings need not include all the unions involved in the settlement, and no minutes would be kept of such discussions. The main purpose of these meetings was to find some basis for the (larger) formal sessions. From the management's side the core of the negotiating team consists of the Personnel Director of Unilever Netherlands, the Industrial Relations Manager and two of his assistants. Where the coverage or bargaining unit is smaller, as with the Shell agreements for Pernis and Moerdijk, negotiations might be conducted by only one union with a team composed of the district official and the chairman of each plant union committee: just three negotiators.

The highly centralised character of Dutch negotiating practices was strongly criticised by some employees from Fokker.

> Most of the time management negotiates with the four trade unions' representatives. So you have the FNV, the Christian trade union leadership, and then you have at Fokker level two trade unions for the higher personnel. The biggest trade union is the FNV and most of the time they lead the negotiations. So the company has enough room for manoeuvre to divide those four trade unions. The trade union negotiator of our union has to negotiate along with the others, but without the committee of twenty people who prepare for negotiations.
> 'How much do workers actually know of what is going on in the negotiations?'
> 'It's hierarchical. We are activists, but we hardly know what is happening when they are negotiating.'
> 'Is it not possible for you to try and find out?'
> 'Yes, but you have to put pressure and sometimes you succeed but very often you don't. The concern negotiator negotiates individually. Often there aren't official negotiations, but he has dinner, or lunch, or brunch or whatever with our management, and after that he says, well, now I'm going to negotiate' (interview).

2.1.2 Styles of unionism: Bombay

In Bombay unionism, there are at least three dimensions which concretely determine bargaining relationships:

> *Type of union*: there are three types of unions: (*a*) employees' unions which are *purely internal* in the sense that no outsiders are involved on the managing committee or negotiating committee; (*b*) unions which are *largely internal* in the sense that they call themselves employees' unions or workers' unions but retain an outside adviser who tends to play a major role in negotiations; (*c*) units which are *affiliated to* an outside union whose name appears on the settlement.
> *Degree of bargaining autonomy*: referring to the precise degree to which local committees can and do run their own affairs, in particular negotiate independently of or jointly with or entirely through an outsider. In general, it would be sufficient to distinguish three degrees here: Low (L) for committees which succumb to management or which are *controlled by* or depend totally on outside leadership; Medium (M) for committees which *participate in* negotiations but cannot or would not want to settle without the outside adviser. In such cases the crucial sessions will be handled by the latter; High (H) for committees which negotiate entirely or largely *on their own* even when they retain an external adviser.
> *General form of bargaining strategy*: this depends on whether a union relies mainly on *discussion* to settle its demands, attempting as far as possible to avoid conflict even though certain forms of bargaining pressure may be applied (DISC); or whether it is willing to press its demands even at the risk of considerable *conflict*, or consciously adopts those types of bargaining tactics which entail high levels of conflict (CONF).[8]

This allows for a three-dimensional matrix as the most precise description of the range of negotiating styles at work in the actual experience of unionism in Bombay. Table 2.1 illustrates this.

This is a purely schematic description but a useful one. The matrix throws up a whole series of contrasting styles; for example, A-L-DISC (i.e., internal unions with low bargaining autonomy and prone to discussion) reflects the case of unions confronting

TABLE 2.1

A Model of Bargaining Autonomy for Bombay Unions (Examples)

Type of Union:	A		B		C	
Strategy:	DISC	CONF	DISC	CONF	DISC	CONF
Autonomy						
Low	Telco Godrej Tata Electric		Firestone		Bayer Searle Gabriel Ralliwolf	Johnson & Johnson
Medium	Parke-Davis		Herdillia Siemens	Hindustan Lever	Roussel Larsen & Toubro	Ciba-Geigy
High	Hoechst Glaxo Wyeth SKF	Philips Tomco	Nocil Mahindra Auto			

managements who leave them no room for independent assertion (this is certainly a conscious policy for labour relations in the Tata group, even if they are not always successful in reducing their unions to a purely subaltern existence, for example, Tomco). A-H-DISC differs in only one dimension, namely, that here there are no restrictions on the bargaining autonomy of the committee, but the model which results could not be further removed from the subaltern type. These are some of the most mature and fiercely independent employees' unions anywhere in the country, run by extremely conscious and technically competent leaderships and found almost always in international companies with reputations for being among the most professional, well-managed companies in India; there is a sense in which these are companies which have to buy their reputation for stable industrial relations (by providing above-average pay and work conditions). Here the option to discuss rather than head for conflict is crucial to the bargaining strategy consciously pursued by these unions, but their style of negotiating does not exclude selective use of the less disruptive forms of agitation. The style of unionism in the Philips establishments is similar but characterised by greater conflict—A-H-CONF.

In B-H-DISC, the union regards itself as internal but retains an

outside adviser who in some cases is involved in negotiations.
Nocil, one of Shell's two major involvements in Bombay industry,
is a somewhat unusual case where the committee chooses to retain
an outsider for legal advice or to help with drafting but feels
competent enough to handle its own negotiations. In B-M-DISC,
the outside leader plays a much more important role in bargaining;
the style would be characterised by close and frequent contacts
between the committee and the union's outside adviser; no major
decisions would be made by the committee on its own. But since
these are unions which have opted for a strategy of discussion, this
would certainly reflect in their choice of an adviser, many unions
of this sort showing a preference for G.R. Khanolkar who leads
the Dyes and Chemicals Workers' Union and who is rated as one
of the best negotiators in Bombay unionism. Khanolkar tends to
encourage initiative and independence in his committees, unlike
those professionals in Bombay trade unionism whose style is largely
authoritarian in the sense that they cannot tolerate opposition
from their committees and might even insist on negotiating alone.
The Hindustan Lever factory at Sewree falls under B-M-CONF;
most of the day-to-day bargaining activity is handled by the local
committee but the union's president, Samant, plays a major role in
important negotiations. The committee has retained its independence because the bargaining strategy it opted for involved forms of
struggle which could only be directed internally through a network
of department leaders. At a certain stage in discussions for the
1983 settlement, bargaining proceeded simultaneously at two levels,
Lever management having decided its best chances of a rapid
settlement lay with Samant, while the committee continued to
bargain through shop-floor actions more or less every day.

The most obvious characteristic of affiliated unions (C) is the
severe limitation of their bargaining autonomy—their ability to
back up their own claims or their ability to take important bargaining decisions—by the control exercised by an outside leadership
which may or may not be the trade union wing of a larger political
grouping. Where a committee has built up considerable expertise
in negotiating, largely through the accumulation of experience in
dealing with its management, attempts to enforce control from the
outside can lead to major conflicts between the union committee
and the outside leadership, which is what happened in the large
engineering complex run by Larsen and Toubro, where the union

was otherwise more or less solidly controlled by the Shiv Sena. In a sense there is a resemblance here to the bargaining situation in Dutch industry. But the greater independence of the local union committee ('managing committee') in Bombay companies, even in affiliated unions, is demonstrated by those cases where the committee has decided to leave an outside leader in favour of an adviser who encourages greater autonomy.

To sum up, it may be said that in terms of bargaining characteristics, the lack of formal bargaining rights at the plant level in Dutch industry and the possession of such rights in Bombay companies is probably *the single most important overall contrast* between Dutch and Bombay unionism. Workers in Bombay have much greater control over the bargaining process than their counterparts working for the same companies in the Netherlands. There is also much more complexity in the bargaining relationships in Bombay industry (apart from huge variations in the size of negotiating teams). The whole style of union leadership is more personal, much less bureaucratic, even if this style is sometimes characterised by deep authoritarianism and personal submissiveness and usually displays the male dominance which goes with contemporary unionism almost everywhere.

2.1.3 Decentralising tendencies

Yet, while centralisation remains a fundamental theme in Dutch union discussions, it would be wrong to ignore the conflicting tendencies which have pulled and still pull in the opposite direction. Through the general movement called 'factory-level work' it became possible for the more advanced sectors of the union movement to establish reserves of active union support on the shop floor in a whole range of individual workplaces. Union activity within the works councils and workers' research at the plant level constitute two partial solutions to the contradiction between centralisation and decentralising tendencies.

A Managements in Dutch industry have increasingly accepted a limited bargaining role for the works councils, both because these structures have been in existence for much longer and because they have, in the theory of the *ondernemingsraad*, allowed for more employer control.[9]

Dealing with works councils in this way would be a strategy

allowing them (employers) to stave off the evolution of a formal bargaining process at the plant level. On the other hand, it was also possible that the union cadre at the factory level could move into the works councils and increasingly influence developments from within those structures. There is some evidence to suggest that this is precisely what happened, especially in the eighties. Because of the significant legal rights possessed by the works councils under Dutch labour law, especially with regard to rights to information disclosure, the right of veto in the event of major organisational changes and the right to call in outside consultants, local union activists tried to influence developments in the company through the works councils, constituting a trade union fraction (the '*OR-fractie*') within them to argue union policy. This shift was in fact part of a conscious strategy of relying more on the works councils, working within and through the OR, as one way of coping with the lack of an independent negotiating position at the plant level.[10]

B   A lot of union committees in plants in the Netherlands became increasingly involved in trying to influence plant developments through their own union-supported *investigations* into local grievances, working conditions, personnel policies, company policy and the local union presence. Buitelaar and Vreeman, who have described these activities in detail, argue that the more recent types of research activity have roots in a much earlier tradition in the Netherlands going back to workplace investigations encouraged by the radical union movement EVC in the immediate post-war years. But workers' research only really becomes more widespread from the mid-seventies, once the FNV is confronted by the massive reorganisation process and huge job losses initiated by big companies like Akzo and Philips. In this crisis it has become vitally important for the unions not only to be able to monitor this process, to keep track of declining job opportunities and analyse the sources of such decline, but also, even more importantly, to be able to *respond* in an effective way to the policies which have led and are still leading to job losses. As this movement (known in the Netherlands as *Werknemersonderzoek* or 'workers' investigations') has far-reaching implications for union strategy, signifying the beginnings of a conscious union initiative in the areas of employment and technology, it is worth describing in some detail.

In the mid-sixties, as part of the metal-workers' unions' efforts to build a stronger base in the plants, district officials were encouraged to make a series of 'company X-rays,' surveys which were based on some twenty to thirty interviews with union activists in the plant and which highlighted essential aspects of the company and its policies. This involved the union researching:

1. History of the undertaking: expansions, management changes, changes in the production programme;
2. Legal aspects in any way relevant to the concern: its statutes, mergers and joint ventures, collective agreements, relevant provisions of the Factories Act;
3. Economic data: product structure, market position, company results, future plans proposed by management;
4. Organisation of the plant: personnel information department-wise, different job groups, jobs in relation to plant technology, ways in which productivity has increased or can increase, product development;
5. Social aspects of the company: service conditions and personnel policies as they operate in practice (recruitment, payment systems, merit rating, promotion, retrenchment);
6. Consultative structures in the company;
7. The company and the union: rate of organisation, plant activists, contacts between union and members, labour relations in the company.

Unions in Bombay, especially internal unions, have made occasional attempts which take up one or two of the aspects outlined here, for example when the Pfizer Employees' Union or the Philips Workers' Union highlighted declining employment opportunities and threats to job security in cyclostyled pamphlets or short printed brochures. Another example is the investigation made by the Hoechst Employees' Union into what workers felt about the union; this was based on a questionnaire which the union circulated among Hoechst employees. Again, there was the remarkably detailed information put together and published by the Philips Employees' Union (i.e., Bombay staff) on practices involving managerial corruption and misuse of company resources. But these examples also suggest that generally Bombay unions would concentrate on a particular aspect and not make an overall survey of the type outlined in the schema described above.

The Dutch employee reports (*werknemersverslagen*) written in the seventies are the most immediate precursors of the more developed type of research activity which emerged later. As a phase in the evolution of union-sponsored plant-level research, the *werknemersverslagen* were a sort of workers' counterpart to the 'social reports' published annually by the companies themselves. Personnel policies were one of the major issues discussed in them. The significant feature of these efforts and the more advanced ones which developed in the eighties in centres like Rotterdam, especially around the docks, and in companies like Akzo, ICI, Dupont, Michelin, Unichema (Unilever) and Philips Data Systems, is that they represent the beginnings of a 'New Unionism' in Dutch industry, one which corresponds perfectly to the forms and objectives of radical unionism elsewhere. The central idea behind all these efforts is that unless employees and their unions fight to influence and gain some basic control over *company policies*, rationalisation and job loss will mean not only drastic reductions in the labour force but intensified domination at workplaces and tighter employer control over the labour market.

But of course neither of these two solutions—union activity in the works councils and plant-level research—actually resolve the conflict they express. For on the one hand, if Dutch employers ever conceded bargaining rights at the shop floor to the works councils, this would only be part of a more general employer strategy to contain an organised *union* presence in their plants. As it stands, the collapse of union membership which is currently under way means that they are under no compulsion to do even that. On the other hand, regarding the second solution, investigating issues like personnel policies, health and safety, job losses or changing skill structures cannot be a substitute for actually *negotiating* these issues in some form where employees, ordinary men and women, have maximal control over the process. The law of combined and uneven development reveals its peculiar force once again: what Bombay factories have and Dutch factories lack (namely, the ability to influence developments through a union presence on the shop floor, in other words, not just the existence of trade union organisation in the plants but the formal recognition and practical confirmation of bargaining rights for such structures) remains the biggest lacuna of the Dutch trade union movement.

2.2 BARGAINING STRUCTURE

The term 'bargaining structure' is now generally used to refer to the main level or levels at which collective agreements are negotiated.[11] Of course, not all employees have their terms and conditions determined by collective bargaining; but where workforces are covered by bargaining arrangements, agreements can be negotiated at three levels. Where there is a clear tendency for agreements to be negotiated primarily or mainly at one of these levels, that would be referred to as the most important level of bargaining, although where agreements are signed at more than one level the term could also mean 'the level at which the largest proportion of the pay increase was agreed' (Daniel and Millward [1983], p. 183). The usual levels are (*a*) an industry or particular type of employment (e.g., public services), (*b*) all or some establishments of a multi-plant company, and (*c*) individual plants or other establishments such as head offices or research centres. The descriptive complexity of bargaining structures arises from the fact that at each of these levels important variations are possible. For example, agreements negotiated for an entire industry may be either national or regional in scope (contrast the Netherlands and Britain with France and West Germany). Another possible source of variation at this level is the nature of the agreement itself, in the sense of the degree to which it seeks to determine terms and conditions of employment, alternatively the scope it allows for further bargaining at more decentralised levels. Again, where companies negotiate their own agreements, such agreements might apply to all plants and establishments regardless of product divisions (as is the case in Philips), or separate agreements might be negotiated for separate product divisions (as for manual employees in Akzo) or the extent of coverage might be limited in some way, whose exact basis is not always clear (as in Unilever). Finally, even where a company negotiates separate agreements for different groups of establishments, higher personnel may be covered by just one common agreement (as in Akzo).

While the level of bargaining defines the form of agreements, the specific combination of bargaining levels, that is, the bargaining structure as a whole, is a complicated expression of the degree of centralisation within a bargaining system. Highly centralised bargaining systems such as those in the Scandinavian countries or in the Netherlands are systems where most of the bargaining activity is concentrated at the higher, national or industry, levels. One obvious consequence of such systems is the lower relative dispersion of pay levels. The almost purely decentralised bargaining structure of Bombay industry is matched by considerable pay dispersion. (This refers to the spread in wage levels for similar types of jobs even between plants in the same area.)

Although most workers in the Netherlands are covered by industry-wide agreements, some years ago there were some 400 company agreements in operation (Bomers [1976], p. 84). A Philips manager with some forty years' experience in this field felt that Holland could pass as a pure case of company bargaining. Within the Netherlands, Philips itself forms the purest example of company bargaining, with complete centralisation of pay scales across all establishments in the Philips group. Unilever deviates from this norm in at least two ways. Firstly, although the ARU (the Unilever agreement for Holland) covers over thirty companies in the Unilever group, the proportion of the total labour force covered by this agreement is only just over 70 per cent; some 2,200 employees fall under other agreements. Secondly, even within the main Unilever agreement there are actually three distinct pay scales, starting at different levels for each grade (the job classification is of course the same); the margarine factory in Rotterdam, v.d. Bergh en Jurgens, is on the highest scales, Lever Sunlight, Unichema and two other plants are on intermediate scales, and so on. But, in fact, the difference in pay is not remarkable. Discussions with the district official from Rotterdam confirmed that in Unilever pay differences within the company are a product of the historical circumstances under which it built up its structure, namely, through the incorporation and takeover of plants belonging to other companies. The common agreement for the Unilever group was a recent introduction.

The Unilever management explained the transition to a single company-wide bargaining structure largely in terms of trade union preferences: 'In the sixties it wasn't just that Unilever wanted a central agreement, this was also the case with the unions, they wanted to have a central agreement because we were a big company then . . .' (interview). On the other hand, within the Unilever management there has always been latent pressure for a reversion to decentralised bargaining: 'The companies who make a big profit

normally want decentralised bargaining, because they can pay.
. . .There's no such pressure at this moment, but if such pressure
comes, I think it will come from the richest companies we have.'
This was so because by paying more they would be able to attract
the best people. The partial decentralisation of the Akzo bargaining
structure is also largely a reflection of a growth process built on
acquisitions, with variations mostly explicable in terms of an area
determination of pay. But whereas in Unilever, apart from minor
differences in pay, all other terms and conditions are the same, in
Akzo, because separate agreements are negotiated for each division,
even other terms such as leave entitlements can display differences
in the group as a whole.

Not all big companies in the Netherlands have opted for company
bargaining. For example, Fokker, with a workforce of almost
10,000 spread over five factories, falls under the metal industry
agreement. Within the Philips group, the employees of NKF are
likewise covered by the metal industry agreement. And deviations
are also possible in the opposite direction: the Stella Artois brewery
at Dommelen has a plant agreement (*bedrijfs-cao*), and so does
the M & T Chemicals plant at Vlissingen, both with workforces of
less than 200.

In the sharpest possible contrast to this general pattern, one
dominated by a strong tradition of centralism, the bargaining
structure of Bombay industry (with the exception of textiles) is
decentralised and fragmented. Philips and Hindustan Lever are in
fact prime examples of this. With the exception of those terms
which the Philips federation has compelled the company to negotiate collectively for all its establishments, employees at the light
factory in Kalwa, staff employed at the Bombay head office,
showroom and service centres, and the Pune establishments are
covered by separate agreements. In Hindustan Lever, the fragmentation is even more extreme: separate agreements for the
soaps and detergents plant at Sewree, the fine chemicals plant at
Andheri, the research centre next to it, the ossein factory at Taloja
and the Bombay head office staff (if the management had been
willing to sign a bilateral settlement here); finally, in the Sewree
factory, separate agreements for staff and workers. When Britain's
trade unionists discussed Unilever at a seminar held in October
1985, this strategy was called 'plant segregation' (TUC [1985],
p. 5). In the UK, 'there is no national organisation, and no national

negotiations with Unilever. Instead the unions have to bargain at either group, company or plant level. This makes it difficult to construct an overall picture of employment levels, pay and conditions' (TICL, 'Unilever'). But in Bombay the policy of plant segregation takes an even more intensified form.

The most striking consequence of this fragmentation of bargaining is the dispersion of pay levels between individual establishments of the same company. By contrast with the domestic practice of their parent firms, *the Philips and Unilever subsidiaries in India enforce pay structures where there is considerable internal inequality*. (For the overall contrast, see Table 2.2). The unions in these companies are the only force which could bring about more standardised and uniform pay scales to ensure greater equality of pay between plants. This means discarding the largely imaginary arguments which managements bring forward to justify pay dispersion in terms of area differences. But at a deeper level it also presupposes an important evolution in union structure: the company-wide federations such as those in the electrical engineering industry (Voltas, Blue Star, Siemens and Philips itself) or the weaker federations in Lever and other companies are the only forms of union structure which could compel managements to negotiate common agreements for most or all of the company's establishments. In Philips, the Mahaunion (federation) settlements, negotiated since 1979, cover bonus, leave travel allowance (LTA), house rent allowance (HRA), gratuity and provident fund; other terms are negotiated separately. But every move towards the formation of company-wide federations and less dispersed bargaining structures or greater coordination of bargaining within the same companies encounters massive opposition from Bombay managements. Philips itself is an obvious case of this since there has been considerable conflict with the federation in the past few years. In Blue Star, controlled by the Advanis, the management forced a lockout of 311 days on its employees (in 1984–85) in order to exclude its new manufacturing unit in Gujarat from the federation settlement. Another company where there has been massive conflict between management and a federation organising employees throughout the country is Tomco (Tata Oil Mills). Here the federation was formed in the mid-sixties and consists of some twenty-seven unions including sales offices, cattle feed plants and a hard core of six factory units. In late 1979, federation demands

TABLE 2.2
Outline of Main Bargaining Characteristics

Dimension	Netherlands	Bombay
Locations	dispersed with some geographical concentrations	a few heavy concentrations
Base of large companies	electrical engineering, chemicals, food	electrical and other types of engineering, chemicals, pharmaceuticals, oil
Bargaining system	coordinated, highly centralised	decentralised, fragmented, major role for courts
Bargaining structure	industry and company levels	plant level, almost no company-wide agreements
Duration of agreements	one or two years	three years, sometimes four
Main pay components	basics, shift payments	dearness allowance, bonus
Pay dispersion	low	considerable
Formal job evaluation	widespread coverage, points rating	limited to a few large concerns
Working hours	38→36 hours	40–48 hours
Consultative rights	extensive, formalised in law on works councils	limited, determined by collective bargaining
Information disclosure	significant legal rights	almost non-existent
Job security	under pressure, massive job losses	natural wastage
Union movement	pluralism	fragmentation and rivalry
Type of unionism	industrial, union committees at plant level	plant unionism, partly independent, otherwise competing political control
Union density	31.7 per cent and declining	high in large-scale manufacturing
Union presence at plant level	weak, no formal status	widespread, formal acceptance
Major union objectives	job creation through shorter working hours, more control over company policies	higher benefits, job security, no subcontracting, housing loans
Conflict levels	generally low	high

led to a strike of 141 days, and violent clashes with a scab union the following year when the company declared a lockout which closed production for another 49 days. Tata management's stubborn refusal to settle those demands with the federation meant eventual arbitration, and the Joshi Award which resulted in 1980 was the first settlement to introduce any of the major fringe benefits which most comparable concerns, especially international companies, had been paying for at least ten years.

If over-centralisation has limited the development of plant bargaining in Dutch industry and reduced the control which most ordinary union members have over the bargaining process, total decentralisation—that is, decentralisation without any form of coordination—has been a major and continuing source of weakness in Bombay unionism. This has now become obvious in at least two ways. First, plant unions which lack any durable collective solidarity or shared coordination have proved completely defence-less in the face of generalised employer attacks. In the seventies these attacks were concentrated on two fronts. Most Bombay managements had decided on the need for strong pay controls and concluded that ceilings on dearness allowance would have to be the crux of this strategy. This was not a decision they could enforce unilaterally. It was something they would have to negotiate. The fact that most managements in the larger companies were success-ful in negotiating ceilings of one form or another shows not only the lack of an effective union strategy on pay, but the inability to fight ceilings in a unified or coordinated way. The other front on which Bombay employers scored repeated victories was in getting unions to accept differential employment statuses, that is, vastly different degrees of job protection for different sections of the workforce. Thus, by the late seventies it was by no means unusual for the bigger plants to employ not only casual workers for inci-dental jobs, but temporaries, sometimes (as in Pfizer or the Mahindra jeep factory) large reserves of them, for in-plant pro-duction jobs and/or contract workers for a whole range of jobs whose scope was not always precisely specified. These categories of workers were almost always excluded from the collective agree-ments which companies negotiated with their permanent employees. Both these movements, consequences of the lack of any coordina-tion between unions, of their hopeless isolation in innumerable factories throughout the city, of their mutual indifference and sometimes even competitive hostilities, were destined to have a serious impact on Bombay unionism in the course of the eighties.

The second way in which fragmentation has been a source of weakness for the Bombay unions is the persistence of sharp trade union rivalries. Increased rank-and-file control over pay bargaining in the form of a totally decentralised and uncoordinated bargaining structure, such as characterises most types of manufacturing in Bombay, also means much more room for conflict *within* the union movement. This accounts for the incomparably greater instability of union affiliation, repeated outbreak of union rivalries (Siemens, Pfizer, Glaxo, Hoechst, CAFI/ICI, Sandoz, Larsen and Toubro, all involving physical clashes), and divided workforces which are typical of Indian trade unionism in centres like Bombay and Madras—as opposed to the stable union structures (but with lower densities) characteristic of most European countries, even those like Belgium or the Netherlands which have several union traditions, Catholic, Protestant and Socialist.

2.3 BARGAINING CYCLES AND MANAGEMENT DEMANDS

In the Netherlands, when Philips signed a famous agreement in the mid-sixties, introducing a cost-of-living index escalator clause allowing for a rise of 2 per cent per year, the agreement was signed for three years. It seems to have aroused considerable opposition among Dutch employers at the time because 'the escalator clause was an undesirable and dangerous precedent for national wage policy' (Windmuller [1969], p. 374) in the sense tnat it allowed for pay increases in this, for that period comparatively novel, inflation-linked form. But

> the company's principal argument in favor of approval of the agreement was its enhanced ability to predict its labor costs. The wage explosions of recent years had made the task of company planning and cost estimation more difficult than ever before. The ability to calculate labor costs over a three-year period with reasonable accuracy made it worthwhile for the company, so it said, to conclude a settlement on terms exceeding the limits set by the national bargain (p. 373).

In other words, in the mid-sixties Philips was prepared to pay more to secure a longer duration agreement in the interests of what it called the enhanced predictability of labour costs. In a recent interview, Philips managers stated that the duration they go for depends mainly on two factors: the 'typical economic situation' prevailing at a given time, and 'discussion with other employers'. Most recent agreements signed in Philips have been for one-year periods, although, 'on the whole, when we talk on a more abstract level,' the manager said, 'two years is better' because the outcomes were more predictable for them as well as for the workers. What was interesting in this discussion was the statement that the duration of an agreement is itself an issue for bargaining.

An additional reason why managements might prefer longer duration agreements is the possibility this offers of reducing the frequency of possible unrest. Each new bargaining cycle could involve actions in support of claims, like the series of short strikes in Unilever plants around Rotterdam in the middle of 1986. Fokker's pressure for a two-year agreement was explained by employees from the Schiphol plant as an attempt to reduce the incidence of industrial action in support of claims: 'Now there's a fight and it happens every year, so management would prefer it every two years instead. In every agreement there's a clause that there will be no strikes for the period of the agreement—so that way they have no trouble' (interview). There are in fact similar no-strike clauses in the Philips (cl. 36.1, p. 37) and Unilever (cl. 3.2, p. 11) settlements: the first rules out strikes and 'disruption of industrial peace,' the second refers to strikes and 'actions aimed at bringing about any change in this settlement'.

One-year agreements appear to be the norm in a large section of Netherlands industry. However, an FNV official, asked about union preferences on duration, felt there were advantages in having a three-year agreement because 'in those three years you can stabilise your position in the factory, because then you have more time for other issues,' i.e., issues apart from the next settlement. In ICI Holland, where they have alternated between one- and two-year agreements, the local union committee said that a one-year agreement would be signed by the union only if there were several issues still pending. In this sense the one-year agreement was described as 'a result of disagreements between the unions and employers'; the rule the ICI union committee advocated was that if only half your issues have been settled in the course of negotiations, opt for a one-year settlement because you can always take up the other issues the following year. However, the management wanted even longer-term agreements: 'last time we asked for a two-year agreement and management said, let's sign for three years.' The union refused, because a three-year agreement would mean that 'they can keep the union out for three years'.

Table 2.3 summarises settlement durations for companies in the Netherlands, the Indian plants of Philips, and Unilever subsidiaries internationally. Bombay unions have generally tended to accept the normality of three-year agreements. A major reason for this is that earnings do in fact increase during the period of the settlement due to the inflation-linked component of wages (dearness allowance). On the other hand, Bombay managements have been pressing for even longer durations, with some success. The 1985 agreement for Philips Kalwa was a four-year agreement, and the Mahaunion (federation) settlement had a duration of five years.

TABLE 2.3
Duration of Agreements

Company/Plant	Year	Duration (in Years)
Philips (Netherlands)	1985	1
Unilever (Netherlands)	1985	1
Shell (Netherlands)	1985	2
ICI Holland	1985	1
Philips Kalwa	1985	4
Philips Pune	1985	3
Philips federation (India)	1979	5
Hindustan Lever (Sewree)	1983	3
Lever Bros. USA	1983	3.5
Philippine Refining Co.	1983	3
Lever Iberica (Spain)	1982	2
Unilever Australia	1981	1

The bargaining cycle is the time which elapses between the date when a union forwards its demands to the company and the date on which those claims are finally settled. Differences in the bargaining cycles of individual companies are an important indication of management labour policies in the sense of the resistance which is actually posed to union demands, and of the relative strength of unions and workforces in the sense of their ability to hold out successfully.

One of the most interesting differences between conditions in India and those in the Netherlands relates to this dimension of the time it takes to reach a settlement. In negotiations in Holland, at least in those companies where we asked this question, agreements are generally reached within three to five months. This contrasts with an average bargaining cycle in Bombay (based on 112 settlements) of 12.97 or almost thirteen months. In other words, on average it takes three times as long to reach a settlement in Bombay as it does in the Netherlands. One factor which immediately accounts for this difference is the *duration* of agreements. Since most Dutch agreements are valid for one year, the nature of the agreement itself forms a silent pressure to settle with some degree of rapidity. Conversely, in India, longer durations allow the bargaining cycle to fluctuate around just over a year. As Table 2.4 shows, the average cycle for foreign-controlled plants is almost the same as the overall average bargaining cycle for Bombay.

TABLE 2.4
Bargaining Cycles in Domestic and Bombay Plants

Plant	Cycle (in Months)
Unilever (Netherlands)	4–5
Shell (Netherlands)	4
Bombay average (n=112)	12.97
Bombay foreign plants (n=40)	12.95
Philips Kalwa	15.80
Hindustan Lever Sewree	20.60

This is an interesting result because it emphasises once more the strong influence of local practice on the labour relations of foreign companies. Indeed, as the figures in Table 2.4 show, in the Bombay plants of both Philips and Hindustan Lever their last settlements took longer than average, which implies strong resistance from their managements as well as a determined workforce capable of holding out in the face of such resistance.

Recently, long bargaining cycles in Bombay industry have resulted from management's practice of presenting its own demands and insisting that they be discussed along with those of the union. This aspect has been crucial to recent conflicts in the Philips plants in India. In the preamble to the 1981 settlement for the Pune factories the company states:

> WHEREAS the Philips Employees' Union, Regd. No. 4206 (hereinafter referred to as the 'Union') . . . submitted a Charter of Demands to the Company vide their letter No. (etc.) . . . . AND WHEREAS the Company submitted their Charter of Demands to the Philips Employees' Union vide their letter No. . . .

This style of intervention was well in advance of most management thinking at that time. In fact, these demands were at the heart of the eighty-one-day lockout which hit the Pune factories in April 1981, the conclusion of which was the settlement cited above. The main issue behind this conflict, a turning-point in the history of labour relations in Philips India and prelude to even sharper conflicts in the future, was the management's demand for tight control over standards of production with the productivity levels established through time study forming 'rated levels of production,' i.e., norms, and with the management free to establish revised rated levels of production in case of changes on existing product lines. In short, more or less absolute management control over the whole area of deployment, manning and work standards was what Philips wanted from the 1981 settlement for Pune.[12]

Not only did the company lose eighty-one days' production in its drive to enforce these demands against strong resistance, but Philips management in other locations continued to press demands of a similar character even at the risk of considerable disruption and renewed conflict. In 1985, in the light factory at Kalwa, management demands for flexibility would lead to a strike of 105 days. Here the trouble started because the management, who presented their own charter initially but dropped their demands in the course of negotiations, then decided to enforce those demands unilaterally in the period after a settlement was reached. Even after the strike was called off early in 1986, it seems that the same attitude of unilateralism prevailed, compelling the union to protest in a letter to the factory manager:

It was mutually agreed that the issue regarding revision of the manning pattern (in the Olivotto plant) would be sorted out by the parties mutually. [But] management . . . did not bother to discuss the issue of revision of manning pattern of the Olivotto plant . . . . It appears that the management is very conveniently construing the term cooperation as the union's consent to anything and everything the management proposes . . . . (S.K. Lotlikar, Philips Workers' Union, letter dated 22 May 1986).

Lever management in India has always proceeded more cautiously but with even greater unilateralism. Instead of placing formal demands on the unions (e.g., in the Sewree factory demands regarding the introduction of high speed machines on the packing lines and redeployment of staff), Hindustan Lever prefers to write into the agreement for manual grades a general statement to the effect that 'The workmen and the Union will cooperate with the Company in carrying out modernisation programme and work to the company norms,' and then specifies in an annexure to the agreement precisely what equipment it proposes to install, listing the machines in detail. The agreement also says that 'The Company stated that approximately 150 workmen would be redeployed in the factory . . . .' In the head office, the management has pressed its demands for computerisation and a ceiling on DA by refusing to settle staff claims for years on end—charters submitted around 1968 were finally settled in 1977, through adjudication; demands forwarded in the late seventies were finally adjudicated in December 1985—and always forcing a settlement of issues in court.

Tables 2.5 and 2.6 summarise information gathered on the kinds of demands managements have been pressing on unions in the last few years and the priorities underlying those demands. As in Philips Pune, *standards of work intensity* continued to rate highest in what managements were after in the early eighties, against the background of a general drive to enforce cost reductions, reduce staff, increase flexibility and introduce higher levels of automation. *Flexibility* on the shop floor was wanted mainly to allow for the reorganisation of workloads and manning levels following the introduction of new high-speed equipment, the creation of 'surplus' staff, and their redeployment elsewhere in the factory. *Ceilings on dearness allowance* were directed mainly against employees in companies where a double linkage DA scheme (see p. 63) would

TABLE 2.5

Management Demands in Recent Rounds of Negotiation in Some Foreign-controlled Firms Around Bombay

SKF (Pune)	Increased work intensity, 25 per cent more production, pay rise linked to equalisation of efficiency levels
Philips (Pune)	Determination of manning levels to achieve management rated levels of production, introduction of new processes, equipment, machines, interchange-ability, continuous working, elimination of wasteful practices
Otis (Bombay)	Subcontracting, abolition of restrictive practices such as refusal to operate new machines, production norms
Metal Box (Bombay)	Increase in productivity in General Line and Open Top divisions
Philips (Kalwa)	Flexibility across jobs and departments, management control over man-to-man relieving, tight control over leave facilities, increased working hours following new schedule of transport timings, restrictions on late coming, compulsory overtime in essential services
Hindustan Lever (Bombay staff)	Drastic ceiling on dearness allownace as a curb on staff pay levels
ICI (Bombay staff)	Computerisation and reorganisation of office, ceiling on dearness allowance, abolition of specific staff practices
May & Baker (Bombay)	Abolition of fifteen-minutes grace period, 180 days attendance as eligibility for fringe benefits, 5–15 per cent increase in production on individual lines, restrictions on casual and maternity leave
Hoechst (Bombay)	Restrictions on leave availability, late attendance, early off, increased working hours, automation, outside contracts for maintenance

Source: Ascertained directly from unions, in some instances from annexures to agreements.

have been negotiated or introduced by an award at some stage in the sixties, with the result that in the inflation of the seventies the major part of earnings had outstripped management control. But employers could have a more specific motive in trying to establish ceilings: since the operation of double linkage schemes would have the result that employees on high basics, e.g., certain staff categories or workers in the higher production grades, could be earning as much as the lower management categories on consolidated scales, the demand for a ceiling could reflect the purely normative consideration that certain pay differentials are appropriate and

TABLE 2.6

Management Priorities: The Distribution of Management Demands According to Main Objectives (No. of demands = 116)

Management Objective	Per cent of All Demands Mentioned/Listed
Higher production standards incl. extra jobs, demanning, etc.	24.1
Increased flexibility and control over work practices	14.7
Ceilings on dearness allowance (DA)	14.7
Demands related to working hours, leave, time, shift-work, etc.	15.5
Automation and modernisation	10.3
Workforce reduction	7.8
Subcontracting explicitly wanted	2.6
Others	10.3
	100.0

Source: As in Table 2.5.

that payment formulas which threaten to erode such differentials are fundamentally opposed to the interests of employers.

To sum up: both in their way of using management demands and in their enforcement of long bargaining cycles and a decentralised bargaining structure, we find the managements of Philips and Unilever as well as other international companies *confirming*, not modifying, the general pattern of Bombay industrial relations, with no discernible influence from the parent concerns.

PAY AND BENEFITS

3.1 EARNINGS STRUCTURE

Like the bargaining structure, the actual structuring of pay is deeply fragmented on national and regional lines; in the Bombay subsidiaries of multinational companies, the earnings structure is determined by local practice and there is no resemblance between this and the domestic practices of those companies. In this context, 'pay structuring' refers to the relative weight of the various components which make up the gross pay of employees. One of the most interesting issues here is what differences in earnings structure mean for the degree of *management control* over pay. For the Netherlands, Leijnse has argued that collective bargaining in fact has less influence on pay determination than decisions which are at management's discretion and not regulated in the contract. Control over job classification, the operation of performance appraisal schemes and the freedom to promote and transfer are 'only the most striking mechanisms in a whole series of possibilities which employers have to fix the pay of "their" employees unilaterally' [1981, p. 122]. Teulings has also shown how a company like Philips has been able to minimise the impact of bargaining on pay determination.

Much of the ground is controlled through job grading and merit rating, matters which in practice are still completely controlled by management but which from one year to the next are at least as important for the pay packet of a Philips employee as the outcome of discussions with the unions [1977, p. 269].

3.1.1 Annual increments: seniority versus merit rating

This dimension of the pay structure summarises an important difference in pay structuring between Dutch and Indian industry, especially within the Philips group.[13] In most Bombay establishments, indeed, in any which are covered by some form of collective agreement, there is an automatic progression in basic pay due to annual increments. The distribution of these increments across the salary range for individual grades and between different grades is structured so as to allow for the influence of job levels as well as increasing seniority (length of service in the company). In other words, higher grades receive higher annual increments and within grades the increment increases for higher steps in the scale. A similar system is used in the Netherlands. Unilever has automatic increments, and for the middle grades where most of the workforce is found the average incremental rate varies from 1.9 to 2.5 per cent. This is certainly better than Philips and probably above the average for most companies, for example ICI, where for the main operator grades the average varies from 1.7 to 1.9 per cent, or Shell, where the variation is similar. However, there are at least three forms in which the seniority impact is modified in Dutch pay scales. First, for an important group of young workers who might account for over 10 per cent of a company's labour force, the level of pay depends on the employee's *age*. This is generally true of workers in the age-group 16–22. For example, in the Unilever pay scales, if you are 16 and you join the company in one of the bargainable grades, your basic is 55 per cent of the base salary for the grade; at 17 this becomes 60 per cent and so on, till you get 95 per cent at the age of 22. In the metal industry agreement, this cut-off point is called the 'age of vocational maturity,' and defined as 'the age by which employees have generally gained enough experience to be able to perform their jobs independently'. But seniority in the purely industrial sense of 'length of service' is a more egalitarian principle since it is directly related to industrial experience whereas biological age does not necessarily correlate with industrial experience in any precise way. Biological age has no place in the determination of pay in Bombay companies.

Secondly, the span over which annual increments extend in Dutch pay scales tends to be shorter than the corresponding range in Bombay. For example, annual increments operate for eleven years at the most in the Unilever scales. Most workers in the Dutch establishments of Unilever come under grades 3–6, and in these grades the ceiling is reached after just seven or eight years. Further increase in pay will then not be automatic but will depend on promotions. In Bombay pay structures, the span is at least twice as long as this, and recently there has been a general drive to negotiate even longer grade spans as a form of pay increase. This happened in the last agreement for the Philips fatory at Kalwa. In Philips Netherlands, it is not possible to determine precisely what the span of the grade is, but in view of the differential in pay between the start and the end of the grade and in view of the average rate of increment conceded to employees in the grade, workers in grade 20, one of the major production grades in Philips, would reach the maximum within five years. Contrast this with the movement of a worker in SS-2 (the main corresponding job group at Kalwa) who starts on a basic of Rs 110 and takes thirty-five years to reach the grade maximum of Rs 501. Again, whereas Unilever allows at most eleven years for its domestic plants, Hindustan Lever scales for hourly-rated workmen extend for a length of eighteen years. And whereas middle grades in ICI Holland reach the maximum in eight years, the corresponding groups at ICI's Terene works in Bombay have a grade span of twenty-three years. So employees in Holland lose their seniority payments (increments) much sooner.

Thirdly, in Philips at any rate, management determines salary progression through merit rating. Annual increments are not automatic payments, but pay increases which depend on the company's appraisal of an employee's performance. Thus, the influence of seniority on the pay structure is drastically reduced in this case through a form of unilateral determination of pay by the management. Pay information for Philips reveals that the average increment for workers who have not yet reached the base salary for the grade is 1.7 per cent, and the average for those (the majority) who are moving between the base salary and the maximum for their grade is 1.8 per cent. (The range of possible increments is 0, 1 per cent, 1.5 per cent and 2 per cent.) These rates are an expression of Philips management's overall evaluation of Philips workers' performance and 'contribution' to the company. For the lower grades it tends to be lower, 1.5 per cent for grade 20 where most of the 'semi-skilled' work is concentrated, and generally (on average) 2 per cent for the highest skilled grades. There is considerable employee dissatisfaction about the workings of this system in some of the Philips establishments. When van Vliet studied conditions at NKF-Delft in the mid-seventies, he found that one of the problems there 'concerned pay differences resulting from differences in performance appraisal (*beoordeling*). This mainly affected employees classified in the higher grades, 6–11. For the lower job groups management had abolished the system under union pressure' [1979, p. 317]. At the Philips factory in Nijmegen there was a strong feeling among workers that payment and performance appraisal should be delinked, that appraisal should be used only for promotions, and that 'there has to be equal pay for equal work' (Buitelaar and Vreeman [1985], p. 209). And at the Drachten plant, one of the demands mentioned in the *werknemersverslag* reads as follows: 'The people whose performance is rated should also have the chance to rate the performance of the performance raters' (p. 214). What workers were challenging here was the purely hierarchical basis of the whole merit-rating system. Why does the rating always proceed from the top downwards? The same objections have been stated by the Philips employees in other parts of the world. For example, one of the points made about Philips UK by the ASTMS is that 'Pay structures, particularly the Hay senior staff one, allow too much unilateral management control in the form of the merit increments. Automatic incremental progression is the trade union objective' (ASTMS, *Tackling a Multinational*).

Of course, Philips is not the only company in Holland where there are employee grievances about merit rating. In Fokker, a major grievance concerns 'the way people are treated at the end of the year when they get their performance bonus' (interview), but here it was also claimed that there is underlying support for a system of this sort in the greater individualism of workers' ideas about pay.

3.1.2 Dearness allowance

The main difference in the earnings structure between the Netherlands and Bombay plants concerns the enormously greater weight in Bombay of that portion of earnings which is linked to the consumer price index. The portion is known as 'dearness allowance' (equivalent to the Dutch 'price compensation' payments), and forms the single most important component of pay in most Bombay companies. The actual amount of DA depends on the type of the DA scheme: in 'flat rate' schemes it is linked only to the consumer price index (CPI) and not to basic pay; in 'percentage' or 'double linkage' schemes it is proportional to basic pay as well as to the CPI, so that 'every paisa' of basic is said to attract DA; and in 'salary group' schemes it is linked to basic pay in a looser form. Since fluctuations in the level of consumer prices are not something employers can directly control (even if they can influence the computation of the index), DA is an area of pay determination initially outside management control. This has crucial implications for labour relations in a city like Bombay because it means that in periods of rapid or anticipated inflation, managements are likely to press for greater determination of this part of pay by modifying the schemes which govern the actual payment of DA. Efforts of this sort have involved a drive to enforce ceilings or reductions in the amount of DA negotiated under previous settlements (as in Lever's Bombay head office and Garden Reach factory in Calcutta, and so many other foreign-controlled companies) or get employees to accept consolidated scales (as in Parke-Davis and Hoechst).

3.1.3 Shift payments

Payments for shift-work have greater relative significance for Dutch pay levels. The rates of shift allowance actually paid in some big companies are summarised in Table 3.1. There is a considerable difference in the level of shift payments, which stems from the greater opposition to shift-working of workers in Holland in contrast with India. For example, a famous survey conducted by Philips in the fifties revealed that 41 per cent of employees working shifts preferred to opt out of shift-work, even if this meant a reduction in pay. Thirty-six per cent said they accepted shift-work only because of the extra earnings. Around 50–77 per cent of workers complained of loss of sleep, headaches, backaches, poor appetite and so on (Teulings [1977], p. 217). Since the whole tendency of Dutch industry involves the extension of shift-work and more widespread application of those forms of shift-work which are likely to impose the maximum strain on its workforce, employers realise that extremely high payments for shift-work are

TABLE 3.1
Rates of Shift Allowance in the Netherlands and Bombay

| A. NETHERLANDS | Per cent of gross salary paid for working on: | | | |
	2-shift system	3-shift system	continuous shifts 4/5	5
Shell	15	21	30	
ICI Holland	10–13*	20	28.5	
Unilever	12	19	22–27†	
Philips	16	19.5	39	24

| B. BOMBAY | 3-shift system: Rs per shift worked | | |
	first	second	third
Nocil	5.00	10.00	15.00
ICI/CAFI	1.00	2.00	4.00
Hindustan Lever	0.50	0.50	2.50**
Philips Kalwa	0	2.00	4.00
Philips Pune	0	2.00	5.00
Philips head office	0	5.00	7.00
Sandoz	2.25	3.75	5.25
BASF	2.00	3.00	6.00
Bayer	2.00	4.00	6.00
Roche	1.00	2.50	3.50
Metal Box	0	0	1.00
SKF Pune	0	1.50	1.50
	Per cent of gross salary		
Ciba-Geigy	4	10	12
Hoechst	2	8	12
Roussel	4.5	5	6

Source: The most recent settlements available for each company; for Bombay, cf.
             URG, no. 5, 1984, and URG, no. 8, 1986.
Notes: * varying according to inclusion/exclusion of Saturday work.
             † varies according to the number of shifts worked on Saturday or Sunday,
               with 27% for more than 45 such shifts, 24% for 31–45 shifts and 22%
               for less than 31.
             ** the formula is 12.5% of basic only + Rs 2.00 for the night shift.

the only means by which they can ensure that people work shifts.
In companies like Shell and ICI Holland, plant operators on
continuous shifts could conceivably earn f1000 or more as shift
allowance (*ploegentoeslag*), whereas the maximum which equivalent job groups are likely to earn in Bombay chemical plants is at
least twenty times less than that. Most companies in India pay shift
allowance at a flat rate and the rates are consistently low. Another
crucial difference is that in Dutch practice the shift payment is
usually *included* in the gross salary which counts for payment of

another important benefit, the *vacantietoeslag* or what Bombay settlements call 'leave travel assistance'. This, of course, is not the case in Bombay where the only components of pay which generally count for calculations of this sort are basic and dearness allowance.

The massive difference in rates of shift allowance is a strong argument for unions in subsidiary plants of international firms to press for a substantial increase in those rates. High shift payments are not a peculiarity of Dutch industry but appear to be common to most European countries. For example, plants controlled by Unilever in the UK (van den Bergh & Jurgens at Bromborough or plants in Walls Ice Cream) pay night shift allowance at the rate of 33 per cent of basic pay, a UK basic being comparable to what in India would be called gross salary. Let us take a concrete example of what an application of this sort of rate would mean for workers in the Unilever factory at Sewree. Take an F grade operator whose job title is 'Attendant—filling machine' in the shampoo department, or a 'Feeder' in hard soaps. If they were entitled to a night shift allowance which is 33 per cent of their gross salary as this is defined in the agreement for Lever, then the contrast would look like this, calculated in rupees:

	Shift allowance for F grade operator on	
	present basis	*hypothetical basis*
Hourly basic for worker at 15th step in scale	0.74	0.74
Basic converted into rate per day (8 hrs.)	5.92	5.92
DA earned on ii. at CPI no. 2600	59.08	59.08
Settlement wages per day (÷ 26)	2.69	2.69
Gross salary per day	67.69	67.69
Payment for night shift	*2.74*	*22.34*

But, of course, one is not likely to see anything comparable in terms of payments for shift-work in countries like India until the union movements in these countries reflect the same general and widespread opposition to shift-working which prevails in countries like Holland.

3.1.4 Vacation payments

Leave Travel Assistance (LTA) is another area where considerable disparity exists. In part this is due to the fact that under Dutch law (and specifically the law governing minimum wages and minimum vacation allowance) there is a *prescribed minimum payment for vacations*, but there is nothing comparable in India. Indeed, till the early seventies the level of earnings depended entirely on the basic and DA since benefits like LTA and house rent allowance (HRA) were simply unknown in Bombay. HRA had only just been introduced in the late sixties and LTA was probably first negotiated in the ICI and Glaxo settlements for 1971. Even these were early breakthroughs pioneered in companies with a union tradition, and the movement introducing supplementary benefits suffered a sharp decline with the recession and Emergency of the middle seventies. Generalisation of fringe benefits to most companies really only started as recently as 1978, and in the early eighties these items of pay rapidly increased in value as Bombay unions began to encounter stiff management opposition in the core areas (revision of basic pay or improvements in DA).

Whereas in Holland the vacation allowance is always expressed as a percentage of the annual salary (except for a specified minimum which is stated as an absolute amount), in Bombay settlements LTA is generally paid as an absolute amount, though not always at a single rate. One formula which has become popular recently is payment of LTA at the rate of 'one month's gross'; in percentage terms this is of course 8.33 per cent, in cash terms at least five times as high as the rate applicable to most Philips employees in India. Table 3.2 shows that the rates of LTA paid by Philips are quite abysmal *even by local standards*. The rates in Hindustan Lever are also below average.

3.1.5 Bonus

In the Netherlands, it emerged from discussions with the union that in Unilever there used to be a profit-sharing bonus till quite recently but that this has now been merged with the salary. In Philips, workers receive a profit bonus equivalent to 6 per cent of gross salary for a base dividend payment of 18 per cent; for each per cent above 18 the bonus increases by 0.15 per cent, and for each per cent below the base decreases by 0.10 per cent (Philips cl. 26, pp. 28–29). It appears from local discussions that in cash terms an average payment of this bonus might be around *f*2000 per year. Thus, for Philips there is a precise estimate of how much the main fringe benefits bring workers: 10 per cent paid as the vacation

TABLE 3.2
Vacation Allowance Internationally and Locally

	Per cent of Annual Salary	Minimum (in f)	
Philips	10	2,838	(c. Rs. 10,785)
ICI Holland	8	2,766	(c. Rs. 10,500)
Unilever	7.5	2,375	(c. Rs. 9,025)
	(in Rs)	(in Rs)	
Philips Kalwa	360	360	
Philips staff	850	850	
Hindustan Lever	600	500	
ICI/CAFI	690	690	
Roussel	1,800	1,500	
Roussel staff	2,425	2,425	
Bayer	2,400	2,160	
Ralliwolf	1,500	1,500	
Atlas Copco	1,300	1,000	
SKF	1,680	900	
Sandvik Asia	1,440	1,440	
	Per cent of gross annual salary		
Nocil	12.5		

Source: The latest settlements for each company; where the rate of LTA varies according to grade, length of service, level of basic and so on, the figure cited on the left is an estimated average.

allowance (called the 'June and December payment' since it is paid in two instalments, 7 per cent in June and 3 per cent in December), and 6 per cent paid as the profit-sharing bonus. In ICI, the bonus payment is called the '13th month,' and as its name implies works out to 8.33 per cent of the gross. If the vacation allowance is added to this, the main supplementary payments work out to around 16 per cent of the gross, as in Philips. Finally, in the Shell agreement a distinction is drawn between the 'basic salary' for the year and the annual 'contractual income' which includes fringe benefits, and the difference between them is two months' gross or 16.66 per cent. This suggests that there is considerable *standardisation* in Dutch industry, at least with respect to the level of the major fringe benefits, in sharp contrast to the enormous *dispersion* of fringe benefit levels within the Bombay labour market area.

In India, before recent amendments to the Bonus Act, a statutory ceiling restricted the payment of bonus to a maximum of Rs 1,800.

This was vastly out of line with what many companies could in fact afford to pay and progressively, under union pressure, companies in Bombay paid the extra amounts as 'ex gratia'. In most cases the ex gratia would have been either equal to or far in excess of the bonus amount. Since this practice became more or less general, it was clear that the Act would have to be modified. This happened recently and involved two crucial modifications: first, the ceiling was raised to Rs 3,840; secondly, coverage by the Act, i.e., entitlement to bonus payments according to the terms of the Act, was extended quite substantially, from Rs 1,600 gross salary as the upper limit, to Rs 2,500.

Nothing is more indicative of the general tenor of the management's labour relations policy in Hindustan Lever and Philips than the ways in which they have chosen to use the Bonus Act, or interpretations of the Act, to impose restrictions on pay. In Lever's case this meant that staff members whose gross was in excess of Rs 1,600, obviously the majority, were denied any bonus payment at all, contrary to the evolving custom and practice of large concerns who were settling the bonus claims of their employees with ex gratia payments running into several thousands of rupees. In taking this line with its clerical employees, Hindustan Lever earned the dubious distinction of being one of only three companies paying no bonus at all in an overall survey of almost two hundred bonus settlements (URG, *Bulletin* no. 5, 1984). Since in the case of employees at the Sewree factory, management paid the bonus amount of Rs 1,800 as ex gratia, it seems that there is some basis for the claim made by the head office staff union that the Lever management have always had a policy of 'divide and rule,' 'splitting staff and workers over issues like bonus' (interview).

The recent amendments to the Act threw bargaining over bonus into considerable confusion since disputes arose over (*a*) interpretation of the valid financial year for payment of bonus at the new rates, (*b*) the level of ex gratia payments, and (*c*) payment of arrears where employees had already received bonus. In this welter of confusion, Philips management actually pressed for the *recovery* of an amount of Rs 200 from the payments already made to each employee, on the grounds that against an actual disbursement of Rs 1,800, the company felt unable to pay more than the minimum bonus of Rs 1,600 under amendments to the Act. Bonus thus became a further ground of dispute in Philips India.[14]

Payment practices with respect to bonus/ex gratia are an excellent criterion in terms of which to describe management characteristics or the overall style of labour relations policies. They generally form the dividing line between progressive companies with stable relations and firms where managements have declared lockouts over the issue (in Mukand recently), or imposed an enormous strain on already tense relations (in Philips), or relied on a superior bargaining position to back up refusal to pay any bonus at all (in Bharat Petroleum, formerly Burmah-Shell but now run by the central government). Foreign as well as Indian firms can be found on both sides of the divide; while firms like Philips and Hindustan Lever, on the international side, restrict the level of their payments by using the Bonus Act as a pretext, the Mahindra plants in Kandivli or the engineering plants in the Rallis group have disbursed ex gratia amounts well in excess of Rs 3,000, at levels comparable to Boots, Burroughs Wellcome, Hoechst or Pfizer, and certainly higher than the payments made by Bayer, BASF, Union Carbide and many other foreign companies.

In short, by contrast with the standardisation characteristic of similar payments in Dutch industry, there is considerable variation in the overall level of payments received by workers in Bombay as fringe benefits and this variation is at least partly rooted in management characteristics of a more general type.

3.1.6 Acting allowance

This is the term for an allowance paid to employees for performing a job assignment in a grade higher than his/her own. Such assignments are usually for short periods, but managements may sometimes use them on a more long-term basis as a way of reducing the rate of promotions. Differences in minimum qualifying periods and the payment formulas used lead to considerable diversity between plants: in the Netherlands, Shell pays an acting allowance of 1 per cent of the gross for assignments in the next higher grade or 2 per cent for anything higher per unit of five days, with an important proviso about rounding off (e.g., six days would count as ten) (Shell, cl. 11, pp. 35–36). ICI Holland stipulates a minimum qualifying period of ten continuous days, and pays according to a formula common in Bombay companies: the difference between the minima of the grades concerned (ICI, cl. 7.1b, p. 14); in

Unilever, workers receive 0.23 per cent of the gross for acting one grade higher, 0.46 per cent for anything higher than that, and the qualifying period is half a shift.

In the Siemens plant at Kalwa, the qualifying period is a shift of eight hours with fixed rates per 'officiating level'; in the Richardson factory on the same road, the qualifying period is half a shift as in Unilever, with Rs 5 as the rate for a full shift; in Pfizer, five continuous days and 50 per cent of the difference between the two salaries. That managements may in fact make illicit use of acting assignments is shown by Philips practice in India; for example, the Pune settlement of 1981 says that workers who have officiated for an aggregate period of 120 days in a calender year will be considered for promotion, clearly implying that where use is made of acting, this can be for fairly long stretches, whereas earnings from such assignments are restricted to a maximum of Rs 35 per month (Philips Pune, cl. 14, p. 9).

3.1.7 Payment by results (PBR)

With two striking exceptions—the Firestone plant in Bombay which the Americans started in the forties and the SKF plant in Pune—PBR systems have never been of much significance in Bombay except in textiles. In companies which use incentive schemes of one form or another (GKW, Metal Box, Siemens and Hindustan Lever among foreign-controlled companies; Indian employers make more extensive use of such schemes as in Kirloskar Cummins, Mukand, Tomco, Kamani Engineering, etc.), payments would not exceed a few hundred rupees per month. In the Netherlands, such forms of payment systems, though fairly widespread at one time, have declined considerably since then so that among the main EEC countries the Netherlands actually accounts for the lowest proportion of workers on PBR (see Colenbrander [1982], p. 101, where for the late seventies the proportion cited is 15 per cent against 35 per cent in France and 45 per cent in the UK).

3.1.8 Overtime rates

Whereas in the Netherlands the share of fringe benefits in overall earnings displays a certain uniformity, the contribution of overtime varies much more due to variations in the *extent* of overtime working between establishments and between groups of employees, even if the *rates* are highly standardised. For overtime rates in Dutch plants see Table 3.3, where rates in the region of 0.87 per cent correspond to time-and-a-half, 1.16 per cent to double time, etc. In India, most types of overtime working are paid at twice the 'ordinary rate of wages,' which is restricted to the basic and DA.

TABLE 3.3
Overtime Rates in Dutch Agreements
(Per cent of gross monthly salary per hour of overtime)

ICI	Monday to Saturday inclusive	0.87	
	Sunday	1.16	*1.74*
	Paid holidays	1.74	*2.32*
	Monday to Friday inclusive		*1.16*
	Saturday		*1.45*
Shell	Monday to Saturday inclusive	0.87	*1.16*
	Sundays or paid holidays falling on weekdays	1.16	*1.45*
	Paid holidays falling on Saturday or Sunday	1.74	*2.03*
Unilever	Monday 6.00 a.m. to Saturday 2 p.m.	0.80	
	Saturday 2 p.m. to Monday 6 a.m.	1.07	
	Paid holidays	1.60	*2.14*
	Monday to Friday		*1.07*
	Saturday		*1.33*
	Sunday		*1.60*
Philips	*Minimum base rate for overtime payment calculation = f1,973 p.m.*		
	First two hours of overtime	0.72	
	More than two hours of overtime	0.86	
	Saturday, Sunday and paid holidays	1.15	

Source: CAOs for the companies concerned.
Note: Figures in italics are the overtime rates paid to workers on continuous shifts (*volcontinu*) for the roster-free days.

Overall, differences with respect to basic pay (its proportion as a part of the total pay packet) are the crucial form of inequality in the earnings structure of multinationals. Whereas in Holland, as in most Western countries, basic pay accounts for the major part of earnings, in Bombay it is common for basic to be less than Rs 100 at the start of lower grades. This suggests that one reason why it may be useful for multinational companies to decentralise labour relations is because it enables them to take advantage of the possibility of enforcing much lower basic rates in their plants in countries like India. However, unions in most big companies in the Bombay area have to a large extent succeeded in offsetting the abysmally low level of basic pay by obtaining DA rates which far outweigh the basic within the total wage. In the past few years, some companies have responded by negotiating for the consolidation of DA into the basic wage in order to reduce the rapid increase of the price index-linked component. This results in a wage structure more closely resembling the pattern in Holland and other Western countries.

The disparity in the weight of shift payments is another striking difference. There is no possible basis for this disparity since the disruptive effects of shift-work are the same everywhere in the world. But lack of standardisation allows multinational companies to take advantage of the lower resistance to shift-work in countries like India by paying allowances which are miserable by Western standards.

On the other hand, Bombay workforces have succeeded in limiting management control over pay by obtaining automatic annual increments with long grade spans; in this case, decentralising labour relations enables managements to retain greater control over wage progression in Holland through the use of short grade spans and merit rating.

3.2 RELATIVE PAY

This section deals with *levels* of pay as opposed to differences in the structure of earnings or individual pay components. How much more do Philips and Unilever pay workforces in their domestic plants as compared to workers in their Bombay subsidiaries? It might be argued that international differences in pay partly reflect differences in the cost of living; but before we can decide how much of the difference in one is due to the difference in the other, we would have to have a more precise conception of the order of magnitude of the differences themselves: is the international differential between plants in the Netherlands and plants of the same company in Bombay or Pune 3:1, or is it 6:1 or even 10:1? We have attempted to obtain an approximate answer to this question by comparing average gross pay for Philips and Unilever in the Netherlands with average total pay for the Philips plant in Kalwa and the Hindustan Lever plant in Sewree.

A second comparison (pay differences between Philips'

establishments in Holland) shows that in contrast to the pattern in India, there is very low pay dispersion in Dutch pay levels. Finally, how do Philips and Hindustan Lever rate in terms of Bombay-area pay levels? And how do Philips and Unilever compare with other large companies in the Netherlands? The first comparison is made in terms of 130 plants in and around Bombay. The second comparison is not one we can make in any precise way, but it has been possible to secure reliable pay information about two other companies and so some comparison has been attempted.

3.2.1 The scale of international differences: an indication

A problem arises in deciding which components of pay to use in an international comparison. In Bombay usage, 'gross salary' generally includes only basic and DA, except in cases where certain special allowances are explicitly said to attract overtime, etc.; i.e., the base for calculation of overtime payments and those supplementary benefits which are expressed as a percentage of gross salary is these two, or possibly three, components of pay. On the other hand, in the Netherlands the gross or 'bruto' amount includes payments for shift-work, the vacation allowance and end-of-year bonus. Thus, what is called 'total pay' in Bombay, which includes the main supplementary benefits, is a closer equivalent to 'gross pay' in the Netherlands. Table 3.6 (see p. 75) summarises the calculation of average total pay for Philips Kalwa and Hindustan Lever Sewree, and Table 3.4 compares these figures with gross pay for Philips and Unilever in the Netherlands.

TABLE 3.4
International Pay Differences in Philips and Unilever

	Average Pay				
	Netherlands		Bombay		International Differential
	f per month	Rs per month	f per month	Rs per month	
Philips	4,068.25	15,459.35	641.76	2,438.70	6.34:1
Unilever	4,516.67	17,163.33	620.83	2,359.14	7.28:1

Source: Philips, 'Inkomensspreiding 1984 in decielen'; Nederlandse Unilever Bedrijven b.v., *Personeeljaarverslag 1985*, bijlage p. 2.
Note: Conversion at Rs. 3.8 to the guilder.

According to Table 3.4, Philips' international differential is 6.34:1, Unilever's is 7.28:1. As we show below for Philips, low pay dispersion in the Netherlands implies that individual establishments have levels of pay close to the average. In India, by contrast, most companies display high pay dispersion even within restricted geographical zones (e.g., in Bombay between the Kalwa and Pune plants of Philips, or the Sewree and Taloja plants of Hindustan Lever). It is, therefore, likely that a comparison with these other plants would yield a much higher international differential.

3.2.2 Pay characteristics within the Philips group in Holland

Table 3.5 compares pay across the Dutch establishments/divisions of Philips. In each case the figures refer to the average pay of the grade at the start of the year indicated. The Philips pay structure, in the sense of the pay relationships which prevail in the company as a whole across all product divisions and individual plants, displays two very significant features: (*a*) *extremely low pay dispersion*, which is strong proof of the tight centralisation of pay levels imposed by Philips through the kind of bargaining structure it has; and (*b*) *huge intra-establishment differentials between manual grades and higher personnel*; this refers in particular to the difference in pay between grades 15–45, covered by the agreement for the bulk of the Philips labour force (some 70 per cent), and grades 50–80 who are covered by a separate agreement where the main union involved is the Federation of Philips Higher Personnel. In the Light and Glass groups these grades earn *over twice as much* as the main production grades taken as a whole, and the differential between the lower job groups and the qualified grades is even sharper; the ratio of the highest to lowest grade (80/15) in the light group is 4.8:1.

3.2.3 Bombay plants: local pay relationships

The first exercise one could perform on the data pertaining to pay scales in Bombay involves comparing the average total pay at Philips Kalwa and Hindustan Lever Sewree (see Table 3.6 for the calculation) across the whole Bombay labour market with all sorts of other companies, foreign and local, regardless of their specific type of production or industrial classification. This is one valid

TABLE 3.5
Relative Pay in the Dutch Philips Plants

Main Industry Group or Establishment	Year	Grade	Annual Pay in f
Terneuzen light factory	1985	20	26,196
		25	28,290
Machinefabrieken Eindhoven	1984	15–45	34,008
HIG Glas	1984	20	29,383
		25	30,796
		15–45	34,412
		50–80	70,673
HIG Licht	1984	15	28,142
		20	29,027
		25	30,730
		15–45	33,370
		50–80	70,250
		80	136,435
Weert light factory	1984	20	26,604
		15–45	29,472
Elcoma Display Systems	1985	20	26,844
		25	28,512
		45	45,048
		15–45	32,232

Source: Philips, *Sociaal Jaarverslagen*, SOBE files.

TABLE 3.6
A Calculation of Average Total Pay of Philips and Hindustan Lever
(Rs per month at CPI No. 2600)

	Philips	Hindustan Lever
Basic + DA	1,780.21	1,637.14
Special allowances	90.00	222.00
Leave Travel Assistance	30.00	50.00
House Rent Allowance	93.50	130.00
Education Allowance	20.00	0
Incentive payment	0	170.00
Bonus	133.33	150.00
Ex gratia	291.66	0
Total	2,438.70	2,359.14

Note: For Philips the special allowance (personal allowance) and ex gratia figures, for Hindustan Lever the incentive payment are averages estimated by the union.

comparison since it tells us which firms pay the most in the local area. The only criteria in terms of which plants enter this sample are their general form of manufacturing and their location within a fairly massive approximately defined geographical area.[15]

The results of this comparison are as follows: out of a total of 130 plants, mostly in the Bombay area, Philips ranks nineteenth, Hindustan Lever twenty-eighth. When we average the pay of the top five (Herdillia, Boots, Ralliwolf, Roussel and Burroughs Wellcome—at CPI No. 2600 their average works out to Rs 2,925 per month)[16] they are found to pay precisely 20 per cent more than Philips and 24 per cent more than Hindustan Lever.

A second form of comparison involves restricting the size of our sample to those concerns which are arguably most 'comparable' in terms of size and industry characteristics, reducing the definition of pay to the more primordial elements defined in Bombay companies as 'gross salary' and concentrating only on those production grades within the factory which account for the largest share of the workforce. Gross pay for these grades is compared at the start of the grade and after 15 years' service. The overall effect of this comparison should reinforce the impressions gained from the first one since both claim to be accurate in their own ways.

Table 3.7 summarises the results of this more reductive and disaggregated comparison. Here the light factory at Kalwa is compared with eight comparable concerns, not all of them foreign-controlled. The comparison is on gross salary (as defined in Bombay) for the *major production grade* in the sense just indicated. The particular grades which have been used for this comparison are identified in column 2 by their name in the company's classification scheme. On average close to a third of the production workforce (excluding clerical, administrative and technical grades) falls under the grade selected for comparison, so these grades are certainly quite representative of plant wage levels. On the other hand, because representativeness in this sense was thought more significant, it is not always the case that precisely the same job groups are being compared; by and large, however, the production grades whose pay is compared here are semi-skilled groups in the middle ranges of the plant grade structure. For Hindustan Lever the most obvious comparison is with Tomco because of similar product structures, jobs and job groups, and because of the close physical proximity of these plants. Three grades are compared for

TABLE 3.7

Relative Pay: Pay Comparisons for Comparable Concerns in Sectors where Philips and Unilever Operate in Bombay
(calculated at CPI number 2600)

Company	Grade Name	Per cent Share*	Start of Scale				After 15 Years' Service			
			Basic	DA	PA†	Total	Basic	DA	PA	Total
Comparisons valid for Philips (Kalwa)										
Ralliwolf	IA	26	286	1711.50		1997.50	841.10	1816.00		2657.10
Tata Electric	VI	30	345	1161.61		1506.61	630	1973.25		2603.25
Mahindra Auto	Sk'B'	31.5	84.50	1256.95	100	1441.45	198.90	2107.79	200	2506.69
Rallifan	III	36	126.10	1586.00		1712.10	274.30	1646.00		1920.30
Voltas	4	40	110	1270.50		1380.50	305	1815.00		2120.00
Philips	SS-2	33	110	1319.75		1429.75	257	1650.00	90**	1997.00
Otis	Sk'B'	21	84.50	1409.90		1494.40	214.50	1622.50		1837.00
Larsen & Toubro	SSK'A'	33	74.10	942.67	190	1206.77	195.78	1809.26	205	2210.04
Siemens	3	30	175	1134.00	125	1434.00	375.00	1512.00	210	2097.00
Comparisons valid for Hindustan Lever (Sewree)										
Tata Oil Mills	E	36.5	83.20	1049.20		1132.40	200.20	1832.11		2032.31
Colgate	III	72	80	972.00		1052.00	210	1738.40		1948.40
Hindustan Lever	C	20.5	69.68	984.58	70	1124.26	126.88	1372.62	70	1569.50
Tata Oil Mills	D	37.5	109.20	1280.80		1390.00	249.60	1982.90		2232.50
Hindustan Lever	E	22	74.88	984.58	70	1129.46	137.28	1435.54	70	1642.82
Tata Oil Mills	C	15	124.80	1375.41		1500.21	284.70	2090.25		2374.95
Hindustan Lever	F	22	81.12	984.58	70	1135.70	153.92	1536.22	70	1760.14

Source: The most recent settlements available for each company

* percentage share of the grade concerned in the total production workforce. In each case the largest production grade in the company.

† P.A. = Personal allowance, or Special Allowance (LT), or Special Pay + Service Pay (Mahindra), or Settlement wages (H.L.) included in these cases because they form part of 'gross salary', and count for the calculation of other benefits.

** an average cited by the Union, and not included for the start of the scale because new recruits into these grades would not receive any such allowance.

these plants, and Grade III of Colgate, containing 72 per cent of
the workforce, is also included in the comparison.

Even on this more restricted comparison, Hindustan Lever pays
less than Colgate and Tomco, especially at the more senior level
where Tomco employees earn as much as 35 per cent more than
Hindustan Lever employees. Philips ranks 7 out of 9 on both
starting pay and senior pay; in other words, Philips has the lowest
average rank in a group of nine comparable concerns, as Table 3.8
shows.

TABLE 3.8
**Philips and Comparable Concerns: Rankings on Relative Pay
for Main Production Grades**

Company	Starting Pay	Senior Pay
Ralliwolf	1	1
Tata Electric	3	2
Mahindra Auto	5	3
Rallifan	2	8
Siemens	6	6
Larsen & Toubro	9	4
Voltas	8	5
Otis	4	9
Philips	7	7

Note: The rankings relate to the calculations in Table 3.7.

Since the results are shown in a disaggregated form (cf. Table 3.7),
it is possible to comment on this ranking by identifying some
features responsible for it.

The first factor which could account for a ranking on average
pay is the way workers have been *classified*. If the majority of
workers are in low grades, the average grade level will be low (see
pp. 95-98); and the lower the average grade level, i.e., the worse
the classification from the point of view of the employees holding
the classified jobs, the greater the probability of low relative pay.
Both Philips and Hindustan Lever have very low average grade
levels.

Secondly, since the biggest part of earnings in much of Bombay
industry accrues under dearness allowance, the specific DA formula
or scheme which has been negotiated will obviously influence the
overall level of pay. Here the most important aspects are:

1. The *type of DA scheme* a union has accepted and whether or not this allows for linkage with the price index as well as basic pay. In the last round of negotiations at Kalwa, the Philips Workers' Union pressed for replacement of the existing salary group scheme by double linkage or percentage DA. This was a major union demand which the company successfully staved off, realising perfectly the implications of a move from one type of scheme to the other.

2. The other dimension in terms of which DA schemes can yield quite different amounts of pay is the possibility that management has been successful in negotiating a *ceiling* or overall restriction on DA. In the seventies ceilings on DA were a crucial management objective in several Bombay companies, and there developed a widespread and coordinated attack on double linkage DA which most unions failed to resist. Hindustan Lever is one of the few companies where double linkage survives without a ceiling, but management has been fighting a tenacious battle to have a ceiling imposed on head office staff. The Dongre Award of 1985 in fact gave the company a DA ceiling for basics above Rs 500, despite the observation that, 'It is contended (by the Company) that the financial position of the Company is sound and it *can afford to pay dearness allowance* as per the existing scheme . . . .' However the union appealed against the tribunal award and obtained a stay, basing its confidence on

> the judgement of the Supreme Court of India in the Indian Hume Pipe case, which has upheld . . . the principle of the payment of DA in accordance with the percentage system . . . . The Supreme Court went a step further when it stated, *Courts and Tribunals have necessarily to keep their hands off from upsetting a wage structure that has satisfactorily worked for a long time* (V. Ramnathan for the staff union).

Thirdly, since dearness allowance is linked to basic pay, the level of base rates is also a crucial consideration in the determination of average pay. Higher basics attract more DA, and it is important for unions to negotiate not just a good DA scheme but higher basics as well, since without the latter even a good DA scheme remains without much practical significance. One of the underlying reasons for Lever management's contrasting behaviour with respect to the ceiling on staff DA and proposals for a ceiling in the Sewree factory, the aggressiveness and persistence with which it went for the former by contrast with the lack of emphasis on the latter, is clearly related to the much lower levels of basic pay among manual grades. It has been the traditional practice of employers in India to fix starting basics at the lowest possible levels. For example, it is hard to believe but unfortunately true that even today a worker recruited into grade C in Unilever's Bombay factory would actually start on a basic of 33.5 paise per hour, which works out to Rs 2.68 per day or Rs 69.68 per month. In Philips the basic on which an 'unskilled' worker starts is Rs 85 per month. On the other hand, although the overall level is low, there is considerable dispersion in these rates between companies.

With the general framework constructed on these three factors, it is easier to explain why Philips and Hindustan Lever pay less than comparable concerns:

	PHILIPS	**HINDUSTAN LEVER**
1. Average grade level:	very low (rank 75/85)	very low (rank 82/85)
2. DA scheme:	a salary group scheme which disadvantages workers on higher basics by compressing differentials	an excellent double linkage scheme whose effect is nullified by the low basics workers are on
3. Level of basic:	on the whole below average, cf. Siemens	abysmally low, which is why Tomco ranks higher

The discussion has been dry and a bit technical, but some sense of its importance comes through when we translate it into the actual relationships at work in Bombay companies. This involves working out some conception of *strategies* on pay and of the ways in which managements have attempted to curb 'wage inflation'. These strategies can involve (*a*) strong *resistance to any increase in basic pay* during discussions for a new settlement; this has been the case with Hindustan Lever where the management was totally opposed to any modifications in the basic pay scales so that much of the increase in the last settlement was finally taken in a series of allowances with peculiar names like 'special allowance,' 'social security allowance,' 'ad hoc allowance' and 'settlement wages'. The net result: the continued existence of abysmally low levels of basic pay; (*b*) tight *control over grading* so as to keep the average grade level as low as possible: this has been the strategy followed by both Philips and Hindustan Lever; (*c*) finally, *attacks on DA schemes* which bring in high earnings, precipitating prolonged struggles to modify such schemes or enforce ceilings as a general form of pay control.

Few international companies operating in the Bombay area could afford to pay substantially below the average, so there is a sense in which their being international or foreign-controlled keeps both Philips Kalwa and Hindustan Lever Sewree wage levels somewhat above the average for Bombay private-sector manufacturing. Not right at the top, however. Both companies, like many other Bombay employers, have used low average grade levels, low basics and restrictions on DA to control pay levels; and consequently there are other multinational subsidiaries as well as purely Indian companies which pay more than they do.

3.2.4 Relative pay in the Netherlands

Table 3.9 produces figures on gross annual pay of Philips, Unilever and two comparable large multinationals, one of them British. Here what is significant is the fact that Philips pay compares with the pay in companies like ICI and Unilever only when the higher, technically qualified grades are included in the calculation, the section of the labour force which is classified in grades 50–80 and covered by a separate agreement negotiated with the Federation of Philips Higher Personnel (FHPP) (mainly). When these higher groups are excluded from the comparison and only manual pay is considered, from packers and assemblers at the lower end to skilled craftsmen and lower supervisory personnel in grade 45, the position is quite different.

As the table shows, companies like Shell and ICI pay almost 30 per cent more than Philips. Of course, to some extent this differential could be ascribed to differences in company job structures, with a more obvious predominance of the so-called 'unskilled' groups in Philips plants, but even for comparable job groups there appears to be a significant difference. On the basis of data supplied by the NKV in Eindhoven, Teulings claimed that

TABLE 3.9

Relative Pay: Pay Comparisons for Large Companies in the Netherlands

Company/Plant	Year	Pay Groups Covered	Gross Annual Pay (in f)
Shell Pernis	1984	fg 8–1 (mgt.)	75,317
	1985	fg 8–1 (mgt.)	78,850
Shell Pernis	1984	fg 15–9 (CAO)	46,191
	1985	fg 15–9 (CAO)	48,502
Shell Moerdijk	1985	fg 15–1	64,880
Unilever (NUB)	1982	ARU	48,904
	1985	ARU	54,200
ICI Holland	1984	III–VIII (CAO)	c.49,000
Philips	1984	15–80	48,819
	1984	15–45	c.38,000

Source: Shell Nederland Raffinaderij bv, *Sociaal verslag 1985*, p. 7–8; Shell Nederland Chemie bv, vestiging Moerdijk, *Sociaal jaarverslag 1985*, p. 8; Nederlandse Unilever Bedrijven bv, *Sociaal jaarverslag 1982*, p. 5, *Personeelsjaarverslag 1985*, bijlage p. 2; ICI Holland bv, *Personeelverslag 1984*, p. 22, p. 17; Philips, company pay statistic supplied by the Industriebond/FNV, 'Inkomensspreiding 1984 in decielen' and 'Statistiek beloningsbeleid funktiegroepen per Januari 1985'.

For years members complained that the pay was less in Philips. Lower even than in other undertakings in the Eindhoven region. A grade-wise comparison enables one to see that the pay of lower grades in Philips—those where the great majority of factory personnel are found—lies significantly below the rest of the metal industry. Comparison with DAF leads to the same conclusion . . . . [In local union enquiries], Nijmegen district for example came to the conclusion in 1973 that unskilled personnel (grades 10–15) in Philips-Nijmegen received around f1200 less per year than their counterparts in the metal industry . . . . In the 1975 negotiations this was openly acknowledged by the company

and Teulings finally quotes from annual reports of the metal workers' union going back to the late forties and early fifties to show that even in that period Philips paid consistently below the average for the Dutch engineering industry [1981, pp. 163–66].

When Philips managers were asked how they rated themselves on relative pay, they were quite straightforward about the issue;

after clarifying that we were talking about pay for manual grades they stated,

'Just below the average'.
'Not in the top ten?'
'No, I think we have our own agreement because we don't want to be at the top' (interview).

This is an interesting response not only for its admirable frankness (few Bombay managements would openly admit that their companies are not in the highest brackets for pay, indeed almost all of them consistently claim to be there) but also for the light it throws on the possible relationships between bargaining structures and relative pay.[17]

For a more recent period it was possible to locate figures which show that one of the important ways in which Philips has been able to hold its manual pay below the engineering average is by consistently pegging the level of its 'price compensation' payments below the average paid by the metal industry. The figures are in Table 3.10.

TABLE 3.10
Price Compensation Rates: Philips and the Metal Industry (Per cent of gross pay)

	Metal	Philips
January 1979	2.21	1.55
July 1979	1.83	1.75
January 1980	2.54	1.95
January 1981	1.78	1.17
July 1981	3.23	3.11
January 1982	3.57	3.22

Source: Union papers in SOBE files.

This is a pay strategy which corresponds to the general movement among Bombay managements to attack and uproot DA schemes under which a major part of workers' earnings escapes management control.

4

GRADING PRACTICES

Grading determines pay through the almost universal fact that different pay scales correspond to different grades (jobs which are graded differently receive different rates of pay)—a relationship which is most explicit in the form of job evaluation schemes. But because of this fairly obvious influence, something which is perhaps not so obvious tends to follow: the average pay of an establishment or group of establishments will partly depend on the average distribution of the workforce into grades. Following work done by the URG for Bombay, this distribution will be called the 'grade structure' of the establishment or product group.

4.1 THE NUMBER OF GRADES

There is considerably more 'harmonisation' of jobs in Dutch companies than in companies operating in Bombay or elsewhere in India, even when the latter are actually subsidiaries of multinationals based in the Netherlands. 'Harmonisation' refers to the application of the same job classification to manual and non-manual employees, or to workers and staff, with no formal distinction between their jobs in terms of the grades which apply to them. The usual practice in Bombay is to have separate grades for staff categories, and in some of the larger companies like Hindustan Lever to divide staff into 'clerical,' 'technical' and 'subordinate,' with separate grades for each of these groups. One consequence of this form of classification is the large number of individual grades that results; for example, a total of 16 grades in Philips Kalwa, or 17 in ICI's plant on the same road. The Dutch pattern merges staff jobs into the general classification applied to manual employees with no formal discrimination between them. This makes for fewer grades overall, and probably also for a greater sense of equality within establishments.

However, there are interesting differences between establishments within the Netherlands and within Bombay. This is clear from Table 4.1 which reveals the number of grades in operation in various companies controlled by the same multinationals. Within the Bombay area, Nocil diverges sharply from the usual pattern in having a harmonised classification scheme, introduced in the early seventies through a formal job evaluation plan undoubtedly influenced by Shell. Thus Nocil has only 5 grades, incorporating both

TABLE 4.1
Grading Schemes: Number of Grades

Company	Main Grades	Staff Grades*	Higher Personnel†
NETHERLANDS			
Philips	10**		4
Unilever	11		3‡
Metal industry	11		
ICI	8		9
Shell refinery	7		8
Heineken	7		3
UK			
ICI	7		
Shell Chemicals	8	5***	
Wellcome Foundation	8	12	
BOMBAY			
Philips Kalwa	8	8	
Philips Pune	6	16†††	
Hindustan Lever Sewree	8		
ICI/CAFI	9	8	
Nocil/Shell	5		
Union Carbide	5		
Burroughs Wellcome	12		
Hoechst	12	11****	

Notes:
 * where avilable and if separate from the main grades;
 † not available for the UK and Bombay;
 ** plus four probationary grades;
 ‡ for assistant managers;
 *** basic clerical grades 63–67;
 ††† subordinate, clerical, technical and supervisory staff;
 **** head office staff grades.

staff and operator jobs. In the Netherlands, this type of grading pattern is most evident in process industry, where the number of distinct grades is 7 to 8 as opposed to the standard metal industry scheme with 11 grades or the 14 grades in Philips.

How many grades a plant has is at least partly a variable quantity open to the influence of bargaining pressures; even if *job* structures are determined by the technical characteristics of plants, *grading* structures are certainly less explicable in terms of such influences.[18] In CAFI, ICI's chemical operation in the Bombay area, the last settlement reduced the number of process operators' grades from 7 to 5, following union pressure for a reduction to 3 grades. This was done by merging the lowest grades 1 and 2 into a revised grade E and grades 3 and 4 into a revised grade D. In Hindustan Lever, following massive pressure from stronger groups in the lowest (packers') grade and hopelessly divided judgements on the evaluation of a whole range of jobs, the company finally agreed to split the lowest grade and create a new grade E through upgradation of almost 50 per cent of C grade employees. Unilever in the Netherlands has witnessed an even more dramatic increase in the number of grades, having started in the immediate post-war period with 5 grades, increased these to 8 and then introduced a further increase to 11. Here it seems that most of the pressure for greater differentiation came from the workers themselves, although according to Tophoven, who handles job classification issues for the Industriebond, 'Now, in the last five years, people are unhappy with the system, they have been saying we must go back to 8 grades because the differences are too big' (interview). In the ICI plant at Rozenburg there were initially 12 grades and a reduction occurred because workers wanted fewer grades. The specific reason why workers at ICI preferred a smaller number of grades is that otherwise it took too long to reach the possible maximum levels. 'You need most money when you're in your late thirties, when you have growing children and mortgage payments, not when you're sixty and ready for retirement,' was the fascinating observation they made about this—a remark which opens up many possibilities for research into pay dissatisfaction among different groups of workers, since it implies that age and family responsibilities correlate strongly with the extent of dissatisfaction; it also shows how discontent over pay can influence the number of grades in a plant.

The number of grades has been a variable entity in the history of

Philips pay relationships too. When the company first introduced job classification there were 14 grades. In 1949 this was reduced to 12. Later, when staff jobs were merged into the overall scheme and Philips switched from talking about 'werkclassificatie' to talking about 'functieclassificatie,' the manual grades were further reduced to 6. By the mid-seventies, expansion of grades had occurred and finally, in 1984, largely under the pressure of skilled groups in the middle grades, two extra grades were created on the usual pattern of splitting grades: a large proportion of grade 25 went into a new grade 27 and part of 35 into 37.[19] The background to this particular restructuring is rather interesting because it shows how managements redefine the number of job levels rather than make any fundamental alterations in the existing job evaluation. A young metal worker then in grade 30 (one of the skilled grades) in Machinefabrieken, Eindhoven, describes what was actually going on.

> At the time I was there, in the beginning we had no power because there wasn't enough work, but after a few years there was more production and then the position was a little bit stronger. The point of action changed to another job classification system. Our point of view was, if skilled workers can work on different machines, they must be placed in a higher *functiegroep*. There was a lot of resistance by the workers against the old job classification system; they said, we now have to do a greater variety of jobs, we must get a high grade. We said, change the whole job classification system. That was a general point, for Philips as a whole. The Industriebond had a joint committee with the company, years passed, a lot of studies were made. We said, it must be possible for the best skilled workers to go to 40. Simple! But no. Philips management and the unions made one group here and one there, 27 and 37, more groups, more differences . . . . We said, there are enough groups, it's *not* necessary to make any more (interview).

But ultimately Philips did increase the number of grades. The actual differences in pay involved in the creation of the new grades were not very significant.

In the last Hindustan Lever settlement, the highest grade ('O' in the hourly-rated classification scheme) was abolished by the company on the grounds that 'There is no person in this grade'. But managements have been reluctant to adopt the same reasoning with respect to lower grades when these have been depleted. Depletion of the lowest grades is a characteristic of Dutch grading patterns which is worth emphasising. As of today, in companies like Unilever, ICI and Shell and in some Philips factories like Machinefabrieken in Eindhoven, there is practically no one in the lowest grade or in the two or three lowest grades. For Unilever one manager explained this in terms of the impact of automation on skill requirements within the company. In Heineken's highly automated brewery at Zoeterwoude, where there is almost no one in the two lowest grades, depletion occurred because of upgradings which were linked to management's plan for increased job mobility. But in none of these cases are managements proposing to abolish the lowest grades on the grounds that 'there is no person in these grades'. On the other hand, this is precisely what happened in Tata Oil Mills in Bombay when an Industrial Tribunal award abolished the lowest grade in 1980.

Not all management influences on the number of grades are purely retrograde. One example which reflects the more progressive thinking of process industry managements was the compression of a ten-grade job classification into a seven-grade scheme through the grades consolidation which occurred in the Burmah-Shell refinery at Trombay in the late sixties when management introduced the concept of 'extended duties' to achieve what it called 'task-orientation'.[20] In short, when we look at manufacturing as a whole, conflicting movements in the evolution of job levels, with expansion of grades in some companies and their simultaneous contraction in others, have to be related not only to technical characteristics in some general sense but also to bargaining pressures and to ideas about work organisation.[21]

4.2 HOW JOBS ARE GRADED

A basic contrast with respect to grading practices in Bombay and Holland concerns the much greater extent to which job evaluation is applied in, or has been introduced into, Dutch industry. It appears from a management survey that by 1950 about 60 per cent of manual employee jobs were subject to some form of job evaluation, and that today this proportion is likely to be well over 80 per cent. This contrasts sharply with the situation in Bombay, where although the vast majority of firms would of course have some form of job classification in their establishments, only a small minority would have introduced this or had it reorganised through a *formal* job evaluation plan. Of those plants which do have a formal plan, only a handful (GKW and Hindustan Lever among them) would have used formal methods of job evaluation before the sixties; most of the plans were introduced in the seventies when Indian industry as a whole went through its first phase of rationalisation.

4.2.1 Job classification systems

Unilever uses three job classification systems, including one for managers. 'The first system is the Unilever special system—they made it for themselves,' according to Tophoven. 'The second system is the universal system we use here in Holland: we call it the "normalised method" ' (interview). Traditionally it was the Unilever method which was used as the basis for grading jobs in the company's plants, but more recently, following an agreement signed in 1973, there has been an extension of the normalised system (UGM) and a uniform set of salary scales for manual and non-manual employees. This is an interesting agreement, because among other things it gave workers some degree of control over the drafting of job descriptions, and also because it established an appeals procedure in case workers wanted to dispute either their description or the points allocation.[22] The chief difference between the Unilever method and the normalised system UGM seems to be the much greater spread of points possible under the latter. Whereas grade 1 jobs correspond to roughly 10.5 Unilever points, the equivalent limit under UGM is 30 points; grade 2 jobs extend at most to 14.75 Unilever points but 50 UGM points, and so on.

A third system which is a more refined form of UGM has been expanding recently, and this is called ORBA. GM, UGM and ORBA represent three definite phases in the evolution of job evaluation in Dutch industry. They are all points rating systems, but there are differences both in the number of factor degrees used by each, the number of levels of complexity or frequency for each factor and the maximum points allotted to them. These have been summarised in Table 4.2.

The scheme about which least information could be gathered is

TABLE 4.2

The Structure of Three Job Evaluation Methods Used in the Netherlands: Job Factors

Job Factor/Method	No. of Factor Degrees			Levels of Complexity, Frequency, etc.			Max. Points		
	GM	UGM	ORBA	GM	UGM	ORBA	GM	UGM	ORBA
1. Knowledge	6	6	6	4	6	6	8	18	36
2. Independence	5	6	7	5	5	6	7	16	39
3. Risk of damage	8	8	8	6	6	6	8	12	34
4. Authority	4			5			7		
a) hierarchical		3	3		6	8		14	40
b) non-hierarchical		2	3		4	4		7	21
5. Articulateness	3	4	4	3	4	4	6	11	27
6. Contact	4	4	5	4	4	5	7	12	28
7. Dexterity	5	5	5	3	3	3	13	13	15
8. Attention/accuracy	6	6	5	4	4	4	8	8	11
9. Special demands		2	2	3	2	2		9	20
10. Physical effort	4	4	5	3	3	4	8	8	24
11. Posture	4	4	4	3	3	4	8	8	17
12. Personal risk	4	4	4	5	5	5	8	8	16

Source: Composed from 'graderingstabellen' supplied by the Industriebond/FNV.

Note: 'Levels of complexity, etc.' would refer to, for Knowledge, the nature of, from 'very simple' to 'extremely complicated'; Independence, degree of dependence on instructions, from 'precise instructions' to 'general guidelines'; Risk of damage, the likely occurrence of for a given situation, from 'very low' to 'great'; Authority (hierarchical), the number of subordinates for whom total responsibility is assumed from '2' to '500+'; Articulateness, the quality required, from 'no special demands' to 'of a high quality'; Contact, distance over which contact is maintained, from 'same sphere, under common supervisor' to 'opposite sphere'; Dexterity, nature of movements in terms of speed and exertion; Attention, degree of difficulty in sustaining; Physical effort, frequency and duration of the exertion, from 'now and then' to 'regularly (c.4 hours per day)'; Posture, as for Physical effort; Personal risk, the chances of occurrence of an accident or occupational disease, from 'very low' to 'great'.

the Philips grading system. According to one official, 'The union
has tried to introduce the UGM system, but we haven't succeeded
because Philips is very strong. Philips uses factors like Knowledge,
Responsibility, Hierarchy and *beinvloeding* which means how you
can influence your job, which is typical of Philips' (interview). At
least four features of the Philips system are clear. First, points
values are expressed on a scale closer to the Unilever method, for
example, 10 for computer operator as against 106 in ORBA,
although a lower scale is quite compatible with a greater dispersion
of points, for example, compare the Philips distance between
computer operators and programmers with the corresponding
ORBA distance:

	ORBA Points	Philips Points
packer	22	
sorter	30	
forklift driver	43	
group leader	63	
data typist	68	10
carpenter	95.5	
computer operator	106	10
shift leader	136	
junior programmer	130	
programmer	149	30
senior programmer	176	
systems analyst	190	

Secondly, a management survey of job evaluation schemes in
operation in the Netherlands points to another feature when it
suggests that in going for job evaluation, 'greater simplicity can be
promoted among other things by a reduction in the number of job
factors (as in the Philips system)'. Thirdly, the same management
survey tells us that 'In the Philips scheme conditions of work are
left out of the classification system; they are evaluated by means of
a separate table'. And finally, in the minutes of the Philips CKK
meetings, that is, meetings of the highest-level union body for
Philips, one comes across the following statement: 'There are no
possibilities of making Monotony a separate factor. This issue has
been brought up on several occasions in the job evaluation committee. It has always ended in strong resistance from Philips.' This
is quite consistent with the general policy of having fewer rather
than more job factors; after all, job factors are an expression of

dimensions of job experience, and the smaller the range of factors involved in a scheme, the more restricted one's conception of what jobs actually involve or mean for people.

By contrast with the Philips system, ORBA gives considerable weightage (18 per cent) to working conditions—more, in fact, than any other scheme (e.g., IFA or the Integral Job Analysis Method assigns a weightage of 7 per cent). ORBA distinguishes nineteen specific aspects of such conditions, defines each of them, and then allows for the usual two-way matrix built around degree/intensity and frequency of occurrence. The aspects are:

- hazardous ventilation
- dryness, for below-average levels of humidity
- exposure to weather
- lighting
- noise
- dust
- smoke
- stench
- damp/humidity
- heat
- cold
- temperature fluctuations
- dirt
- wetness
- unpleasant substances
- vibration
- protective clothing which causes discomfort
- nervous tension which arises from job characteristics such as restrictions on mobility, time pressure,[23] short-cycle repetitive tasks, etc.
- depressing circumstances such as work in isolation, in confined spaces, monotony, and so on.

Each of these aspects is concretely illustrated with examples of jobs and the characteristics they involve, e.g., 'depressing circumstances' is illustrated by reference to the slaughter of stunned animals in meat-processing plants.

In Hindustan Lever, the demand for a new job evaluation goes back to 1975 when the union asked workers to give in their names if they felt unhappy about their grades. Applications were then scrutinised and some 95 per cent eventually admitted; these were the grievances that formed the basis of the demand for re-evaluation. It turned out that out of a total of some 300 classified jobs, around 40 per cent were being disputed. Lever management continued to stress the position that job evaluation is a scientific technique. By 1979 a job evaluation committee was formed with two representatives from each side. This committee was scheduled to start its work after training and to work for two years. It was agreed that in the event of a dispute, the committee would appeal to the General Factory Manager; if his decision left either side dissatisfied, the issue could be referred to court as an industrial dispute. Training was done by the company's industrial engineers. The plan was based on points rating: the factor weightings were those which management had fixed in 1956; from each grade two 'bench jobs' were selected with designated points, and other jobs rated in relation to these key jobs.

From the beginning there were disagreements; for example, the union argued that the level of mechanisation characterising different jobs should be taken into account for points rating, but management was opposed to this and eventually got their way. The job descriptions drafted by management were shown to workers by the union, but there were no major disagreements about this: apparently workers felt that upgrading would be easier if they did not object to the inclusion of 'informal' tasks in the description. However, after two years the two sides found themselves supporting sharply divergent ratings, largely due to differences in scoring. On management's proposal, seventeen jobs would be upgraded, another four downgraded; the jobs earmarked for upgrading involved less than 200 workers in a workforce of over 3,000. Disputed classifications were then referred to the GFM; he ruled that the management's proposals were correct. A new committee now led the union, and 'some people on the committee felt we should go to court over the evaluation. We opposed this and argued we should use our bargaining strength. The committee agreed with this because most people felt a court decision would take months or even years, and was in any case not predictable.' The job evaluation committee had left enough room for bargaining—at least two grades for each disputed classification. The union first proposed that they should work out the 'average difference' in evaluation and use that as a common principle for all grades; in practice this would mean one grade higher for everyone, and management disagreed. The union then proposed that they should adopt Tomco's grading as a model, but the company objected to Lever being 'led by Tomco'. Lever management maintained that the points values of individual jobs were not negotiable—'this is not something you can settle by pressure'—but proposed that the way the grade lines were drawn *could* be changed. It was a strategy which allowed for the resolution of a possible deadlock without obliging management to negotiate on the assigned values: 'this proposal was made because management was basically concerned to *avoid breaking the system*'. The union agreed, even though this exercise was restricted to grade C. A new grade E was established, and the company agreed to upgrade between 700 and 800 workers.[24]

Presumably by the device of creating a new grade to accommodate the strong pressures in some of the job groups in C, Lever management saw itself keeping the system intact and immune to any modifications. In practice, because grade E had no clear cut-off points of its own and there were jobs with the same ratings in C and E, to some of the more perceptive workers this only emphasised the arbitrary character of management grading practices.

Not all Bombay managements make the same claims or have the same illusions about the scientific character of methods like job evaluation. According to one manager of a large Swedish multinational talking about his company's experience with job evaluation, the sort of criteria which actually count in grading are factors such as the assumption that workers expect to move upwards and the feeling of the company that they have to sustain the 'morale' of their employees; job classification systems are 'historical growths,' they contain an 'element of arbitrariness' and reflect bargaining pressures. The scheme followed by this company in its Pune factory did not follow any accepted 'scientific procedures'.

Arbitrariness as a characteristic of points rating was in fact one of the several criticisms which De Metaal, the metal-workers' union affiliated to the radical movement for trade union solidarity EVC, levelled against the new job classification systems which Dutch employers were introducing in the early fifties. De Metaal was especially strong in the larger engineering plants in the west of Holland, and the points it made about the essentially subjective character of the weighting factors (Buitelaar and Vreeman [1985],

p. 113) were only too clearly illustrated in the way these factors were actually modified by the bigger employers in the industry when they expanded the points tables for individual job factors in a general competition to attract labour (Teulings [1977], p. 176ff.). A comparable realism about grading practices is evident in the remarks of one union official about the reasons why although as a large aircraft manufacturer Fokker is in fact covered by the metal industry agreement, the company opted for its own grading system.

> Fokker *could* use the metal industry system, but they said they wanted their own system. It looks like the metal system and it's quite good. Knowledge and Responsibility get the most points . . . . In Fokker, since most of the workers are highly skilled, they pay very well, otherwise these workers would go elsewhere. That's why they have their own system. If they use the metal system, they have to use its benchmarks, and then they cannot pay more than the metal industry. So they made an arrangement with us to have another system so that they can pay more (interview).

4.2.2 Grading levels

The notion of an *average grade level* is useful partly because it shows that control over this level could be a major management objective, especially in plants or industries where labour costs are an important consideration and there is continuous management pressure for control on pay. The practical significance of arguing that grading patterns, in the sense of workforce distributions across grades, are not just passive emanations of some objective force called 'technology,' that their specific form reflects both management strategies and union pressures, begins to emerge when we compare grade levels. The results displayed in Tables 4.3, 4.4 and 4.5 bear the same general title, 'Grading disparities'. A disparity in grading level, in the sense in which this term is being used here, means a significant difference in the average grade level of two or more establishments. 'Average grade level' is an intuitive notion of how well or badly workforces are classified. Intuitive ideas of this sort are present in almost any workforce, in the sense that the workers of a plant or department usually have definite feelings about whether their jobs are properly graded or about the kind of

TABLE 4.3

Grading Disparities in Four Large International Companies with Bombay Plants: Grade Structures (%)

Company/Plant	Year	No. Covered	Grade-wise Distributions								
			Gr 15	19+20	25	27	29+30	35	37	39+40	45
Philips overall	1/85	51,596	4.24	19.45	15.57	6.55	13.14	14.29	5.70	11.40	9.64
Philips Light dvn.	1/84	5521/6565	10.03	26.26	16.85	5.96	12.03	11.03	3.60	7.63	6.61
Philips Glass dvn.	1/84	1087/1397	2.30	23.00	25.76	18.77		14.63		8.00	7.54
			US	SS-1	SS-2	SS-3	SK-A	SK-B		HSK-I	HSK-II
Philips Kalwa	1983	877/1124	9.35	21.21	32.84	16.65	9.81	5.36		4.10	0.68
			1	2 3		4	5	6	7 8	9	10 11
Unilever overall	1985	6130	1.3	7.9 14.0		13.8	11.6	12.0	8.9 8.3	9.0	6.6 6.6
			C	E		F	I	J	K M	N	
Hindustan Lever Sewree	1983	3385	20.7	22.2		22.05	13.2	8.55	3.9	8.2	1.2
			I	II	III	IV	V	VI	VII	VIII	
ICI Holland Rozenburg	1/85	1097/1829	0	0.17	2.33	19.17	23.33	19.5	27.17	8.33	
			E	D+CrI		C+CrII		B+CrIII	A+CrIV		
ICI/CAFI Thane-Belapur	1983	/824		22.6	37.6	18.6	13.3	7.9			
			15	14	13	12	11	10	9		
Shell Nederland Chemie Moerdijk	1/86	451/988	0	0	0.44	1.55	16.85	31.04	50.11		
				I	II	III	IV	V			
NOCIL (Shell/Mafatlal) Thane-Belapur	1983	1008		6.0	18.0	45.5	19.2	11.3			

Source: For plants in the Netherlands, calculated from the annual personnel/employee reports of the companies concerned; for plants in the Bombay area, collected from the personnel departments or unions.

TABLE 4.4

Grading Disparities: Rankings According to Average Grade Levels

Company/Plant	Year	WARGI Value	WARGI Rank
Shell Chemie, Moerdijk	1985	82.087	1
ICI Holland, Rozenburg	1984	64.209	2
Philips Netherlands	1984	48.302	3
Nocil, Thane-Belapur	1983	47.234	4
Unilever Netherlands	1985	45.293	5
Philips Glass Group	1983	42.927	6
Philips Pune, Loni	1986	40.984	7
Philips Light Group	1983	34.027	8
Philips Pune, Pimpri	1986	32.746	9
Philips Kalwa	1983	31.779	10
ICI/CAFI, Thane-Belapur	1983	28.025	11
Hindustan Lever, Sewree*	1983	28.018	12

Source: Computed from the grade structures shown in Table 4.3, following a
method outlined by Union Research Group, *Bulletin*, nos. 6–7, 1985; data
for Philips Pune supplied by management.

Note: Figures for the month of January are taken to express the situation in tne
previous year.
* See note 26, p. 218.

TABLE 4.5

Grading Disparities in Philips Netherlands

	Year	WARGI Value	WARGI Rank
Machinefabrieken	1983	54.066	1
Science & Industry	1980	50.983	2
Philips overall	1984	48.302	3
Elcoma Display Systems	1984	43.904	4
Philips Glass Group	1983	42.927	5
Elcoma Group	1981	38.224	6
Philips Light Group	1983	34.027	7
Philips Audio Group	1982	29.446	8
Weert light factory	1983	27.447	9
Terneuzen light factory	1984	24.516	10
Johan de Wit	1982	23.413	11

Source: Grading data contained in the *Sociaal Jaarverslag* for individual establishments or divisions.

Note: Figures relating to the month of January are taken to express the previous
year's situation.

inequities which flow from the way their jobs have been graded. Such ideas may not always manifest themselves in a direct or simple form.

The purely intuitive notion of an average grade level has a precise *quantitative* expression in something called the 'weighted average relative grade indicator,' or WARGI for short. For each grade structure (labour force distribution into grades), WARGI assigns a precise value which is a quantified expression of our intuitive notions of how well or badly jobs have been classified.[25] In Tables 4.4 and 4.5 the WARGI values have been ordered into rankings, with the highest values expressing the *best grading situations*, (*a*) for plants controlled by four major companies in the Netherlands and in the Bombay area, or groups of plants in a major product division, or the company as a whole, (*b*) for divisions and establishments within the Philips group in Holland.

Results

In general, domestic plants of international companies have considerably higher average grade levels than plants controlled by those companies in the Bombay labour market area, but this overall pattern is not true of these companies to the same degree. The difference in grading levels is most apparent in the case of ICI, where the average grade level of the production workforce in the Rozenburg plant is over twice as high as the average level of the workforce in ICI's Bombay factory. There is also a big disparity in Shell's case, but this would be due not to the low average classification of the Bombay plant (Nocil would in fact rank high by Bombay standards) but to the exceptionally high WARGI of the chemical plant at Moerdijk where there is almost no one in the three lowest job groups and where 50 per cent of the bargainable staff comes in the highest bargainable grade (grade VIII). In Unilever's case, the average grade level of the company's Netherlands labour force is over 61 per cent higher than the average grading of workers in Hindustan Lever's Bombay factory.[26] So in these three cases (ICI, Shell and Unilever) one is dealing with differences in average grading which are quite considerable.

Philips deviates from this general pattern in displaying *much less disparity* internationally. For Kalwa the obvious comparison is with plants in the light division. But as Table 4.4 shows, the disparity is slight (about 7 per cent), while the Pune plants (where the values are taken from a later date) could conceivably have higher average gradations than most Philips domestic establishments in the Light and Audio divisions. The chief reason for this is not something that could conceivably count as high overall gradings in the company's Indian plants—in fact Philips Kalwa comes close to the bottom in an overall Bombay ranking (cf. the histograms in Union Research Group, *Bulletin*, nos. 6–7, 1985, where its rank is 75/85)—but the exceptionally *low* grade levels which Philips has successfully enforced in the domestic plants of key product groups.

To argue that the international disparities are of no significance, managements of groups like Unilever, Shell and ICI would need to show that there are significant technological differences between domestic and Third World plants which determine corresponding differences in job structures, including the types of qualifications and skills required, *and also assume that* higher levels of automation mean higher levels of skill or technical qualification *within the bargainable categories*. Now it is true that domestic plants would in general have higher levels of automation, but the assumption about skills is not so obvious. At least there is no study which establishes this result in any direct way, and some evidence to suggest that in fact the modern forms of automation are leading to sharper polarisation within workforces.

Some industrial influence is apparent in the grading distributions. Chemical plants generally have better grade structure than plants involved in the mass production of discrete parts with significant manual assembly of components and products. The car industry is an obvious example of a technological process of the latter type: if one takes the data cited in the remarkable book by Friedman and Meredeen ([1980], p. 68), the WARGI value for the grade distribution which emerged directly from the job evaluation at Ford Dagenham in 1968 works out to 40.997, which is where Philips mass production groups figure in our tables. But even within the Philips group there is some technological influence at work. Sectors with the most pronounced mass production characteristics such as Elcoma, Light and Audio also have the lowest average gradings compared to the grade levels in MF or Science and Industry, where older or newer types of skills are far more in evidence. Differences of this kind (between process industry and mass production, etc.) have a lot to do with technical characteristics of the general type that Naville, Mallet and Touraine drew attention to in France late in the fifties, when the discussion of a 'new working class' first began.[27] But the example of Unilever shows that process industry characteristics do not automatically result in higher average job classifications, and the case of ICI's Bombay plant shows that even in the process industry you find workforces with remarkably low average grade levels.

An important dimension of the Philips grade level patterns shown in Table 4.5 is the differential/discriminatory grading of women and men. This accounts for a large part of the grading disparities within Philips in Holland, since divisions and establishments with a high proportion of women employees are also consistently ones with the lowest average gradings. There is, of course, independent evidence for this general proposition; for example in 1980, in Philips as a whole, while 35 per cent of all male production workers were classified in the lowest Philips grades 10–25, 75 per cent of women employees were classified there. Again, while the highly skilled grades 39–45 accounted for almost 17 per cent of the male workforce, their share of the female labour force was only 4 per cent. In the factory which comes through with the worst grade structure, Johan de Wit in the Audio group, some 37 per cent of employees belonged to grade 15 in 1982, and 94 per cent of the employees in that grade were women! (SOBE Philips Archives) In Philips' Pune factories where women form around 30 per cent of the labour force and most of them are employed in Radio Assembly and Foil Varco, early in the eighties the great majority of them were classified in the lowest grade but one (Group II in the plant classification, the grade for 'Operator I').

There are at least three ways in which companies enforce low average classifications on women:

A Straightforward *discriminatory grading*, where women and men doing the same jobs are classified differently, with men in higher grades. For example, in one pharmaceutical company, males working on packing machines are classified in the 'skilled' grade while women working on the same machines are classified as 'senior packers'; on the whole, however, this type of discrimination is hardly ever found in large companies in Bombay.

B *Exclusion* of women from high-graded jobs even where women have acquired the skills and experience to handle these jobs, as in this case from Philips in the Netherlands:

I knew the machine inside out. If something was broken, I knew exactly what it was and repaired it myself. I sometimes repaired machines for other women as well. If someone from the technical department was called in, it usually took much longer. One day, the head of my department asked me whether I would be responsible for the repair of all the machines in the department. But when I asked him what I would get for this, he replied that I wasn't eligible for a rise in function as I had no technical training. So I refused his offer. I still repair the machines if I feel like it (*Philips Workers' News*, June 1983, p. 7).

Women workers in Bombay also complain that although 'women operators look after their machines just as much as men do, we can also set up machines and do minor repairs,' yet 'women don't get the grade' (interview). Managements often exclude women from better-paid jobs on the pretext that these jobs may be too strenuous or hazardous for them, but the same arguments do not seem to exempt them from lower-paid jobs. For example, women employees in the Bombay pharmaceutical industry point out that companies assign tasks like the capping and sealing of bottles to women when those tasks are performed manually and involve considerable physical exertion, but the men take over as soon as the same jobs are automated and the work becomes physically less strenuous. In Lever's Sewree factory, a whole range of jobs which were hazardous because they were done manually were assigned to women, but when these jobs were mechanised the recruitment of women for them stopped.

C   *Low evaluation* of the jobs which are assigned to women because the kinds of skills and abilities which are required for doing such jobs are simply not recognised in most job classification schemes. The low average gradings forced on women are an effect of the operation of all these factors, especially the last one.

4.3 SOME ISSUES RELATED TO GRADING

By 'issues' we mean those areas of deployment which interact with grading practices and possible disputes on grading without actually constituting disputes on grading as such. For example, one of us attended a meeting at the Heineken brewery at Zoeterwoude, where the management and union had to decide on a demand for higher grading by a group of three technicians who claimed that they were actually doing the work of a higher grade insofar as their jobs involved, or had involved for several years, the exercise of authority with respect to employees under them. Although this was a dispute about classification, much of the discussion was framed in terms of the job descriptions for grade 7 technicians. These included no reference to the exercise of authority and management chose to contest the claim entirely in these terms, reinforced by the department supervisors who argued that no authority was actually exercised by those workers. Thus this was a case where the *job description* was central to a claim about grades, although the issue itself was not mainly about the job description but about whether the technicians should be upgraded.

4.3.1 Job descriptions

Dutch practice with respect to disclosure of job descriptions is far more liberal than the usual practice of most Bombay managements. Clause 27 of the Unilever agreement states first that the job description forms the basis for the grading of jobs, and next that once the description attains a final form, a text of this is issued to the employees concerned. At the ICI plant in principle the job descriptions are confidential, but you can see your own description if you want to. This was also said to be the case at Heineken, and appears to be the usual practice at least in the bigger companies. You also have the right to ask for a new description if you are not happy with the present one (in Unilever this is regulated by a special appeals procedure). And if changes are introduced in job content, you have the right to be consulted about the new description. Moreover, there is no reference in any of these cases to the description being of a 'purely illustrative' nature. When Philips managers were asked whether employees could see their descriptions, the answer was, 'Yes, of course, when it's there. Not every job has a description.' This bears out one of the numerous grievances on classification described in the workers' report from the Philips Drachten plant, namely, that there are no descriptions for some jobs.

Bombay managements diverge from these practices in at least three ways: by treating job descriptions with greater confidentiality and expressing reluctance to issue descriptions; by not always using the description as the basis for the grading of employees when the same jobs are performed by people in different grades; and by drafting descriptions so as to allow for greater flexibility (or from the employee's point of view greater arbitrariness) in the deployment of labour. The usual form in which Bombay managements achieve this fluidity is by writing a clause into the agreement stating that job descriptions are purely 'illustrative' in nature. In Siemens, management departed from this practice by having a specific formula included in the trade descriptions for various groups of jobs; e.g., the Siemens trade description for 'Machinist B' would read: 'General Duties—Operations on preset mass production machines like presses, turrets, spot welding machines etc. and operating on general purpose machines like hack-saw shearing, drilling, etc. *All general and handling work incidental to his job . . .*' (Siemens 1985, p. 25ff.). This 'General Duties' formula was so loose that it was bound to lead to conflict. Siemens management wanted considerable vertical flexibility, with operators doing helpers' jobs, while workers realised that withholding the kind of flexibility management wanted by appealing to the trade descriptions was an effective form of non-cooperation: while management would use 'General Duties' to increase tasks, workers would refuse job assignments. The 1985 Siemens agreement resolves this conflict through a note called 'Elaboration of General Duties,' where a series of tasks which were previously undefined are now listed explicitly.[28] An additional reason why managements might want such fluid job descriptions is that they could be used against work-to-rules which in many plants are a major form of industrial action.

4.3.2 Possible downgradings

In the Unilever settlement for 1985–86, there is a detailed clause outlining the company's redundancy payments, and Section 1.7.1 states: 'In the event that an employee is placed in a lower grade (*in een lagere functieclasse wordt geplaatst*) on reorganisation . . .' (Unilever, p. 82), i.e., it is assumed that 'reorganisations' may lead to the downgrading of employees. It is interesting that the same section says that in cases of this sort the company will assign the same or a comparable type of job to the employee, because this implies that reorganisations can entail the downgrading of *jobs*, which is never actually said in so many words.

In the ICI agreement the grounds stated for possible downgrading, namely, that an employee can no longer do the work in question, or for disciplinary reasons, or on medical grounds (cl. 7.3, p. 15) implies that the movement need not entail the downgrading of jobs but only a downgrading of employees. But even here there is a reference to 'bedrijfsomstandigheden' ('operational circumstances') which leaves the management free to downgrade jobs as well.

The Philips agreement states,

> Once an employee has been classified in the grade applicable to him, no downgrading shall be possible in his case. This does not apply . . . . b. whenever a lower job level is proposed because an employee's contribution fails to meet the requirements of the job over the long run; c. whenever a measure is proposed involving closure of a factory or department of a factory, major changes in task content (*van het werkpakket*) which are of a permanent nature, a substantial reduction in personnel strength in a factory or department of a factory; in these cases the employer shall establish further rules after discussion with the unions concerned (Philips, cl. 4.1, pp. 47–48).

By contrast, downgrading is almost never mentioned in settlements in Bombay. What these agreements often do give management is the right to get workers to do jobs of a lower grade than their own, but that of course is another issue. One case where management did press for substantial downgrading of jobs was Larsen & Toubro, where the last round of negotiations in 1983 started with the issue of classification. The local union committee on the other hand was pressing for reclassification of the majority of jobs because of the almost continuous modification of job content which the company had brought about over the years through what the committee called 'vertical loading,' that is, adding extra tasks or 'elements' from more highly graded jobs to less highly graded ones.

4.3.3 Promotions and job content

In Bombay agreements, 'seniority-cum-merit' is a common promotion formula and reflects an obvious compromise between management and union control over promotions. There is continuing management emphasis on criteria like 'competence,' 'qualifications,' 'suitability for the job,' 'attendance,' and recently even on the willingness of employees to take on additional responsibilities or tasks. Where managements have a monopoly over promotion decisions, which is often the case workers and unions face considerable uncertainty about the criteria by which promotions are actually determined. The Philips Employees' Union expressed a general feeling when they told the Industrial Relations Manager:

> For promotions the only determinant of relative value should be the job itself—the duties that must be performed, the conditions under which they are performed, and the qualification required to perform them. In our company promotions based only on the so-called 'merits' of the employees resulted in inequities (letter dated 23 November 1983).

This referred specifically to the fact that staff members doing the same work could be found in different grades.

Unilateral management control has been a source of widespread latent dissatisfaction, but unions are quite wary of becoming involved in decisions relating to promotion because of the possible effects this could have on membership solidarity. According to R.R. Mishra who leads the Philips Workers' Union in the factory at Kalwa,

> There was a Supreme Court directive in 1981 which said that the precise yardstick for promotions must be made known to workers. For management simply to say it's their prerogative is not sufficient. On the other hand, if the union gets involved, then the workers feel, if the union doesn't get me a promotion the union is my enemy. If you satisfy two, you dissatisfy a hundred. It creates enmity between workers. In my experience, unions have even broken on this issue.

The most dramatic illustration of this is what actually happened in the Philips Pune plants in 1983 when a conflict over promotions was used by management as the basis for launching a massive attack on the union, involving wholesale dismissal of the local leadership and 148 chargesheets.

On the other hand, there *are* a few examples of Indian companies where the unions have established considerable control in the area of promotions. In Atlas Copco's Pune factory, the union has questioned the appointment of management personnel and on one occasion a promotion decision had to be reversed under union pressure. A more striking example of strong union control over promotions is Lever's Sewree factory. Here, largely due to the enforcement of a complex set of seniority rules on the shop floor by the union, one of the most powerful private-sector managements in the whole of India has been forced to cede control over a crucial area of personnel relations. In the Lever plant, seniority operates in two fundamental forms—departmentally and grade-wise. As between grade and department, priority is assigned to the latter; anyone in the department would get priority even over someone with a higher grade from outside the department. The way the system operates forms a powerful obstacle to the movement of workers between departments, and in this sense it is obviously a fetter on management's flexibility in deployment. When a new manager tried to break the system and held interviews for new jobs, the union told workers that only the senior-most should apply; if the senior-most was not competent to do the job, applications would move down the line in order of seniority. So this is a case where the standard seniority/merit compromise has been broken not in the company's favour but to the advantage of the union.

In the Netherlands, management criteria like 'Education and Performance' (Heineken Zoeterwoude) are used for promotions, and dissatisfaction with their application is often expressed by employees. Some workers at the Hoechst plant in Vlissingen described the company's promotion policy as 'messy,' citing the case of the management's use of reserve operators on certain jobs for months on end but its consistent refusal to give them the grade on grounds of age, lack of experience, lack of qualifications, etc. (Buitelaar and Vreeman [1985], p. 213). In the Philips group, NKF Delft and Drachten are plants where there has been considerable discontent over promotions. At Delft, higher selection norms in most departments meant fewer chances of promotion for the existing personnel; at Drachten, workers complained that promotions depend on your willingness to accept shift-work, and that for women there was no possibility of being promoted to grade 20 (p. 373). Discrimination against women in promotions is a common complaint in Bombay too; a poor promotion policy was the main grievance of Philips women employees in Pune at the time they were interviewed by Pit Gooskens in the early eighties, and women at the Hindustan Lever plant in Sewree complain that some of them are still in the lowest grade (grade C) after having worked for the company for over thirty years.

Management arbitrariness in making promotions is one source of dissatisfaction; lack of promotion possibilities is another. Bombay agreements have dealt with the problem of stagnation in various ways: (*a*) where pay stagnates for a large number of employees because they have reached the end of the grade, unions have negotiated *extension of the grade* or *continuation of the last drawn increment*: here pay increases but both the grade and the job remain the same; (*b*) one method of dealing with grade stagnation has been *mass upgradation* of whole groups of jobs or employees: in these cases the job remains the same; (*c*) more recently, some agreements have introduced *time-bound/automatic reclassification*—i.e., after a certain number of years of service in a company in a given grade, employees are automatically upgraded: here too the job usually continues to be the same.

However, employee grievances about promotion possibilities in the Netherlands suggest that dissatisfaction with jobs and with prospects for the future is rooted in the way jobs are designed. The section on 'Job content' in the workers' enquiry into conditions in the Philips/NKF factory reported:

3. How far does the company make it possible for workers to develop further in their work? This question was answered negatively by all departments. In the last two years almost nothing has been done about employee training. The causes cited were: a. dilution of jobs, b. running down within the factory, c. closure of departments.
4. What about promotion possibilities? All departments react negatively, the possibilities are few.
5. What do you expect in terms of changes in job content? People feel insecure, partly due to increasing automation in the plant.

In the Philips factory at Drachten, workers described the work as dreadfully boring—the precise term used was '*geestdodende*,' which is much more vivid—when they drafted a report on the factory in the mid-seventies. Some years later in the light factory at Deurne, the jobs were described as 'uninteresting and in some places monotonous'. For most of the seventies, before the automation of manual assembly tasks through equipment such as automatic assembly inserters for components assembly in TV production, the great majority of Philips production personnel would have been engaged in jobs involving highly repetitive short-cycle work and far below their average qualification.

In the workers' report on Hoechst Vlissingen (see Table 6.1), criticism of job design is suggested by remarks like: 'boring work, zero promotion chances,' 'few chances for development,' 'deteriorating job content, no possibilities for training due to shortage of personnel on shifts, few or no promotion chances,' 'monotonous jobs, chances of promotion very low,' and to sum it all up: 'The longer you work in Hoechst, the fewer your chances of development.' Presumably it was recognition of this kind of criticism which led to the inclusion of an interesting clause in the last Hoechst settlement for their Bombay employees which states that the existing classification system 'cannot satisfy the aspirations of employees to grow unless there is a qualitative change in the job'. This was a case where the company restructured grades to increase promotional opportunities both to satisfy what it called 'the aspirations of employees to grow,' and to secure greater flexibility, including mobility across departments.

Some differences have emerged in this comparison: greater harmonisation of jobs and more widespread use of formal job evaluation schemes in Holland, lower average grading in Bombay, more liberal practice with respect to disclosure of job descriptions in Holland, the mention of possible downgradings in Dutch agreements, perhaps more use of seniority as a criterion for promotion in Bombay. What is more striking, however, is the similarity between employee grievances on grading and promotion practices in Bombay and the Netherlands. Grade levels and grading patterns are ultimately a product of ideas about, but also strategies with respect to, *the social evaluation of work*. A narrow range of job factors with weightings biased to reflect management's overall evaluation of job characteristics would tend to result in the patterns and levels which actually prevail. A broader range of factors, inclusion of factors which express dimensions of job experience such as monotony, time stress, control skills, hazards of working with new technologies, tension, mental fatigue and so on; unbiased weightings and employee control over the drafting of descriptions are all some obvious ways in which a different evaluation of labour power could result and make for more equitable/higher grade structures. Therefore, even when one allows for the fact that mass production technologies have involved job design practices consciously aimed at reducing (employers' dependence on) skill requirements, it is possible for jobs to be evaluated in a different way, one which reflects and expresses the real experiences and evaluations of those who perform the jobs as opposed to having those experiences abstracted and de-realised in management evaluations. The only factor which accounts for job evaluation generally assuming the form it has today is the general *power relationship* between companies and workforces, and the fact that managements have generally been able to establish and preserve a large measure of control over the ways in which labour is divided into jobs, grades and employment statuses.

With the introduction of new technologies and resulting job changes, unions are doing more than just disputing the way particular jobs are graded: they have begun to think in terms of alternative job designs. The APEX model agreement, for example, says, 'Jobs will be carefully designed to ensure that routine and monotony are minimised,' and suggests that 'Job design' should be redefined as 'the organisation of tasks in such a manner as to structure jobs which will provide job satisfaction, make full use of the ability of job holders and allow access to facilities which ensure proper career progression' (APEX, *Job Design*). This is just one example of the growing opposition to the 'process which oddly is known as "Scientific Management," (which) attempts to reduce the worker to a blind unthinking appendage to the machine or process in which he or she is working' (The Lucas Combine's Corporate Plan).

5

LEAVE, WORKING HOURS AND LABOUR USE

Contrasting the social and labour practices of European-based multinationals in the early seventies, the ILO concluded, 'The main differences noted when comparing conditions in plants in industrialised and developing countries are longer working hours and shorter leave in the latter' (ILO [1976], p. 114). With respect to leave, the gap has narrowed since this was written (except in the case of sick leave) due to the extension of leave facilities in Bombay. But despite some successes in negotiating shorter hours in Bombay, the disparity in working hours remains, and in some cases is growing even wider. This is partly because of stiff resistance from many Bombay managements to a shorter working week, partly because in the context of high unemployment, trade unions in the Netherlands and other European countries have adopted further work-time shortening as a priority. Employers in Europe have responded by demanding more flexible working hours and an extension of shift-working, whereas in India shift-working is already widespread. Employer enforcement of other types of flexibility— especially task flexibility and the use of temporary and contract labour to obtain flexibility of numbers—also began earlier and is more prevalent in India, but is now spreading in countries like Holland and Britain. The new patterns of labour use are having complex effects on the employment of women, increasing some types of employment available to them and reducing others.

5.1 LEAVE

Some essential information on leave entitlements is summarised in Table 5.1. The main area of substantial inequality in leave involves

TABLE 5.1
Leave Entitlements

A. *BASIC LEAVE*

Company	Public Holidays	Annual Holidays
NETHERLANDS		
Philips	7	22
Unilever	9	24–30*
UK		
Philips	8	25
ICI	9	25†
BOMBAY		
Philips	10	28**
ICI/CAFI	10	22
Hindustan Lever	10	23

B. *SICK LEAVE: UK SCHEMES*

ICI Sick Pay Scheme		Philips Sick Pay Scheme	
Length of Service	*Maximum Period of Sickness (weeks)*	*Length of Service*	*Maximum Period of Sickness (weeks)*
6m–1 year	4	less than 1 year	4
1–2 years	8	1–2 years	8
2–3 years	13	2–3 years	16
over 3 years	26	3–4 years	24
		4–5 years	32
		5–6 years	40
		6 years and over	52

C. *SICK LEAVE: BOMBAY*

	Maximum Period of Sickness (days)
Philips	15
ICI/CAFI	15
Hindustan Lever	17
Foreign-controlled average‡	13.8

Source: CAOs, agreements in LRD files, agreements summarised in Union Research Group, *Bulletin*, no. 9, 1986, and *Philips Industries Group Common Conditions of Employment*.

Notes: 　* according to age;
　　　　† from 1987;
　　** calendar days;
　　　‡ thirty-three settlements.

sickness benefit provisions or provisions for sick leave. For example, Philips employees in the Netherlands can sustain sicknesses up to a maximum of three years, while in the UK the Philips sickness payments range up to fifty-two weeks per year with no other limit specified; the company contribution in both cases is the amount necessary to make up state sickness benefits to a sum equal to 100 per cent of net pay. On the other hand, in Kalwa and other Philips establishments in India, employees are entitled to a maximum sick leave of fifteen days. The sickness payment schemes in operation in the UK plants of Philips and ICI are summarised in Table 5.1, which also shows that the average sick leave entitlement of the Bombay plants of large companies of this sort works out to just under two weeks.

Annual leave or basic holiday entitlements show almost no significant disparity, and in terms of paid holidays India could be better off. Finally, regulation of casual leave is tighter in Holland because agreements list the occasions when employees can apply for such leave. In Bombay agreements casual leave varies from seven to ten days, and there is no provision for 'unpaid leave'.

5.2 WORKING HOURS

This is an area of considerable inequality, not only between the Netherlands and Bombay but even between different establishments or groups of employees within Bombay. Hindustan Lever's Sewree factory still works a 48-hour week (at the time of writing), while head office staff are on 36 hours. In the factory, clerical grade clerks and technical grade clerks work completely different hours; when clerical employees promoted to the 'technical' grade had their hours extended and the union took the company to court, management argued, 'There is a mobility between these two grades and although while in clerical grade the employee may be expected to work for 36 hours only, on his transfer to the corresponding technical grade he must put in 48 hours' (*Maharashtra Government Gazette*, 22 May 1980, p. 3777f.). On the other hand, manual employees in Unilever plants in the Netherlands are on their way to 36 hours, which will make the disparity in working hours between the domestic plants and the Sewree factory *a whole twelve hours per week*. Philips Kalwa works 44 hours against 38 in the Philips establishments in Holland (Philips rejected the reduction to 36 in the 1986 negotiations), so here the disparity works out to six hours per week. Overall it would be possible to claim that the working hours disparity between Dutch and Bombay factories varies from just under five hours (for ICI) to twelve hours (for Unilever). Whereas employees of Philips Kalwa work some 16 per cent longer than Philips employees in Holland, once Unilever introduces 36 hours in the 1986 settlement, workers at the Sewree factory will be working 33 per cent longer than their colleagues in Holland (see Table 5.2).

TABLE 5.2
Working Hours: Evolution and Disparity

Company	Year	Working Hours*	
NETHERLANDS			
Unilever	1986–87	36†	
	1985	38	(35.6)
Shell	1987	38.3	(35.2)
	1986	38.6	(35.5)
ICI Holland	1986	37.69	(34.74)
Philips	1985	38**	(33.6)
Holland over 1922–50		48	
Holland 1961		45	
UK			
Shell Chemicals	1985	37.5	
Shell UK Oil	1985	40	
ICI	1985	37.5	
Philips	1985	39	
Birds Eye Walls (Unilever)	1985	39–40	
Lever Bros, Port Sunlight	1985	37.5	
v.d. Bergh & Jurgens	1984	37.5	
Metal Box	1985	37.5	
May & Baker	1985	37.5	
SKF	1985	39	
UK 1968		40.5	
INDIA			
Nocil (Shell/Mafatlal)	1986	39.38	
ICI	1986	42.5	
Philips, Kalwa	1986	44	
Siemens	1986	44	
Metal Box	1986	45	
SKF, Pune	1986	48	
Hindustan Lever, Sewree	1986	48	
UNILEVER ELSEWHERE			
Unilever Australia	1981	37.5‡	

TABLE 5.2 *Continued*

Company	Year	Working Hours*
Sunlight–Vinolia, Denmark	1981	40
Lever Iberica, Spain	1982	40
Philippine Refining	1983	40
Lever Bros USA	1983	40
Unilever S. Africa	1983	43***

Source: CAOs for Unilever, Shell, ICI and Philips in the Netherlands; IDS Reports 446/April 1985, 454/August 1985, 455/August 1985, 456/September 1985, 458/October 1985, 459/October 1985, 461/November 1985, 463/December 1985, IDS Study 349/November 1985, and NBPI, *Hours of Work, Overtime and Shiftworking (Report No. 161)* (London 1970) p. 7 for the UK; URG, 'Leave and working hours', *Bulletin*, no. 9, 1986 for India; *Unilever Information*, no. 11, March 1984.

Notes: * figures in brackets refer to hours of workers on continuous shifts;
         † agreed for two- and three-shift workers;
        ** 35.6 for three-shift workers;
         ‡ 40 for the edible fats division;
       *** for employees working shifts.

Foreign-controlled firms whose Bombay or Pune factories are still on 48 hours include Hindustan Ferodo, Atlas Copco, SKF and Genelec (GEC). But in the Bombay chemical and pharmaceutical industries where a lot of foreign firms are present, the average working week fluctuates around 42 hours. Voltas (Indian-controlled and part of the Tata group) was probably the first major company in the Bombay engineering industry to agree to a five-day week, which meant 42.5 hours for workers at the Thane factory. Again, this shows that service conditions are not always better in the foreign-controlled companies, although the best working hours (40–42.5) are found more often in foreign-controlled plants, while the majority of factories with the worst working hours (45–48) are Indian-controlled.

5.2.1 Working hours reduction

In 1980, when the majority of British establishments were on a 40-hour week, one survey found that '60 per cent of the claims were for an immediate reduction of the working week to 35 hours . . . . In the majority of cases, therefore, the union negotiators at local level were bidding for a substantial reduction' (White [1980], p. 23). By the end of the seventies, labour time shortening had become a major union objective in most countries of Europe. By the early eighties, the whole thrust of Dutch union strategy had shifted to the demand for shorter hours, a phased, long-term reduction to 32. Reduction of working hours is today seen by the unions in Holland as their main strategy for fighting job losses, one basic way in which they can establish their grip over the level of employment and create more jobs through 'redistribution of work'.

There is a second reason why this demand has a basis in the experience of wage-earners in the Netherlands. In the technically advanced productive sectors with high capital-intensity, such as the concentration of refineries and chemical plants in the region south of Rotterdam, continuous shifts have increasingly become the main form of shift-working. Resistance to shift-work in general is something Dutch employers have had to contain through the high level of shift payments discussed in an earlier chapter (p. 63ff.). But high rates of compensation have failed to suppress a key demand of workers in these sectors of industry for a reduction of working hours through the introduction of a five-crew system. This is a case where the demand for shorter hours has practical implications not just for the degree of union control over the number of jobs but also for the physical, psychological and social well-being of workers.

The actual situation with regard to the progress of shorter hours was as follows: by the middle of 1985, twenty-three collective agreements and a further thirty-two agreements of principle had been negotiated introducing 36 hours. These covered something like 9 per cent of the total labour force. For workers on continuous shifts, labour time shortening meant a transition from five-crew working to a hybrid four/five-crew system involving an average reduction from 40 to 36 hours. The Ministry survey reporting these facts also predicted a further expansion of the four/five-crew system, and noted that transition to a complete five-crew system would mean a working week of 34 hours.

To be precise, a five-crew system would mean 33.6 hours. In the 1986 negotiations in Unilever, where workers on continuous shifts worked 35.6 hours, the union was pressing for 34.6 as a transition to a complete five-crew system. Philips put up considerable resistance to any further reduction of working hours below 38, and categorically rejected the demand for 36 in the 1986 negotiations; Unilever, on the other hand, agreed to 36. Philips President

Dekker summed up his company's position on the issue when he told the press 'Labour time shortening as it is now evolving forms a major threat to the competitive position of Dutch industry' (NRC, 2 March 1985). He was also quoted as saying that 36 hours is 'impractical and unreal'. Like Philips, Fokker was holding out against 36, whereas Heineken agreed to the reduction without reducing pay. To some extent this reflects a division among Netherlands employers on the issue of labour time shortening, but it is also partly an expression of the demands which managements want the unions to accept in return for shorter hours.

In some companies—in Philips with respect to higher personnel and more generally in Shell—managements successfully resisted reduction of hours by retaining the option to have part or all of the free time encashed. Thus in Shell the agreement states that for workers on the day shift and people working two- and three-shifts, of the nine extra free days for 1986, five are open to encashment, and of the eleven extra days for 1987, likewise five (Shell, p. 19). It seems that during the negotiations, the Industriebond was opposed to this arrangement and finally agreed only because the company assured the union that it would exercise its option in exceptional cases only. A shortage of trained instrument technicians then led the company to use the encashment option rather more widely than it had promised. Small examples like this show that there is every reason to believe that the general drive to reduce working hours drastically *could* expand job opportunities quite considerably, but for it to have this effect the unions would need to launch a frontal attack on the prevailing rationality of cost reduction.

Since reduction of working hours is by itself only a general process whose concrete forms depend on factors related to the workplace—such as the prevalence of different shift rosters and the duration for which plants are kept open—discussions around the issue have been forced down to a decentralised or plant level. This aspect is explicitly acknowledged in the Unilever agreement which states:

8.6 The parties to this agreement shall have further discussions about the structures through which labour time shortening can be realised . . . . With a view to working out the agreed shortening of labour time by 5 per cent the parties shall conclude a framework agreement (*raamovereenkomst*). This agreement defines the limits within which discussions of this issue may proceed in each individual establishment . . . . From the unions' side the discussions shall involve paid officials who in keeping with clause 1a.6 of this agreement can avail of the support of a delegation comprising one or more members of the union who are employed in the establishment concerned (Unilever, pp. 17–18).

As the local committees saw it, this was a form of bargaining: 'They have given us 36 hours, but we have to negotiate at plant level how it's going to be worked out.' (For the kinds of demands managements were making on unions in return for shorter hours, see below.)

In India the situation is much less homogeneous, the only standardising factor being the maximum limit of 48 hours per week for factories registered under the Factories Act 1948. Over the period 1971–85, working hours were in fact reduced in several establishments, including the Philips factory at Kalwa, where the working week was reduced from 48 to 44 hours in 1980. Even those managements which agreed to the reduction were successful in getting unions to agree that production would be maintained at pre-reduction levels. Other managements refused to negotiate the issue; among these was the management at Hindustan Lever's Sewree plant, which rejected outright the union's demand in their last charter for a reduction of the working week below 48 hours.

5.3 FLEXIBILITY OF TIME

In the bargaining over labour time shortening in the Netherlands, at least three principles have won general acceptance by employers: (*a*) if you're going to accept reduction of hours, go for flexibility: do not be bound by the convention of regular working hours; (*b*) keep the factories open for longer, use the equipment on a more continuous basis; (*c*) fight for control over determination of *how* workers take the free time created by shorter hours.

The last aspect here illustrates the quietly hegemonic role that Philips continues to play in establishing the general lines of evolution of Dutch labour relations. In August 1984, Philips signed a 'Principe-Akkoord' linking the shortening of working hours to flexibilisation of labour time (*flexibilisering van de arbeidsduur*).

Netherlands employers reacted quite favourably to the innovations contained in those discussions. The annual report of the main employers' association stated:

> The substance of these agreements is that factory time and working time are completely delinked, and there is some talk of increased flexibility of work times for the plant. In the agreement for the small metal industry, the workweek can vary from a minimum of 34 hours per week to a maximum of 42.5 hours (with a maximum working day of 9 hours) . . . . In Philips the labour time shortening agreed for 1985 will be realised by means of 26 blocks of roster-free half-days per employee. Management can fix 8 blocks for all or for groups of employees after discussion with the works council. If management wants to fix more than 8 blocks for all or for groups of employees, the consent of the works council is required.

And the employers concluded, 'With the agreements mentioned above, an important step has been taken to a form of labour time shortening which can contribute to the optimal running of plants' (VNO, *Jaarverslag 1984*, pp. 131–32). The Philips negotiator in the 1984 discussions also thought that the agreement was a victory for the company. At the time, *Volkskrant* commented, 'De Lange however sees the real gain in the fact that management now has a free hand in determining when employees can take their roster-free days. Nothing has been agreed about the obligatory spreading of such days throughout the year as in the metal industry agreement' (18 August 1984).

The principle described here is stated more fully in clause 13a of the Philips agreement for 1985 (Philips, p. 19). In the Unilever agreement, in clause 18b which has the interesting title 'Framework agreement on labour time shortening,' it is agreed that from 1985 working hours will be reduced by 5 per cent, which works out to 104 free hours. Of these 104 hours, the company can fix a maximum of four days (32 hours) as 'collective holidays' after local discussion. The same clause on shorter working hours allows for working days of 9 hours after discussion in the factories concerned, and also states that in such cases, overtime starts only with the tenth hour (Unilever, p. 40). Unilever BLG members commented, 'They (i.e. management) want to fix just enough to fill the gaps between our holidays. They don't want to start up the whole factory just for one day if there's a gap between two holidays—that's much too expensive' (interview). In other words, control over the determination of the free days created through labour time reduction would enable management to schedule production so as to ensure maximum continuity in the operation of plants.

'But how do *you* want to take the extra free time?'
'We want it on Friday night. In our three-shift working, we want the free time on Fridays. It's difficult because they don't want that, it costs production, and so they want us to take the time on holidays or other days but not Friday nights. If you don't work on Friday night, you have your Saturday free. If you work Friday nights, you have to sleep on Saturday. So we'd rather sleep on Friday night and have our Saturday free, but I don't think we'll make it.'
'Why not?'
'In most factories because of automation they have overcapacity. They *could* get Friday night's production through the rest of the week. But still they don't want to do this. And we think they want longer factory hours, they want Saturday working, because they are planning to invest in new machines which are very expensive, so they want to use them continuously, or at least on Saturdays. That's their aim' (interview).

Philips management: 'We have invested a lot in machinery, it's better to let the machines run longer than eight hours, possibly sometimes continuously. This is one of the special items at stake within Philips with the union and the works council' (interview).
Keeping the machines running for longer could mean, for example, two crews working four-day weeks 9 hours a day, Monday to Thursday/Wednesday to Saturday. For workers this has obvious drawbacks, including Saturday working. For employers, however, the advantage of formulas of this kind is that working hours reduction is linked to an extension of *factory* hours, of the time that plants are kept open and running. Once we take account of this dimension, the general drive of Dutch employers to use their capital equipment more intensively and extend factory hours, and relate these aspects to the more general fact that employers in the Netherlands are in any case already engaged in a variety of shift

systems, it is clearly true that 'there are dozens of variations possible for combining working hours, factory hours and shift rosters' (Vervoersbond-FNV [February 1985], p. 35).

Maximum continuity in the operation of plants due to investments in expensive capital equipment is one factor in the drive to restructure the pattern of working hours. But the prevalence of strong *cyclicity* in the productive rhythms of some plants is also significant. The cycles do not all have the same specific form but in most cases they have so far meant regular and heavy dependence on overtime. In at least three cases, the cycle takes the form of a well-defined seasonal fluctuation of demand: demand for the GLS lamps produced at Philips' extremely modern light factory at Weert is concentrated in the winter months; demand for ice-creams picks up dramatically in summer, and summer is also the busy beer-drinking season, so both Unilever and Heineken have to concentrate production at those times of the year. In another case the fluctuation is seasonal, but a fluctuation of supply rather than demand: the spinach harvest and its impact on the demand for labour in the frozen foods division of Unilever.

At the Philips Weert factory, works council members said,

> We are just starting talks on flexibility because we want to separate this issue from the issue of labour time shortening; management wants to link them. We know what management wants, because for the GLS lamp most of the turnover is in winter. They're asking that either we should work an hour longer or work on Saturdays, but seven days must be worked longer in winter. And in spring it's the other way around, we'll work that much less (interview).

Unilever management:

> In some companies we want flexibility, for example, for spinach in this season (summer) we need more time for the foods group than we do in winter. But that's just for the foods division, not for margarine. You also have some influence of the seasons in the meat business . . . . Altogether we are offering a 36-hour week, but within this framework of flexibility. That's one of the topics at the moment (interview).

Union activists at the v.d. Bergh en Jurgens factory in Rotterdam said:

> We want shorter working hours because of the high unemployment. We want to share work with more people . . . . Management is trying to take advantage of our struggle for shorter hours by introducing flexibility. We are usually paid overtime for the extra hours, and now they are trying to reduce that through flexibility, to convert them into normal hours.

Militants at Fokker's Schiphol plant made a similar point:

> Management wants us working longer when they need it and shorter when they don't. In Fokker we are very dependent on customers. If some American customer says, 'We want five planes in three months,' everyone has to work very hard to get those five planes. Then for two months there isn't any customer, so we just make our regular planes, but it's on a very low schedule. So flexibility is very important, I think it's the most important thing going on. Because when you work overtime you get paid extra, it costs a lot of money, so they want to abolish the extra payment for overtime. They won't say so, but that's what they are after (interviews).

Hence, extension of factory hours to keep the equipment running for longer, and reduction of overtime through schedules allowing for a flexible distribution through the year. On the other hand, the increase in total operating hours leads to an extension of shift-working. There's some evidence to suggest that Philips has made rather careful investigations into the relative profitability of different shift systems and, in two cases at least opted for an extension of factory time to 15 hours on the basis of three five-hour shifts. Here the decisive consideration was the ability of workers to sustain high levels of production in shifts of this sort. A director of the Terneuzen light plant observed, 'A 5-hour shift is most favourable when the labour curve is considered. If people work 8 hours they get tired. The mini-shift exactly covers the time during which one feels best and in which the most work can be done') *Connecta* [October 1985], p. 3).[29] Ria Hermanussen says,

To run these mini-shifts 150 new workers were recruited on part-time contracts of two years. Depending on the pressure of production they work 20 or 25 hours a week in a three-shift system. When they joined, workers could choose between a morning shift (7.00–12.00), an afternoon shift (12.00–17.00) and an evening shift (17.00–22.00); no change of shift was possible thereafter . . . . People are significantly less enthusiastic about the evening shift than about the morning or afternoon shifts. Only 13 per cent of those currently employed on the evening shift would opt for the same shift if the system is continued. The rest would want to be transferred.

Apart from considerations related to performance standards, a major advantage of this form of shift-working for Philips would be the savings in shift payments, since no shift allowance is paid for the mini-shifts. (The Belgian unions got Philips to agree to a small allowance, but only for work after 8.00 p.m. It is estimated that in the Belgian plants the number of employees on part-time contracts expanded from 440 in 1983 to 1000 just a year later.) These are only a few of the forms of flexibilisation that are spreading rapidly in countries in the West and which affect mainly women. (For the effects on women, see below.)

If there have been no comparable developments in Bombay industry, it is because there has been no necessity for them. The Factories Act specifies a limit of 9 hours to the working day, and many establishments with a five-day week have a working day of around this length. Lack of resistance to shift-work means not only that shift payments are negligible but also that three-shift workers could often be working a six-day week. Thus long factory hours and continuity of production are already features of much of industry. Fluctuations in demand are commonly met with the use of casual workers, etc. (see below), or in some cases by the use of overtime. In a sense, therefore, it could be argued that companies in Bombay already have the kind of flexibility which is sought to be achieved by a new pattern of working hours in the Netherlands. Paradoxically, in Bombay the greatest obstacle to this kind of flexibility occurs where there is a large proportion of permanent women employees in the workforce, since they would be covered by protective legislation.

5.4 FLEXIBILITY OF NUMBERS

One of the most disquieting developments in Holland in the eighties has been the spread of temporary contracts and use of labour supplied by employment agencies. In the UK too, the LRD Flexibility Survey found that in 1986 the

> most common of all strategies was the increased use of subcontractors, which was reported by 50 per cent. Frequently mentioned uses for these were general and equipment maintenance (19 replies) and specialist machining or tooling (11 replies). The use of temporaries and short-term contracts was reported by 45 per cent of replies with cleaning and catering being mentioned frequently. (LRD [November 1986], p. 6).

Unilever was one of the companies making use of these types of labour (TICL, 'Unilever').

In the Netherlands, ICI has a clause which gives management the right to use such workers for jobs 'which under normal circumstances cannot be done by the company's staff' and specifies a number of areas where this might be the case, including plant construction, shutdown, jobs of a temporary nature, jobs for which no employees are immediately available and reserves to cover shortfalls (ICI, cl. 21.3a, p. 38). However, this clause also states that 'The employer shall not get any jobs done through contract labour for a period lasting longer than six months'. The Philips agreement states almost at the very start: 'The employer shall not retain any employees in his service on terms which are less favourable than those stated in this agreement' (Philips, cl. 2.1, p. 9). This is very important because it implies that there is no difference in the terms and conditions of employment between temporary or contract workers and the permanent workforce. By contrast, almost every plant in the Bombay area has some workers on terms which are less favourable than those applied to permanent employees.

In India, managements were able to force this type of control over the labour market throughout the seventies. In Hindustan Lever's soaps and detergents plant at Sewree there were some forty contractors with a contract labour force of around 600; it seems that this was recently reduced to less than 200. Since it is the contractor who deals with the company, Lever would have had around 15 per cent of its workforce working for it but not on its payroll, including a number of skilled groups, especially fitters and welders. In Chemco, Carbide's petrochemical plant at Chembur, about thirteen contractors would supply the company with a labour force of around 150 workers for piping, installation, gardening and some maintenance. And in the large public sector refineries near Chemco, established in the fifties by foreign oil companies and nationalised some twenty years later, management retains a contract labour force running literally into thousands.

Large-scale use of contract labour is a feature of process industry. One advantage of this form of labour use for the companies concerned is the ability to get jobs done without paying workers the benefits and other entitlements due to their permanent employees. But there are other advantages. Much of the most hazardous work is assigned to them, and this makes contract workers a group with a high average rate of accidents, especially fatal ones. Finally, their services can be terminated without legal complications. In Bombay engineering plants, the counterpart to these forms of unprotected labour is the use managements make of temporary workers. In the Philips Pune agreement of 1977, management had pressed for deployment of temporaries, apparently on a large scale, but the agreement finally stated that the company would employ not more than 10 per cent of the total permanent strength of each factory on this basis. It was also agreed that they would be entitled to annual increments and leave facilities if they put in a whole year's continuous service. But it is common practice for managements to break the service periods of temporaries to escape legal obligations they would otherwise be liable to. Some of the biggest engineering plants in Bombay, in particular the Mahindra jeep and tractor manufacturing units on the Akurli Road, employ upto 25 per cent of their labour force as temporaries, mainly to reduce dependence on overtime working. But here, in the jeep factory, a recent agreement succeeded in confirming a large number of these workers.

Flexible use of labour in the specific form of multiple employment statuses within the same establishments gives managements the additional advantage of fragmenting workforces and playing off different groups of workers against each other—not only permanent workers against temporaries and contract workers, but even the latter against each other. One example is Abbott Laboratories, where the employees' union was demanding that temporary workers be made permanent. Management replied that if the temporaries were made permanent, contract workers employed at the same factory could not be made permanent. The result was that the contract workers brought in another union in 1983 and violent clashes followed. Workforce divisions have been a major source of union rivalry in Bombay factories, and one of the main forms of such divisions has been the use of temporary and contract workers.

5.5 FLEXIBILITY OF TASKS

With increasing automation, employers have also wanted flexibility between jobs. This was an important dimension in the productivity bargaining which occurred in Britain in the sixties, and its importance has revived recently. It was not possible to tell whether flexibility agreements have the same significance for Dutch industry, but in their Rozenburg complex, one of ICI's five key production sites in Western Europe, management were preparing a major offensive—the introduction of what they called the 'multifunctional system'. This means more jobs or tasks for the same grade. But whereas ICI Holland management was only beginning to ask for job flexibility, the ICI agreement for its Terene Works on the Thane–Belapur Road already gives management extensive controls in this area:

> (d) The union agrees that the Management may
>   a) carry out rationalisation of jobs and create adequate inter and intra trade/job flexibility,
>   b) redesign and restructure the existing jobs . . . (CAFI/ ICI [1983], cl. 13A, p. 5).

Since Nocil, the Bombay operation partly controlled by Shell, has what would certainly qualify as the most versatile workforce in the whole of Bombay industry, it was worth asking whether Shell had gone for anything similar in domestic plants.

'A multicraft system?
We don't have that, but they talk about it [the union said].

There have been changes on the job. You do a lot more things
now than you did in the late sixties.'
'What happens if operators refuse assignments?'
'They don't refuse; if they do, they can be fired. The company
wants flexibility. For example, the movements operators. Some
of them are going to be head operators. Management has said if
there are going to be new head operators, they have to be plant
operators first. That's the new demand. That means more tasks.
I think in ten years there won't be a movements operator any
more. In Esso one operator runs the plant, he does everything
. . .' (interview).

This may imply higher levels of workforce versatility in the Bombay
petrochemicals plant than in some of Shell's domestic plants.

One plant in Holland where there does seem to have been a
considerable increase in shop floor mobility is Heineken's large
modern brewery at Zoeterwoude, commissioned in the mid-
seventies with a total staff of 2,000 and producing five million
hectolitres of beer every year. There are seven manual grades in
the brewery, the bargainable category, and another three for
higher personnel. When asked how much flexibility Heineken
had, the manager responsible for job classification said,

'A lot of flexibility, almost 100 per cent.'
'How? Did they have overlapping jobs?'
'No, we have made the operators do more jobs, they are more
versatile. Previously there were at least ten distinct job descriptions on the shop floor, now there are only two. Machine
operators are the main job category, and they can be shifted
from one machine to another.'
'How did you get so much flexibility? What did you give in
return?'
'We upgraded all the operators who were in the two lowest
grades, and this gave them more money. We said the upgradation was necessary because their work now involved greater
responsibility, which is true' (interview).

In other words, here increased flexibility was related to actual
changes in job descriptions and grading. Today there are almost
no employees in the two lowest grades, while grades 3, 4 and 5–7
account for roughly equal shares of the workforce.

In the Unilever settlement for Holland, the general clause on employees' obligations towards the company includes a brief statement to the effect that 'an employee may be required to work temporarily in a place other than his usual place of work. Such employment shall not exceed a period of six months at one stretch . . .' (Unilever, cl. 4.2, p. 12). In the Philips agreement a similar clause states, 'The employee shall follow all reasonable instructions, even when this involves performance of jobs which do not belong to his normal work' (Philips, cl. 5.2, p. 10). In the Philips cable factory at Delft, when the local union committee drafted a report on employment conditions in the factory in the early eighties,

> workers in almost all departments felt generally insecure over task content, an insecurity one could trace to the shifting of personnel within and between departments. Taken together with changes in task content, this implies multifunctionality of work: 'For management starts from the idea that no one is 100 per cent occupied by one's job, and if you're only 80 per cent occupied, then it's a question of making you productive for the remaining 20 per cent somewhere else . . .' (Buitelaar and Vreeman [1985], p. 373).

In Bombay industry, flexibility has been a major management objective. Most Tata plants in Bombay have got unions to sign flexibility clauses in recent rounds of bargaining.[30] As Table 2.6 shows, demands for flexibility formed around 15 per cent of the main management demands listed for a group of bigger companies. Like other employers in Bombay electrical engineering, Philips was in the forefront of the general drive to enforce tighter control over deployment. The agreement for Philips' Pune factories has a clause entitled 'Interchangeability' according to which, 'In order to take care of the changes in the planning and exigencies of work, Management may allocate any job/machine to any workman or change his/her job depending on requirements in his/her section/ department or another section/department.' This gives considerable freedom of deployment since it allows for unrestricted mobility between jobs, machines and departments. For permanent transfers, management has to take into account the 'seniority and trade of the concerned workman,' and the agreement adds, 'This clause is not intended to harass/victimise any workman' (Philips Pune, cl. 17, p. 12).

The drive for flexibility is equally apparent in the light factory at Kalwa. Here a 'Work Requirements' clause in the 1985 agreement states, 'The Union will cooperate in the movement of workmen within the department,' and 'The existing practice of movement of workmen from one department to another after discussion and agreement with the Union shall continue' (Philips Kalwa, cl. 20a-b, p. 10). In other words, there is *mobility* both within departments and between them. The settlement also includes a note to the effect that 'Workmen shall do additional jobs within their department and skill, wherever time is available' (letter of the Plant Manager to the Union, 28 February 1985). However, the interchangeability agreements for Kalwa also restricted management's freedom to use acting assignments to cover for absenteeism, since the General Reserve was agreed as an alternative. The 1982 agreement states, '2. Out of the total (permanent) operators in the sections where interchangeability is applicable, 16 per cent of them will be called General Reserves . . . . 4. The minimum grade of the General Reserve operators in the Lamp Factory shall be SS.III. 5. To fulfil the requirement of minimum grade, the General Reserves will be upgraded . . . .' The reserves would have to be able to perform a variety of tasks; on days of low absenteeism, they would work in fixed positions, otherwise be mobile on the understanding that 'movement of General Reserves will be normally restricted to two occasions per shift.' But management was not satisfied with the degree of flexibility it obtained through the interchangeability agreements. In 1985, one of the factors behind the strike was the company's attempts to cut the size of the General Reserve and deploy other workers in violation of their agreement.

Thus the emphasis on flexibility is much more explicit in agreements for Bombay than anything which comes through in the settlements for domestic plants, although Bombay has nothing comparable to the agreements on flexibility which companies have negotiated in the UK.[31] The evolution of a modern industrial culture in Bombay was entirely the work of foreign companies. It was these companies which first brought into the country management techniques which were still 'modern' by international standards. By the early sixties, Hindustan Lever made use of work study, Indian Oxygen (a British Oxygen subsidiary) had introduced 'Systems & Methods Study,' Murphy had a job evaluation agreement, Stanvac wanted-multicraft jobs. Once productivity bargaining was in full swing in Britain, equivalent concepts were being imported into plants controlled by British firms or firms with experience in the UK: there would be no other way of explaining the detailed emphasis on interchangeability in the Indian Oxygen agreement of 1967 (British Oxygen was then in the forefront of productivity bargaining), or the 'crafts consolidation scheme' negotiated as part of the Esso agreement some months later. It was, therefore, only to be expected that when the general movement to enforce tighter standards of performance developed in the course of the seventies, it was led by international firms. The demand for flexibility became widespread in the Bombay chemical industry by the early eighties, but in what was then the Burmah-Shell Refinery it had been in operation a whole decade earlier. Clauses on redeployment of staff, clauses on transfer, rotation and mobility within and between departments, the insistence on flexible job descriptions, trades consolidation schemes and amalgamation of crafts, control over job assignments, etc., were so many norms managements were evolving with respect to the efficient utilisation of labour.

5.6 FLEXIBLE WOMEN?

In the Netherlands, far fewer women employees are organised into unions than elsewhere in Europe; according to Visser's estimates for the early eighties, only 16.3 per cent as against 35.4 per cent in Britain, 50.6 per cent in Denmark or 77.2 per cent in Sweden ('Die Mitgliederentwicklung', Table 7, p. 19). The only occupational unions with a substantial proportion of women were the union of teachers (ABOP, 51.9 per cent), employees in public services (Dienstenbond, 32.6 per cent), artists (Kunstenbond, 30 per cent) and government employees (Abvakabo, 24.3 per cent). The main reason for this low overall presence within unions is the low labour force participation rates of women in Holland, the fact that traditionally Dutch women were discouraged from seeking employment. It was an integral part of the policy of Dutch patriarchalism that instead of encouraging women to seek paid employment, employers should pay higher allowances to the male breadwinner. One indication of the strong underlying resistance to women's employment is the lack of any provision for creches within workplaces and the low availability of places in day-care centres in a country where the unions have otherwise succeeded in establishing a wide range of welfare benefits.

In India, by contrast, both the government and trade unions have always accepted that many women will take up paid employment. One consequence is the requirement in the Factories Act that any factory employing thirty or more women (initially fifty or more women) should provide a creche for their children. Unions have fought for implementation of this legislation in most large workplaces in the Bombay area, and have been successful in most places. Not everywhere, however. The Philips plant at Kalwa is one factory where management has so far resisted the demand. In 1964, Philips had its factory at Mazagaon in the heart of old Bombay, and about 200 women worked there. In 1965–66, when Philips relocated to Kalwa outside the municipal limits of Bombay, most of the women were told to leave. Apparently some fifty women continued to work in the factory even after relocation. But there was no creche in the new plant, and the number of women was gradually run down until in the late seventies there were only thirty of them left. When an amendment to the Factories Act made creche facilities statutory for establishments with thirty or more women, the Philips Personnel Manager is reported to have pressurised one of the women at Kalwa to accept a transfer to the head office in Bombay so that the company could escape its legal obligation to provide a creche. She accepted the transfer, and Philips continued to be one of the very few foreign-controlled companies with the doubtful distinction of denying creche facilities to its women employees. It seems that the Personnel Manager was promoted for this minor achievement.[32] During negotiations for the 1985 agreement, the union again pressed for a creche but were again met with refusal by management and had to settle instead for a 'creche allowance' of Rs 25 per month, subject to a maximum of two children. This is hardly an adequate substitute, since most creches would charge four times as much or more.

Despite the provision of workplace creches, however, in Bombay as in the Netherlands it is assumed that women will take primary responsibility for housework and childcare even if they go out to work. One indication of this is the fact that there is no provision for *male* employees to bring their children to a creche. As in the Netherlands, women in India are entitled to 12 weeks' fully paid maternity leave and are prohibited from doing night work, but provisions for paternity leave are negligible, and there are no restrictions of any sort on night work for men. Consequently, permanent women employees are not only more expensive than men, but also less flexible. Many employers have responded by ceasing to recruit women. At Lever's factory in Sewree, management has cut the proportion of women from 30 per cent to less than 5 per cent, and their numbers continue to fall. 'The last recruitment of women took place back in 1952.' 'As far as women are concerned, their policy is this: they don't want women to be employed in this company.' Even the agreed policy of recruiting employees' children was consistently violated where the child happened to be a daughter. 'They will act very benevolent, they'll go out of their way to have programmes, one for the wives, one for the daughters. But they will never bother to recruit even one daughter into the company' (interview). One consequence of this was management's closing down of the once-flourishing creche, since the children of the women employees were all grown up and some even had children of their own!

The assumption that housework and childcare are women's work leads to protective legislation which makes permanent, full-time women employees covered by such laws less flexible than men. But the corollary of that assumption, i.e., that women are merely secondary or supplementary wage-earners, can make part-time, temporary or other women employees who are not covered by protective legislation far more flexible than men. In Bombay, the main form in which cheap and flexible female labour is exploited by big companies is through subcontracting to the unorganised sector which is not covered by the Factories Act. In the Netherlands, part-time, temporary and contract workers provide a highly flexible labour force. According to Ria Hermanussen, Philips is a company which has made use of all three types of female labour. We have already referred to the mini-shifts staffed by women. One element of flexibility here is the fact that weekly hours can vary from 20 to 25 hours, even for permanent employees: a union official from Terneuzen said that although the company was supposed to inform employees about their schedule four weeks in advance, often they gave no more than one day's notice. Another is that many of the new workers taken on for the mini-shifts were on two-year temporary contracts. At Sittard, 140 women were hired from a labour agency for work on three shifts (7.00–15.00,

15.00–23.00, 23.00–7.00; Philips obtained permission from the government to get the women to work on the night shift). These contracts were initially for three months, extendable for another three months and then for one year. If the women survived that long without being retrenched, they would be made permanent; but this could be bypassed because the one-year contract contained a clause that they could be retrenched if there was no work, and this often happened, so that the women lost their permanency rights even if they were subsequently rehired in another department.

Flexible contracts for women have been spreading rapidly in the Netherlands. Women on *min-max contracts* could be working anywhere from 0 to 30 hours or from 12 to 24, the contract specifying not how may hours you actually work but how many you *might* work. A more extreme form of this uncertainty is the *on-call contract*, where women have to be ready to work at any time but have no guarantee that they will get any work at all in a given week; some unions even described the rate of increase of this type of contract as 'explosive' (Roozemond, 'Flexibilisering: flexibele vrouwenarbeid'). Since people wait at the phone for a call from the employer, there is a sense in which the on-call finally brings out the deepest determination of wage labour for capital, namely, the underlying fact that it is always there, at the employer's disposal.

The low proportion of women members in unions in the Netherlands is partly due to their low participation in the workforce as a whole, but it could also be due to reluctance to join or be active in unions for fear of victimisation. A woman worker in Philips said,

> I was asked by the union district official to bring some women to a union meeting and so I went to the department and asked, does anyone want to come, you have the chance if you want to. But women who belong to the union didn't want to come because they were scared. They are scared of the repercussions—they may get even less opportunity for job change and things like that than they get now. And when I went to the department to ask women to join up, the department manager said, 'What are you planning to do?' and made it quite plain that he didn't like what I was doing. The women said, 'Well, we'll come,' but no one did (interview).

Having more women in the unions would certainly make a difference to the unions' radicalism: the most left-wing unions in the FNV–ABOP, the Dienstenbond and the Voedingsbond—are all unions with a comparatively greater proportion of women members. The Voedingsbond, which represents workers in the food industry and is one of the most radical unions in Holland, is led by a woman and is one of the few unions opposed to the idea that employees should subsidise the reduction of working hours by giving up some part of their pay (*Solidariteit* [April 1986], pp. 4–5).

In Bombay, union membership among women in the organised sector is high, and there have been occasions when they have participated actively and militantly in union struggles. One indication of the relatively high level of confidence of women workers in this sector is the fact that they never tolerate sexual harassment and it has virtually been eradicated. However, their occupation of leadership positions in the unions is very far from being proportional to their numbers in the workforce. This is related not so much to fears of victimisation as to lack of time (given their double burden of wage work and domestic labour), lack of opportunities to obtain the training and experience necessary for union work, and often also opposition from family members.

One blatant form of discrimination against women which has been practised by managements in Bombay was their dismissal when they got married. The pharmaceutical employees' unions took up struggles against the notorious 'marriage clause' in the late fifties, and expanded these into a coordinated campaign when they formed themselves into a Federation in the sixties. They took the case of one woman worker all the way up to the Supreme Court, and simultaneously staged a variety of public demonstrations against the practice. After several years they won their fight when the Supreme Court ruled that the practice was illegal. Since then, explicitly discriminatory clauses have not been included in collective agreements or individual contracts; yet other forms of discrimination continue to be practised, and unions have not attempted to incorporate into agreements *positive* Equal Opportunities clauses which would go some way towards ruling out discrimination against women and other sections of the workforce.

The Unilever settlement for Holland has a clause which says:

The employer undertakes to conduct a policy aimed at equal
opportunities at work and equal opportunities in the organisation of work for employees of equivalent level (*gelijkwaardige
werknemers*), regardless of sex, sexual disposition, civil status,
creed or convictions, colour, race or ethnic origin, nationality
and political choice (*politieke keuze*), in each case applied in
such a way that no conflict arises with the objective requirements
of the job (Unilever, cl. 1a.2, p. 4).

One of the best clauses comes from Pye Telecom, which is part of
the Philips group in the UK. Here the 'Equal Opportunities Policy'
states:

1. . . . The company has an established policy of equal opportunities, regardless of sex, race, colour, ethnic origin, religion
or marital status. 2. Responsibility within establishments for the
application of this policy is with the Establishment Heads, and
Managers and Supervisors have a particular responsibility to
ensure, within their own departments and sections, that this
policy is applied . . . . 3. Within this policy, recruitment and
selection are carried out according to specific job-related criteria.
Job specifications include only requirements that are necessary
and justifiable for the effective performance of the job. Training
and promotion opportunities are related only to the individual's
suitability to fulfil the work requirements. 4. The principle of
Equal Opportunities applies in respect of payment practices,
other terms and conditions of employment, and the application
of all company employment policies and procedures . . .
(ASTMS, *Tackling a Multinational*, section 4, pp. 9–10)

One aspect of unionism in the Netherlands which has no real
equivalent in Bombay is the autonomous organisation of women
within the union movement, in forms such as the women's cells in
some of the larger unions, women's committees and women's
groups in several plants (like the *Vrouwengroep Hoogovens* in the
country's biggest steel plant), local activity by trade union women
and finally, certainly the most interesting initiative of this type, the
Vrouwenbond (Women's Union), membership of which is open to
any woman living in Holland, *including housewives*. This means
that apart from being organised as women within other unions,

women who could not otherwise belong to a union because they have no formal contract with an employer are also drawn into the union movement.

The Women's Union has taken up the problem of women being forced into insecure, badly-paid jobs in various ways. Firstly, it has started schools which run nine-month diploma courses to train women in advanced computer skills so that their jobs are not jeopardised when workplaces automate or when they re-enter the labour force after leaving paid employment to get married or have children. The first schools to be started were the Alida de Jong school in Utrecht and the Annie van Dieren school in Tilburg, half the costs of which were met through the EEC and half by local government. The courses were free, and the women who attended them got free childcare while they were on the course. Since they were highly successful—80 per cent of the women who took the diploma later went into qualified jobs—the union was setting up more schools in Assen, Zeeland and The Hague. Secondly, for women forced into paid employment on adverse contracts, it attempts to increase the degree of contractual protection by improving the terms of the contract and welfare benefits, for example, by ensuring that women on '0–40' contracts get at least five hours of work per week and that social security payments are linked to a minimum working week of five hours and not thirteen-and-a-half hours as at present. For sections of the labour force not covered by a formal contract, the Women's Union has set up a support centre in Hengelo called 'Steunpunt Thuiswerk' to organise and help homeworkers to improve their conditions. For housewives the union is campaigning for better social security benefits which also take account of their role as working women—for example, housewives who have had an accident and cannot do their usual work should receive home help without having to pay for it.

On the other hand, neither the Women's Union nor Steunpunt is empowered to negotiate with employers on behalf of their members, and this limits their ability to represent important sections of women who are also most dependent on them because they cannot belong to any other union. As a voting member of the FNV since 1982, the Vrouwenbond can influence the policies of other unions. In fact, within the FNV women have been actively involved in shaping bargaining objectives and demands through a coordination involving several unions. Concretely this means that groups of women who are not necessarily connected through their industries or workplaces and the Women's Secretariat of the FNV have been able to draft 'model clauses' for the union negotiators to try and incorporate in the agreements they sign. These *vrouwenpunten* (women's points) cover the following areas:

1. declarations of intent to take positive action to promote equal opportunities for women,
2. clauses combating forms of flexibilisation which mainly affect women,
3. clauses to improve the position of part-time employees,
4. domestic leave for longer periods (unpaid),
5. other forms of domestic leave not involving loss of pay,
6. unwanted intimacies (sexual harassment) at work, and
7. positive discrimination in recruitment and redundancies.

The draft clause on sexual harassment, for example, states that 'The employer shall make it quite plain to all employees that unwanted intimacies will not be tolerated and could lead to sanctions for the persons who are guilty of such intimacies,' and provides for a joint committee to evolve a grievance procedure for complaints against harassment and to enable women to make complaints without threat of reprisal (Roozemond [1985]).

It appears, then, that despite the wider acceptance of women's employment in Bombay, there is still a tendency for employers to treat women simply as a source of cheap and flexible labour. Unions have fought this tendency at the plant level, on at least one occasion in a more coordinated fashion; yet their overall fragmentation has prevented them from taking up women's issues at a level which would begin to tackle the complex interaction of social practices which make for the oppression of women. Nor have working women attempted to organise autonomously in order to take up these issues themselves or to put pressure on trade unions to take them up. The situation in Holland is in some ways worse, with more general social opposition to women's employment and no provision of workplace creches—an indication of a trade union movement which is perhaps even more heavily male-dominated than the movement in Bombay. But working women have found a variety of ways in which to organise themselves and take up issues concerning women at work, and their intervention will inevitably have an impact on the trade union movement as a whole.

In general, while there still remain areas of substantial inequality in working time and labour use—considerably shorter working hours and longer sick leave in Holland than in Bombay, provision of workplace creches in Bombay but not in Holland—the more striking tendency seems to be towards a greater equalisation of conditions. In a few cases, such as the extension of some types of leave entitlements in Bombay, this is to the advantage of employees, but in most cases it is not. It is significant that although decentralisation of labour relations allows companies like Philips and Unilever to have a working week which is six to twelve hours longer in Bombay, sick leave facilities which are much poorer than those in the Netherlands, and no mention of equal opportunities in any agreement, it does *not* prevent them from introducing into their establishments in Holland the unprotected forms of labour and extensive shift-working which have been prevalent in Bombay, nor even from trying to evade the obligation to provide creche facilities for their women employees in Bombay. This is a strategy which leaves international firms free to force on their Bombay establishments working hours which Holland left behind in 1950, yet introduce flexibility of tasks into the same establishments with a rapidity which keeps pace with the most advanced international standards! It is, in other words, a very flexible type of decentralisation indeed.

6

WORKING CONDITIONS, HEALTH AND SAFETY

6.1 WORKING CONDITIONS IN SOME PLANTS IN THE NETHERLANDS

In describing workers' reactions to the ways in which managements utilise labour our best source of information is the kind of report which employees began to draft from the mid-seventies, in the general form called *werknemersverslagen*. It was possible to consult some of these reports directly, for others there are excellent summaries in the book by Buitelaar and Vreeman. While most of the physical concepts are not sufficiently precise to be of practical use, there could not be a more vivid statement of the ways in which workers experience their jobs and working conditions.

In a survey of four factories in the district of Drenthe conducted by the Industriebond/FNV in collaboration with a local group of industrial psychologists, they found that 50 per cent of all the workers surveyed complained of the high noise levels in their immediate place of work, 31 per cent had complaints about explosive sounds; 46–50 per cent complained about backaches and joint pains, especially production staff working on machines, 41–45 per cent about bodyaches of one type or another, 31–35 per cent about severe muscular pains, 16–20 per cent about aches due to unusual postures. The enquiry also revealed that the majority of workers (51 per cent) experienced some discomfort due to low temperatures, temperature fluctuations and draughts, 43 per cent complained of high temperatures in confined spaces, 37 per cent of gas, vapour and stench. Eyestrain was mentioned by 16–20 per cent, 41–45 per cent felt they worked in a polluted atmosphere, 21–25 per cent complained about bad sanitary facilities, 16–20 per cent were troubled by harmful substances. In general, close to half of all workers complained about hazardous working conditions, especially in the Akzo Enka plant. Some 36–40 per cent expressed grievance about having too little control over work speeds, 31–35 per cent found their jobs monotonous, and in jobs involving machine-work, as many as 79 per cent found the work monotonous. Around 57 per cent of machine operators said they could not execute their jobs in a way determined by themselves, 36–40 per cent resented their dependence on an immediate superior, 26–30 per cent felt they were not consulted about the jobs they did (Industriebond/FNV [December 1981]). There were grievances about inadequate safety precautions, unclear operational instructions and so on, but this is enough to show that conditions in the average Dutch factory may not be so different from working conditions in many of the bigger Bombay plants.

This impression is reinforced by a survey which the local FNV committee made into conditions at the Hoechst Vlissingen plant. Table 6.1 summarises their depressing experience.

TABLE 6.1
Working Conditions at the Hoechst Chemical Plant in Vlissingen as Experienced by Workers in 1981

Department	Complaints
DMT plant	boring work, zero promotion chances, undermanning, hazardous working conditions, insecurity about the number of jobs
SKZ	no chances for promotion, high work tempo, machine pacing, sickness rates around 40 per cent, insecurity about number of jobs
Alkaan	hazardous substances, heat, noise, shift strength too small
Sinter plant	heavier workloads, poisonous vapours, risk of explosions, few chances for development, grading too low, dust, noise, sharp temperature fluctuations, reduction in shift strength, high sickness absenteeism, poor canteen facilities, poor facilities for washing and changing clothes, undermanning in shifts, poor training in department
Oven house	deteriorating job content, no possibilities for training due to shortage of personnel on shifts, few or no promotion chances, working conditions conducive to sickness with sickness rates of 20 per cent, vacancies left unfilled or only filled too late

TABLE 6.1 *Continued*

Department	Complaints
Salt & Acid plant	heavier workloads, decline in job quality, higher work tempo in future, noise, vapours, gases, dust, worsening working conditions, poor canteen facilities, undermanning
Acid purification	more work and heavier work, zero promotion possibilities, working conditions which make you fall sick, poor health and safety provisions, vacancies filled late or not filled, high labour turnover
Phosphorus lab	shift-work, monotonous jobs, chances of promotion very low, conditions leading to sickness, hopeless canteen facilities, work tempo machine-paced
Office	few promotion chances, too much control from Amsterdam head office, undermanning, insecurity about job numbers, irrational pay system, fear of legal curbs on phosphate
Electrical	dirty and dusty work, regular undermanning due to high turnover, pay too low
T.M.R.	conditions which lead to sickness, poor sanitation, bureaucratic organisation
T.W.P.	no promotion chances, monotonous work, dust, noise
Security	few or no chances of promotion, low appreciation, no diploma allowance, minimal staff strength
Energy	no promotion chances, work involving hazardous substances, poor canteen facilities
Stores	high sickness absenteeism, 25 per cent, undermanning, bad payment system
Port	few chances for personal care during work, no promotion chances, 'voluntary overtime', problems with free days, pre-war conditions in the unloading of hazardous products
Drawing office	stench and draught

Source: Hoechst Holland BLG-FNV, *'Werknemersonderzoek naar de Kwaliteit van de Arbeid bij Hoechst Holland NV, vestiging Vlissingen'*, April 1981.

   A striking indication of conditions in at least some of the Dutch Philips establishments is the fact that in Philips as a whole the number of employees reporting sick increased by 53 per cent between 1955 and 1971. 'The average number of days that Philips employees stayed away due to sickness increased in this period from 13.2 to 25.2 days, thus by 91 per cent. The percentage of the workforce reporting no sickness at any stage in the year has since 1955 declined from 52.9 to 25.6' (Teulings [1977], p. 241). In his book on Philips, certainly the best account of what working for Philips means for a lot of Philips employees in the Netherlands,

Teulings characterises high turnover rates and sickness absenteeism as largely 'a reaction to the degradation of work, work intensification and incomplete remuneration for qualified labour power' (p. 223). In the late sixties, not only did the supply of unskilled labour on the Dutch labour market actually begin to contract drastically, but more interesting, even among the unskilled workers who could ·still be found, 'it seems that only 7 per cent have no objections to working on the assembly lines' in Philips (p. 222). These general results can be reinforced by the workers' enquiry which the Industriebond/FNV activists conducted into conditions in the Philips/ NKF cable factory at Delft. Like the Hoechst report this was published in 1981 and involved the same structure. Here is a short excerpt:

Working times and work tempo
1. Which shifts do you work? Day shift, two shifts and three shifts.
2. Do the workers find the work tempo or production norms too high? Yes, certainly in departments 1, 2, 3, 4, 6, 7, 8 and 9. (There are eleven departments at Delft.)
3. Do the workers have longer rest pauses than two years ago? Six departments answered this question negatively, viz., departments 1, 2, 4, 6, 8 and 9.
4. Do the workers have to work harder than they did two years ago? In most departments people said yes to this question . . . .

Working conditions
1. What conditions constitute a danger in one's work or make one sick? A major problem was draughty departments . . ., hazardous substances in departments 4, 5 and 11, tensions in departments 3 and 5, lifting heavy materials in departments 2 and 6.
2. What is the rate of sickness in different departments? At least three departments reported rates of 20 per cent or more.
3. Are there more accidents today than there were two years ago? Departments 2 and 8 answered this positively.
4.• Do workers fall sick more often than they did two years ago? In six departments people felt sure there was more sickness today.
5. Are working conditions better or worse than they were two years ago? In departments 1–3 and 7–10 people said 'worse,' but

they also gave the reason for this, namely due to reduction of staff.

6. What conditions account for loss of job satisfaction? Blackmail and pressure, said department 7, shift-working in department 6 and psychological pressure from the top in 2, 3, 5 and 8.

7. What are the health and safety provisions like for workers? The responses were distinctly negative in two departments where people said 'poor' or 'nothing'.

At the time of the survey, NKF-Delft had lost about 22 per cent of its labour force in just two years, and all departments complained of chronic undermanning.

In most Dutch factories, employers pay a special allowance for all those aspects of one's job experience which may be regarded as *deprivations* of work.[33] In many agreements this is called an 'inconvenience allowance,' but the precise terminology varies. In the Unilever agreement the allowance is called '*toeslag bezwarende werkomstandigheden*' or the '*bwo toeslag*,' which means 'allowance for troublesome working conditions'. To qualify for this allowance, a job's points total for this factor (under its overall evaluation in the company's job evaluation scheme) must constitute at least 20 per cent of the average points value of all the jobs in the same grade. The allowance is paid once every quarter according to the level of this percentage. For workers aged 23 and above, this works out to f90 per quarter where the inconveniences are 20–30 per cent of the grade points average, f180 where they are 30–40 per cent, and f240 for anything higher. So this works out to at least f360 a year and at most f960 a year. In the Philips agreement, the allowance for deprivations is called '*hindertoeslag*' or 'allowance for hindrances'. Here the clause specifies the aspects regarded as relevant to the allowance, namely, dirt, temperature, air pollution, the need for personal protection and heavy work. Philips then defines four levels, 0 to 3, pays no allowance for level 0, f162 per quarter for level 1, f291 for 2 and f438 for 3. So here the maximum inconvenience allowance works out to f1752 per year and the minimum to f648. When H.B. Colenbrander made his survey into what employees in Holland felt about different aspects of their pay, over half (54 per cent) of the workers surveyed by him thought the inconvenience allowance should amount to at least 8–12 per cent of gross pay, and another 30 per cent thought it should be at least 18 per cent. Colenbrander then worked out that going by the average salary or modal income in his sample, this would mean a majority in favour of about *f*900 per quarter (*f*3600 per year). As he commented, 'People find today's allowances much too low' (Colenbrander [1982], p. 304).

In the more automated process industry, the main characteristics of job experience that people repeatedly referred to were isolation, stress and intensified management control. In the group interviews which Vreeman conducted with operators from ICI, he found that

> Perhaps the most characteristic feature for ICI plant operators working shifts is a *multiple isolation* which is always there in varying degrees: from colleagues elsewhere on the site (because you work in one plant or area), from colleagues within the plant (because of noise or because you work in one place), from colleagues in other shifts, from social interaction (family and social contacts) because you are tied to the roster (Buitelaar and Vreeman [1985], p. 332).

Before its transfer to the American company Archer Daniels Midland, Unilever's oil extraction plant at Europoort, southwest of Rotterdam, was quite conceivably its most automated operation. Paul Elshof said that at UniMills,

> people work in much greater isolation, there's quite a lot of stress, the workload isn't physical, it's psychological. You're responsible for a lot of equipment, management makes it only too obvious how much it will cost if something goes wrong in the process. It's a kind of psychological pressure on people to influence them. Because you are working isolated, the pressure is bigger, you can't talk so easily to the people around you . . . . It's more difficult to have regular contact, you have to organise normal day-to-day contact with the other people. If you work five-shifts, even knowing each other and seeing each other gets very difficult (interview).

In Lever Sunlight, where automation involved retraining batches of workers and jobs were changing drastically, 'isolation is a much bigger problem than it was before. They are now ten to twenty yards from each other, and it's much more difficult to communicate and more attention is required,' according to a former plant manager who described the packaging lines. And finally, in the oil extraction plant again, 'All parts of the process are so closely monitored that each hour of production can be viewed on a screen and is put into a computer, so all information is concentrated. Nothing can be done which is unseen.'

6.2 ACCIDENT RATES IN BOMBAY

There are no workers' investigations into working conditions in Bombay comparable to those in the Netherlands, but this is not for lack of employee grievances about working conditions. A study of packing lines in large pharmaceutical and food factories showed that workers had many complaints, for example: 'labelling and sealing boxes is tiring'; 'there are not enough people for carton-packing'; 'too much work for packers'; 'very tiring, especially case-packing; in bottle-filling, hands get cut on broken glass'; 'have to stand all day, very tiring; need more people on the line'; 'not enough people in checking and packing; shoulders ache'; 'checking involves eyestrain'; 'this line is tiring and overcrowded'; 'mixing gum for labels by hand is very tiring—should have a mixer'; 'one operator for bottle filling and sealing is not enough, the work is exhausting'; 'heavy work, hands and feet ache'; 'if the plaster roll is tight, pulling by hand is very strenuous; continual cutting results in corns; carrying rolls causes chest pains'; 'hands get cut while guiding the plaster'; 'eyestrain in checking; filling operator has to stand all day: one more is needed'; 'label checker feels dizzy due to the speed'; 'too fast, very tiring'; 'arm aches when sealing; eyestrain in checking'; 'shrink-packing operator has to keep adjusting polythene; legs and back ache'; 'terrible eyestrain for checkers, shoulders ache; packing is very tiring'; 'too fast, can't check properly, very tiring'; 'hazardous work: causes nausea, dizziness and headaches'; 'hand aches when levelling the cream'; 'have to stand all day; shoulders and chest ache'; 'heavy work for the helper who lifts biscuit tins; more people are needed on the line'; 'too fast; wax-wrapping the biscuits is uncomfortable due to the heat', and so forth (URG, *Bulletin* no. 3, 1983).

In many other factories, conditions are far worse. Yet there is very little recognition of this in agreements—nothing, for example, on the scale of the 'inconvenience allowances' found in Dutch agreements. The 'Hardship Allowance' of Rs 6.25 for 2 hours' work per month in the Fersolate Section of the Tablet Department of Glaxo, the half-litre of milk per day for workers in certain departments and jobs at GKW Sankey, the vitamin tablets and one rupee per day in lieu of milk for workers in some jobs at Larsen & Toubro are the nearest equivalent. The clause in an agreement negotiated by the Hoechst Employees' Union in 1984 which states, 'The company agrees to substitute, wherever possible, monotonous and strenuous manual jobs by introducing mechanisation or automation, thereby reducing physical effort and improving working conditions,' is quite exceptional.

Therefore, in order to get a better picture of working conditions in Bombay plants, it is necessary to look at accident rates. Here the concrete articulation of experience is replaced by numbers, but the emerging picture loses none of its vividness. Table 6.2 describes the rate of infliction of injuries in a few of the more important factories in Bombay where managements were both open and

TABLE 6.2

Working Conditions: Accident Rates for Large Plants in Bombay

Company and Plant	Year	All Injuries (No.)	Lost Time (No.)	Frequency Rate	Severity Rate
GKW Sankey *Bhandup*	1981		21	6.5	94.7
Electrical stampings	1982		40	12.6	171.5
Siemens *Switchgear*,	1981–82		141	c.38.0	250.1
motors, Kalwa	1982–83		119	19.0	110.3
Larsen & Toubro *Powai*	1981	6,940	618	37.1	371.2
*engineering works**	1982	7,259	471	27.7	326.9
Mukand	1982	353	160	37.9	425.3
Rolling mills, Kurla	1983	331	125	29.5	247.5
Voltas *Thane*	1981		596	129.5	790.8
engineering works	1982		643	163.8	953.9
Hindustan Lever *Sewree*	1986	982	47	5.5	184.6
soaps, edible oils	1986C†	232	10	9.2	258.7
ICI UK *weekly staff*	1979	27,884	1254	8.1	—
(no. = 45,512)	1980	24,624	1068	7.3	—

Source: For Bombay, documents supplied by managers responsible for safety; in one case by the safety committee; for ICI UK, LRD files.

Notes: * Excluding lost time cases classified as 'minor'.

      † Contract workers only.

helpful, and for ICI's domestic (UK) establishments. Of the basic columns, the first two are an indication of the scale on which workers sustained injuries in a group of plants for the period mentioned. The first includes both 'reportable' and 'non-reportable' accidents, reportable accidents being those which cause an absence of 48 hours or more (24 hours in Hindustan Lever) and which the table refers to as 'lost time injuries'. The third column is the frequency rate for reportable accidents, defined as the number of lost time *injuries* per million man-hours worked, while the severity rate in the last column is the total number of *man-days lost* per million man-hours worked. For comparative purposes, that is, in contrasting accident rates between plants or with the experience of workplaces elsewhere, severity is the most relevant index, because it accounts for the seriousness of accidents as well as their frequency. Unfortunately, in the only case where international data could be obtained (ICI, UK), this information was not available, and the most we have is a frequency rate.

It is of course quite possible that part of the variation between plants is due to under-reporting in one or two cases (this is known to happen and could even be widespread), but even allowing for this, the extent of the variation between plants is striking. This is partly due to differences between manufacturing processes and the kinds of jobs designed for them, but it is also an expression of differences in the conscientiousness with which safety managers pursue their task. As the Table indicates, it is possible for local companies with tight safety controls to have a record which is comparable with the domestic standards of large international companies. But the general standards are abysmally low, and most managements continue to work with a mental picture of accidents in which consistently high rates are 'institutionalised' by the theory that accidents arise due to short cuts and employee negligence, and that promotional methods are the obvious way of tackling them. With the exception of a few companies where managers responsible for industrial safety have gone about their job with exceptional vigour, there is almost no conscious effort to control the level of job hazards in Bombay. Chronic exposure to hazardous substances, manual handling of molten metals and acids, chronic infliction of injuries in certain jobs or departments (material handling, tyre building, die-casting, furnace, foundry, rolling mills, forges, fabrication shops and dozens of others)—are somehow accepted as integral to the experience of work, part of the normal deprivations entailed by industrial labour.

6.3 HEALTH AND SAFETY: UNION ATTITUDES AND LEGISLATION

Some unions in the Netherlands have negotiated excellent health and safety clauses in their agreements. One of the best general clauses in this area is clause 18 of the ICI Holland agreement, which states:

> Protection of employees. 1. The employer recognises the right of employees to a safe workplace and shall take the necessary steps to ensure a safe workplace within the limits possible. 2. The employer is obliged to ensure that employees are *sufficiently acquainted with the specific hazards related to their work situation* and the safety measures which have been taken on these . . . . 3. The employer shall do his utmost to make sure that research is conducted into the toxic (including genetic) properties of the substances which are used in the company's production processes and about which it is reasonable to suppose that these substances can constitute a danger to employees' health. 4. The employer shall arrange for periodic medical examination of the employees in question. 5. The employer shall do his utmost to avoid exposing employees to substances which are generally acknowledged to be carcinogenic and/or to have genetic effects. 6. *The employee has the right to refuse instructions in the event that safety regulations have not been satisfied* or whenever a situation arises which constitutes an immediate danger to life or health so that it would not be reasonable to require him to comply with instructions . . . (ICI Holland, cl. 18, pp. 34–45).

The Unilever settlement has a clause entitled 'Quality of work, safety, health and hygiene in the factory' which says, among other things,

> 3. The employer *shall give employees information on hazardous substances related to their work and the risks involved in handling these.* The employer shall also keep employees informed

about the consequences of sharp temperature fluctuations. 4. Wherever possible the employer shall take measures to bring the noise level down to acceptable limits . . . (Unilever, cl. 2b.1.3–4, p. 8).

The Philips settlement also contains a clause which allows for the provision of safety information (Philips, cl. 8.2a, p. 13), while a clause on 'Medical care' makes provision for medical investigations where employees have health complaints related to their jobs and for a general check-up for older employees (cl. 31, p. 33).

In the UK too, some unions have been very active over health and safety issues. For example, one ICI establishment near Manchester has an elaborate structure of safety committees, some including management representatives while others consist exclusively of union representatives, which meet frequently at both department and site level. Safety representatives go through a course lasting one day a week for ten weeks, for which management gives them time off.

In Bombay, management indifference is repeatedly cited by workers as a major cause of unsafe working conditions. But lack of regard for safety is not a characteristic of managements in India and other Third World countries alone. The persistent refusal of ICI to extend the chimney of its factory at Huddersfield so as to avoid pouring toxic emissions on local residents, the P & O ferry disaster at Zeebrugge, and a series of other recent catastrophes, all display a familiar pattern of management cost-cutting which economises on safety. However, one reason why such lapses are so widespread and their consequences so drastic in India is that the unions there have failed to launch any consistent or coordinated campaigns on safety issues. Opposition to unsafe working conditions has been spontaneous, sporadic and sometimes violent, and has tended to concentrate on claims for *compensation*. An employee from Firestone reported one conflict of this kind shortly before the Americans pulled out and handed over to the Modis:

The whole of the early part of 1981 was a period of tension in the factory and one day, early in March, there was a massive fight in the canteen . . . . Then in July that year there was a horrible accident when a worker in the Curing section was instantly crushed by a burning hot mould weighing one ton.

This happened on 21 July. Two days later when the Factory Inspector came for his usual inspection, U. demanded that the company pay a compensation of 7 lakhs immediately or the union would be forced to take action. The company stuck by the agreement under which only 50,000/- was payable. The following day workers 'gheraoed' management; both first and second shifts were involved since this happened at 2.45 in the afternoon. Groups of workers smashed up office furniture and one group assaulted Steinmetz. So that day Firestone management declared a lockout, and this lasted for a whole seventy-three days. When the lockout was finally lifted, four workers were kept out and another forty-three had police cases against them. The afternoon Steinmetz was assaulted, the SRP (Special Reserve Police) invaded the factory and attacked workers indiscriminately, fracturing skulls, arms and feet, and in one case inflicting such severe kidney damage that the worker died some months later.[34]

Compensation, however, implies that an injury has already occurred. Measures which might *prevent* accidents are hardly ever mentioned in Bombay agreements, apart from a few stray examples like the reference to management provision of safety shoes in the GKW Sankey agreement. A safety clause like the one in the ICI Holland agreement would prevent, for example, the use in petrochemical plants of massive numbers of contract workers who are completely untrained and ignorant of the properties of the chemicals, thus incurring horrifying injuries and fatalities. The Bhopal disaster might have been averted if employees had a clause in their agreement affirming their right to refuse hazardous job assignments instead of the comprehensive management rights clause which states:

The selection, placement, distribution, transfer, promotion of personnel, fixing of working hours and laying down of working programmes, planning and control of factory operations, introduction of new or improved production methods, expansion of production facilities, establishment of quality standards, determination and assignment of workload, evaluation and classification of jobs and establishment of production standards, maintenance of efficiency, maintenance of discipline in the factory . . . are *exclusive* rights and responsibilities of the management (Union Carbide India Ltd./APD, settlement dated 14 May 1983, pp. 6–7).

In Bhopal, management used their 'exclusive rights' to cut down the workforce, neglect essential maintenance of equipment, and enforce hazardous working practices by charge-sheeting or cutting the pay of workers who refused to comply with them. It is worth contrasting their case with that of the ICI Rozenburg plant because the comparison highlights another crucial difference: the nature of safety legislation in Holland and India.

On 30 November 1983, there was a phosgene leak at the ICI factory at Rozenburg and thirteen persons were admitted to hospital. ICI trade unionists scrutinised the causes of the leak and pressed for changes in the operating procedure; and while management may have resented their intervention, the improvements *were* implemented, by and large, with the result that the next shutdown went without mishap.

On 26 December 1981, there was a phosgene leak at Carbide's plant in Bhopal; some workers were admitted to hospital and one of them died. The causes were similar, but in Bhopal violations of procedure were more blatant. The union 'gheraoed' management and also wrote to the Factory Inspector and other government officials demanding an enquiry into the incident and protesting about the unsafe way in which the factory was being run. Carbide retaliated by dismissing union leaders, and the local government declared the factory to be completely safe. The leaks continued until one night, in December 1984, a reaction occurred which released forty tons of MIC into the atmosphere, killing thousands of people and inflicting lung damage, blindness, miscarriages, etc., on hundreds of thousands.

The union's experience at the ICI Rozenburg factory provides a truly impressive example of workers enforcing their right to a safe workplace through local actions and initiatives. In 1983, they made working conditions the subject of a 45-minute video called 'This is our business' ('Dat zijn onze zaken'), and in 1985 produced a report on working conditions for one of the plants.

In 1984, union representatives on the ICI works council produced some remarkable reports on incidents involving potential disasters which occurred in the MDI plant within four months of each other in the latter part of 1983. In the first incident, a phosgene reactor is said to have 'gone out of control'. The second incident involved a leak during a plant stop when a quantity of phosgene, ten kilograms on management's estimate, escaped from the phosgene buffer tank through a leaking flange

On these incidents the union wrote its first report by February 1984: fifteen pages which concentrate on the phosgene leak, analyse the internal organisation of plant shut-down, then deal with the causes of the leak, the precise sequence of events in the Terylene and MDI plants, the organisation of the several gas alarm systems and practical suggestions for safety improvements during shut-down. In view of the similarities to some of the things which the Bhopal MIC plant operators told the URG (cf. Union Research Group [June 1985]), one section of the ICI report is worth translating. This is the section which reports what the union found out from the process operators in the MDI plant.

> Why did the plant-stop go so badly? According to process operators, there are several causes: (*a*) insufficient experience (*Onervarenheid*) among operators. With the introduction of the 4/5-crew system, on average each crew got two new men. This involved a decline in the knowledge and experience of operators on shifts . . . . (*b*) Too much work in too little time (*Teveel werk in een te korte tijd*) . . . . Before and during the stop you got the feeling that two weeks' work would have to be done in one week of stop. This feeling is further strengthened by the fact that after stop week an incredible lot of overtime was needed to get the plant start clear again. (*c*) Process faults. During the last shutdown, a number of process faults were made as a result of: unclear instructions from management, insufficient experience among operators, an excessive workload because of too few men ('Rapport gevaarlijke gebeurnissen MDI', pp. 4–5).

This first report was then discussed with the management some five weeks later. That the union could take the initiative to raise issues about the accident was evidently a source of some irritation to the management: 'We had no idea that you found our report incomplete,' they said, and, 'Therefore I find it strange that a report appears, at the same time it's circulated externally, without anyone having the chance to discuss it with you.' About what the process operators told the union, the concerned Section Manager said, 'That one has to look at the quantitative extent of the five production crews I agree. Where I have problems is with your remarks about the quality of the crews. By making them you're suggesting that I can't vouch for my operators.' To which the union replied, 'One has to reckon with an assimilation period of a year before you have enough knowledge and experience to handle things properly during a shutdown.'

By September 1984, the union representatives on the works council came up with a second report called 'Evaluation Report, MDI'. This shows that largely under union pressure management had introduced the following changes: in any similar eventuality, the plant support organisation would have to be alerted as soon as possible, 'even if the situation is still vague or unclear'; here the important principle is that a false alarm is better than an alarm given too late (the union's first report had pointed out that 'when it became known that phosgene had leaked, no alarm was given in MDI and in Terylene the alarm was sounded too late,' p. 14). Secondly, the conditions under which the small gas alarm is sounded were redefined to read, 'In case gas is detected on plant premises; information is received from some other department outside MDI that gas has been detected there; the phosgene analysers of the Fume and Caustic Scrubbers set off the alarm.' But the most significant change was the introduction of a new 'job coordinator' with overall responsibility for all the jobs during shut-down: the ICI employees felt this was an important innovation worth applying in chemical plants elsewhere. The evaluation report then gives a short assessment of the May shut-down which was altogether better organised: the small gas alarm was in fact used quite frequently; on the whole there was less use of overtime; the scenario for the shut-down was more logical this time, drafted six weeks before the stop and backed up by a checklist; above all, operators felt they had less pressure on them. In discussions it also emerged that the company had had to initiate process training for every single operator, and that this training is both continuous and intensive. Operators have to know as much as they possibly can about the process they are handling, and it is the company's job to make sure that this happens.

Inadequate training, undermanning and faulty alarm systems lay in the background of the Bhopal disaster too. But there were also operational lapses of a far more serious variety. The worker who died in 1981, for example, had been asked to open a pipe which ought to have been put under vacuum to ensure that it was empty, but this had not been done and the pipe contained liquid phosgene which fell directly on him. This was one case where the union *did* intervene on a safety issue and attempt to bring about changes aimed at preventing future accidents. Their failure cannot be explained solely by the lack of a safety clause in their agreement. What was crucial in this case was the total lack of *legal* rights which would have enabled them to press effectively for the changes to be made.

A crucial resource which the Dutch unions have for struggles on health and safety is the 'Arbowet' (short for *Arbeidsomstandighe-denwet*), the law on working conditions which was passed in November 1980. Arbowet applies to all plants and all workplaces (the army is a notable exception) and thus avoids the whole problem of possible degrees of hazardousness and the criteria used for defining plants as hazardous or not hazardous. Under clause 5 (Arbowet, p. 42), employers are under a statutory obligation to make sure their establishments have a safety report containing:

1. a description of the plant, the substances it contains and their properties;
2. a description of the process and activities conducted in the plant;
3. a description of the hazards which could conceivably arise through disruptions in the process under (2) or through faulty handling during any stage of the process;
4. a description of any further steps that might be required to assess foreseeable hazards and to ensure the safety and health of employees;
5. a description of the technical and organisational provisions which have been made to anticipate all possible disruptions and faults and to restrict as far as possible the seriousness of their consequences.

Apart from seven copies of the safety report which the employer forwards to the chief district inspector, one copy is given to the works council, so Arbowet in fact extends the information disclosure rights which the works councils in particular have secured under Dutch law. Clause 38 of Arbowet says,

An employee is empowered to stop work and to continue a stoppage of work in case and as long as in the employee's rational opinion personal danger threatens and in the employee's rational opinion the threat of such danger is so immediate that the Factory Inspector cannot be present in time. The employee is entitled to receive full pay for the duration of the stoppage . . . (Arbowet, p. 73).

In India, by contrast, health and safety is governed by the Factories Act, which in the first place does not even cover hundreds of thousands of contract workers, workers in very small establishments, etc. Secondly, under the Act workers as such have *no rights*, neither to obtain information, nor to carry out inspections nor to take action. Everything is left in the hands of a Factory Inspectorate which for various reasons has proved totally ineffective, as in Bhopal. Even after the disaster, employers successfully resisted the introduction of such rights. The Factories Act was amended with tighter standards and heavier penalties, but implementation was still to be left to Factory Inspectors. The amended Act contains whole paragraphs which have been taken word for word from the Health and Safety at Work Act, UK, yet the paragraphs specifying the rights and responsibilities of safety representatives, which constitute such an important part of the UK Act, have been carefully omitted.

Given the lack of legal protection for employees in countries like India, it is not surprising that multinational firms prefer decentralised bargaining over working conditions. A safe workplace is inevitably more expensive than an unsafe one, often considerably more expensive; and a rationality of cost-cutting would quite naturally seek all possible opportunities to take advantage of local conditions which allow for economies in this area. Yet this, precisely, is the area where lower standards for some countries make least sense, because they mean loss of sight, hearing, limbs, health, and, ultimately, lives.

7

BACK TO BARGAINING: ATTITUDES, ORGANISATION AND CONFLICT

7.1 MANAGEMENT ATTITUDES

There are probably more differences in overall management attitudes to unionism *within* Bombay or the Netherlands than there are systematic differences between the two places. In both, there are some managements which are seen by employees as being progressive and others which are seen as being anti-union, with a variety of other characterisations besides.

7.1.1 Dutch managements

According to an official from the Industriebond,

> Managements in Holland differ a lot. There are some managements who like to negotiate with unions. Akzo for example. They have the philosophy that it's better to negotiate with a strong union because they know that with a strong union, if you've made an agreement it will be okay, there will be no problems, more people are satisfied. That is the philosophy of the strong modern manager, the sort you have in Unilever. But there are managers who come from the family tradition who say, we must try to split the unions. This is common in the textile industry or with smaller companies . . . . The American companies, most of them, not all, have another style of management, free-style management, they want to do things by themselves, no talking, no negotiating. They have collective

agreements, but not with the unions, the *ondernemingsraad* makes the negotiations. But they can succeed only by paying more than other companies. If you have a higher wage, that's something you can see directly, so it influences workers. Take IBM, Johnson, Dupont, Esso, Dow Chemicals (interview).

Another view:

> In very large multinational companies like Shell and Philips, employers *can* have an anti-union strategy; medium employers wouldn't bother, we don't have the practice as in the United States where you have consultancy firms who do this for you. But Philips does it through what I would call a 'sweet' strategy: they have a very intelligent, highly educated, sophisticated Personnel Department. They really know their stuff. Then there's housing, there's education, grants for the children of their workers; but they don't like unions so much. Shell takes a more American view, in some ways Shell has proved to be rather anti-union. American firms work on a minimalistic interpretation of the law, in the sense that if it can't be avoided they will bargain, if it can't be avoided they will have a works council . . . . I had an interview with someone from IBM, and it's quite certain that among IBM personnel it's not nice to be a union member, it can cost you a promotion, so you keep a low profile if you're a union member. This is perhaps more true of the new technology firms, a few Japanese firms . . . . These kinds of new industries, especially software firms, have a young, skilled, rather mobile labour force, highly educated; they get good training—sometimes you're sent, if you're good, to the United States. All this on the understanding that you don't bother about unions of course, it's understood it's better not to be a union member; certainly if you *are* a union member, to keep a low profile, not to ask for any union leave, for instance (interview).

'We are interested in productivity, not in agreements,' is how the Chairman of Dow Chemicals summed up the American management position on dealing with unions in the Netherlands (cited in Vreeman, *Flexibele*, p. 17).

On the other hand, 'Akzo are proud of their social image, I'd say they have a more social image than Philips. They are not that hard, you can negotiate with them, they are more friendly in negotiations than Philips' (interview). In another discussion:

> 'Someone in the FNV said Fokker management is fairly pro-
> gressive. Is that right?'
> 'I think he's right in the sense that management's ideas are very
> progressive. What I find very striking in comparison with my
> other job is that management doesn't act as an authority, "You
> have to do this, you have to do that"; your group leader, your
> supervisor always asks, "What do you think about this" They
> say they want you to do independent work, take your own initia-
> tives, etc. They try to prevent any conflict, and when there is a
> conflict they try to talk to the workers . . . . The management at
> Fokker is highly educated because it's an industry developing its
> own aeroplanes. There's a technical university in Holland which
> has a faculty for aeronautical engineering, it maintains close
> contact with Fokker.'

Another index of management attitudes, apart from employee and union impressions, is the kind of union rights and facilities clauses they sign in their agreements. Under Dutch labour rela-tions, only works council office-bearers are legally entitled to time off, so local union activists would have time off only in their capacity as works councillors, not in their capacity as trade union representatives. But settlements do contain clauses which entitle the unions to paid leave of different sorts, and to plant facilities. Clause 38 of the Philips settlement states that if requested, the employer shall grant paid leave (called 'union leave') to enable members to participate in training courses or workshops run by the union, in meetings which have been organised according to the statutes of the union and in meetings of the district official with local management. The Unilever settlement reflects the same gen-eral compromise of denying time off for union activities while allowing paid leave to enable BLG members to attend committee meetings (although 'in principle' such meetings are held 'outside working hours'), to consult with members of the union in an office provided for this purpose, and to attend combined meetings of the various BLGs or plant committees in Unilever. Activists can apply for paid leave to attend these company-level meetings 'maximum six times a year' and for one day on each occasion. Time off to attend to local grievances or attend plant committee meetings when the timing of these meetings conflicts with service rosters is restricted to 'a maximum of 50 working hours per year for every 100 employees covered by the Unilever agreement' (Unilever, cl. 2c, pp. 9–10). Leave of absence on full pay to enable activists to participate in other sorts of union meetings including training courses organised by the union is governed by a separate clause in the agreement. This states, 'The union will at the start of each calendar year inform the local management concerned of the estimated number of days of leave to be requested for the coming year' (Unilever, cl. 1a, 5a-b, p. 4).

The general clause on trade union facilities in Unilever establishments includes a section which provides against possible victimisation for union activity: 'The employer shall ensure that the position of union committee members in the undertaking shall depend purely on their observing the rights and obligations under their contract of employment and shall not be influenced by their role as members of the local union committee' (Unilever, cl. 2c.3, p. 9). The same clause permits use of company phones, duplicators and notice-boards for union work. There is a similar provision against victimisation for union activity in the Philips clause dealing with 'Union work in the employer's plants,' stating that the position of an activist as an employee in the company shall in no way be affected by that person's belonging to the union or participating in the union committee (Philips, cl. 39.4, p. 39). But in general the Philips clause is much more reserved in its extension of local union facilities. For example, while use of notice-boards on company premises is allowed, 'whenever the content of these notices goes further than mention of the time, place and subject of proposed meetings, the employer's consent shall be required before publication' (cl. 39.2.b, p. 39). Again, members of the local committee can establish contact with union members only outside working hours unless 'special circumstances' justify such contacts during working hours, and there is careful and precise regulation of meetings between local union committees and district officials: the agreement states,

'To participate in discussions of the district officials of the unions with managements in the company's local establishments: one union activist per union per establishment may participate in such discussions. The district officials shall be given the opportunity to consult with the committee members of the union committee for precisely one hour before and after this meeting (up to a maximum of 3–5 employees)' (Philips, cl. 38, p. 38).

Rather surprisingly, the best union facilities clause we came across in any Dutch settlement occurs as an appendix called 'Facilities for union work in the plant' in the agreement of the American company M & T Chemicals, which has a performance and speciality chemicals plant next to the Hoechst factory in Vlissingen. The clause is both detailed and thorough; apart from extending the usual facilities, including a conference room for BLG meetings and a room where the chairman of the BLG can meet with individual committee members, this states:

Time 9.1 To encourage union work within the plant, for the time being no predetermined limit shall be specified by M & T Chemicals BV to the total time available which can be devoted to union work in the plant. 9.2 Any time which is devoted to union work shall be noted down according to the 'house rules' and kept within reasonable limits . . . . Administration of union membership. 10 M & T Chemicals is prepared to explore how once a year it can extend its cooperation to keep the membership administration of the unions up-to-date [referring, obviously, to use of the company's computer facilities]. To ensure the principle that the privacy of individual employees is not thereby endangered, it shall be understood however that this will not involve supplying a list with the names and addresses of the employees concerned. 11 M & T Chemicals shall make sure that no committee member of the BLG finds himself/herself in any way affected in their position as employees in the course of performing that function, any more than any other employee of M & T Chemicals is affected in this way for his/her participation in internal consultative structures . . . (reproduced in Buitelaar and Vreeman [1985], pp. 351–53).

When the information obtained from discussions and from agreements is put together, the following characterisation of the labour relations policies of large companies in the Netherlands emerges:

1. accepting unions because one accepts the need for a bargaining process—Unilever, Akzo, Fokker, among many others presumably, including some American firms like M & T Chemicals;
2. minimising dealings with the unions or their presence on the shop floor—Philips is the prime example of this strategy, but there are others, e.g., Shell;
3. keeping the unions out, the strategy associated with American companies operating in Europe[35]—IBM, Johnson, Esso, Dow Chemicals, Gillette.

In this classification, the area which requires the most conscious use of an industrial relations strategy is (2). The Philips strategy consists in restricting bargaining with the unions as far as possible to issues of a largely financial nature, while the crucial questions which relate to deployment, workforce reductions, reorganisations, etc., are handled on a decentralised basis by dealing with the works councils. According to the management,

> We also have to choose—this has happened in the last two years—what sort of items we are discussing with which sort of body . . . . About typical economic issues, financial problems say, social costs as a whole, there's more knowledge in the unions, especially knowledge about the total industrial setting in Holland and what's possible or not possible. When we talk with works councils, we are talking with employees of Philips—that's a handicap . . . . We don't want to negotiate with people who have a labour relation with us and we think their knowledge of problems is mostly less. But there are other problems, other items, we choose to negotiate or to discuss with the works councils, especially when there are items which have to be implemented in the plant itself . . . (interview).

According to union members, 'Management always prefers the *ondernemingsraad*, always, because the BLGs are composed only of union members. In the OR there are people who are not members of any union' (interview). The works councils are more amorphous than the union committees; they are less cohesive organisations, divided into union and non-union participants, often dominated by the higher personnel, with massive under-representation of women, lower grades and younger workers. That the Philips works councils have lacked any significant decision-making powers, that they cannot influence the main lines of company policy, that the powers assigned to them by the Law on Works Councils are not a basis for dealing with a management like Philips on equal terms, are constant themes both in literature on Philips labour relations and in reports of what workers have experienced in their own plants. Before the last revision of the Act when the right of companies to appoint the chairman of the council was finally removed, this powerlessness was obviously most apparent. Yet even after the major changes introduced after 1979, the position did not change in any dramatic way. For example, when the works council opposed company proposals for the reorganisation of Elcoma BB in Eindhoven, which involved converting the plant into a 'proeffabriek' and redeployment of 240 employees, and came up with an alternative plan in June 1981, the company went ahead with the reorganisation once the Ondernemingskamer in Amsterdam turned down the employees' case. A former employee of Philips, reflecting his experience in the Machine Factory works council early in the eighties, said, 'If management consults and the OR says "No," management can then go ahead with redundancies because it has complied with legal regulations by asking the OR for its advice' (interview). As Teulings wrote, faced with a redundancy, 'works council members can choose which of their colleagues will be most affected. On the policy as such they can exert no influence' [1977, p. 289].

This relative helplessness of the *ondernemingsraad* in the face of major corporate decisions is not true of Philips alone, however. A union case study of Calvé Delft, one of the Unilever plants, reported that while workers there valued the work done by the works council, they felt that 'the OR was powerless before the important decisions' (van Klaveren and Vaas [1983], p. 45). The committee from Shell's refinery at Pernis felt that 'the OR is very weak; it mainly talks. Management has to *ask* the OR for advice, but they don't have to *follow* the advice . . . . Management tries to dominate the OR.'

7.1.2 Management characteristics in Bombay

In Bombay too there are wide variations in the general style of industrial relations management in different companies, and these clearly contribute more to differences in the conflict experience of individual plants than 'the particular patterns of the industry group' to which plants belong.[36] Philips and Siemens have adjoining plants, recruit from the same labour market, belong to the same industry, yet their labour relations could not be more different. One wonders how much the character of Philips labour relations was ultimately determined by the astonishing crudeness of conception evident in the following remarks of a personnel director: 'Workers in high wage island companies tend to be unwilling to develop the companies they work in or to discharge their social obligations and serve the national interest. However, we are attempting to change these attitudes through training and development programmes' (*Business World*, 5–18 November 1984, p. 55). His counterparts in Siemens obviously didn't feel able to support any such generalisation when they told the same reporter, 'We have maintained very good relations with our Siemen's Workers' Union and with our staff union for almost 30 years,' and 'The unions have been co-operative, they identify with the company's interests and understand its problems' (*Business World*, 15–22 April 1985, p. 49).

The management at Philips Kalwa does negotiate with the union, but does not always abide by the agreements they arrive at. We have already referred to their violation of the interchangeability agreements; another dramatic case is their refusal to honour the 1985 agreement for Kalwa. Clause 19 of this agreement states, 'The Kalwa Factories will observe Sundays as weekly off days instead of Friday as at present' (Philips Kalwa, p. 9), but in the period following the settlement, management backed out of this, 'expressing their unwillingness to implement the settlement in respect of change of weekly off,' according to a union circular ('Communication' dated 6 February 1986). When workers decided to implement the agreement, coming to work one Friday shortly after the agreement was signed and staying away on Sunday, management began to serve charge-sheets on the committee members the following Monday.

In Hindustan Lever, management has on several occasions refused to discuss issues with the union. One example involving a decision which simply bypassed the union was the sudden conversion of a clerical grade into a management category. It is worth quoting from the union circular on this, not least because its style conveys the atmosphere of labour relations in some of the large companies in India with remarkable vividness:

We have just received the 'bombshell' news from our Madras
Unit that the Management has arbitrarily and compulsorily
converted all the C-4 clerks in Madras Branch into 'Officers'
with effect from 1.8.1984, in spite of the fact that the Charter of
Demands for the C-4 workmen is pending adjudication before
the Industrial Tribunal in Madras. The local unit of the Sabha
while recovering from its initial shock is taking the necessary
legal and other steps to protect the interests of the workmen
concerned and they have been assured of active support of the
unions from all centres to stop this illegal and mad action of the
management. Once successful, the management will become
bold enough to follow suit in the other offices as well and these
compulsory conversions may well be extended to other categories as well. In fact, there may well be some truth in the
rumours that while the C-4 clerks will be designated as Administrative Officers, C-3 clerks will be Deputy Administrative
Officers, and C-2 clerks will be Assistant Administrative Officers,
etc. Even for the Service Staff, the likely designations are Auto
Officers for Drivers, Attendant Officers for Sepoys and Sanitary
Officers for Sweepers! The idea seems to be to achieve a truly
egalitarian society in Hindustan Lever, giving status satisfaction
and ego boost to the employees with no Union headaches to
worry about.

Of late there have been overtures made to some employees
belonging to the Clerical Staff to voluntarily accept the 'Officer's'
grade which the Head Office and Bombay Branch employees
have unhesitatingly declined to consider. The Sabha would
remind members that there is an agreement between the Company and the Sabha regarding avenues and procedures for promotions from Clerical to Management and there is no place in
the Agreement for the so-called 'Officer's' grade.

The circular goes on to state that Lever management's other
policies on employment of office staff have been,

not to fill in vacancies occurring due to retirements, etc., but to
spread the work of the erstwhile incumbents amongst the other
employees in the department and overload them; (ii) employ
temporaries and trainees over prolonged periods in permanent
vacancies; (iii) do away with the higher grades when the

employees retire and downgrade their jobs arbitrarily; (iv) arbitrarily convert and divert as many manual jobs to computers and micro-processors which will ultimately store in their memory not only Company data but the employees themselves, though any computerisation or micro-processing should be done only with the consent of the Union as per the Committee appointed by the Government of India as early as 1972 (Hindustan Lever Mazdoor Sabha, circular dated 23 August 1984).

Claiming 'prerogative' is a form in which Hindustan Lever management both refused to discuss and attempted to justify this refusal. Take the issue of subcontracting: 'The company's interested in tonnage, not in finished products. So they want us to remove noodles here and send the stuff to the interior areas of Maharashtra to the unorganised sector where they hardly get minimum wages and working hours are longer; just subcontract and get the soap packed there. There was even a forty-day strike to stop this' (interview). Management took the line that subcontracting was the company's prerogative. Manning was another area where it insisted on retaining absolute control.

Employers in Bombay make frequent and often extensive use of charge-sheeting, suspension and outright dismissal as forms of bargaining pressure, and of lockouts when these prove inadequate. To break go-slows in the Sewree factory in 1981–82, Lever management applied for permission to deduct wages. 'The company went upto the Supreme Court for that wage cut and it was rejected in the Supreme Court, they said you cannot deduct wages. This was one of our major victories' (Franklyn D'Souza). Failing to secure legal backing for a measure that might have crippled the go-slow, the company continued to rely on disciplinary action, and shortly before the settlement the toll stood at five dismissals and twelve suspensions. The conflict in Philips Pune involved ninety-nine suspensions and dismissal of the entire leadership. These are dramatic examples of the use of disciplinary action as part of a bargaining process.

The majority of lockouts arise as managements attempt to recover the initiative in the face of an organised go-slow which cannot be broken or controlled by other means. There have been such lockouts in foreign-controlled as well as Indian-controlled plants; but some lockouts continue for several months, sometimes even extending beyond a year, and this is significant because it expresses the employer's determination to *break the union* rather than just force workers to settle on terms they (the employers) find acceptable. Frequent use of lockouts is a characteristic of those Indian employers, or groups of employers, who are still basically unreconciled to unions or regard unions which are not controlled by them as an infringement of their authority as employers and not just a challenge to their control as managers. This distinction, though subtle, is important, because it implies an even deeper level of resistance to collective bargaining than anything that characterises the behaviour of Philips and Lever.

7.2 ORGANISATION AND CONFLICT

7.2.1 Union organisation

We saw earlier that Dutch unionism is characterised by a high degree of centralisation but low densities and weak representation at the plant level. This is certainly the case in Philips, partly as a result of conscious management strategy. It is striking that the Eindhoven plants have a union density of only around 15 per cent, and the Dutch Philips establishments as a whole something between 20 and 25 per cent.[37] This suggests an extremely weak union position within Philips, especially in Eindhoven. One of the militants from Eindhoven presented a concise and lucid analysis of the main features of Philips strategy. It seems that the location (Eindhoven) was initially selected for a number of reasons, the most important of which were the position of the town in relation to the German market, the hegemony of the Catholic church in that part of the country, and finally the fact that kitchen gardening was widespread and allowed the company to depress wages accordingly. 'Till the sixties it was almost a crime to be a member of a socialist union.' Philips went north only much later when it faced massive shortages of unskilled labour, dispersing locations in what Teulings vividly calls its 'search for the last unskilled' (*Philips*, p. 152). It was the company's conscious policy to avoid plant locations in the traditional strongholds of the working class such as Rotterdam and Amsterdam, and even in countries like Belgium and France, Philips has always gone for the economically under-developed regions—'to avoid unions. Not that Philips has ever openly forbidden union membership. It was also one of the first companies in the country to start working with the *onderneming- sraad*.'[38]

In Bombay, in both Philips and Lever the unions have a *broad base within the factory*. In the sharpest possible contrast to union situations in most of Europe, plant densities are well above 90 per cent. Both unions display excellent internal relations between the leadership and the mass of workers, rooted in a structure spread through all the departments, with a second or even third line leadership. They are both led by humane, competent, democratic and experienced leaderships, people with remarkable personal qualities and with the capacity to survive under the most intense pressure.

The early eighties saw major changes in union organisation at the plant level in the Philips and Hindustan Lever factories. In the Kalwa plant in 1982, the Philips Workers' Union redrafted its constitution to introduce a new form of organisational structure. The plant as a whole was divided into seven groups, and each group would henceforth elect its own joint secretaries and com- mittee representatives or department representatives. Earlier the union 'executives' were elected by the entire factory, but now only four office-bearers would be elected in this way, while the rest would be elected departmentally by the various groups. There is a clear-cut distribution of work, with shop floor problems raised initially at the levels of the department representative and joint secretary for the section concerned; that is, the leadership no longer handles issues at this level, e.g., allocation of overtime, allocation of work, working conditions. Negotiating is done by a team of four chosen by the executives in a managing committee of thirty-seven.

The Philips managing committee is certainly large by the average standards of most Bombay industry, but variations in the size of the committee partly reflect variations in the size of the workforce. The Siemens Kalwa plant has an equivalent group called the 'General Council,' and this consists of some eighty people elected by secret ballot from the individual departments—toolroom, motor machine shop, switchgear assembly and so on—in a 25:1 ratio which is roughly the same as the ratio in Philips.

At Hindustan Lever the essential structure is the same—a 'general council' composed of department leaders elected in a definite ratio to the general workforce. Although unions are not completely consistent about the regularity with which elections are held, drastic changes of committee are not uncommon in Bombay plants. In Lever's Bombay factory, a change of this sort occurred after the bonus agitation of 1980; in the new general council the leadership lay with a group of young workers recruited into Lever from the Siemens Training Centre. In that period, participation increased rapidly; as conflict escalated, meetings were occurring at five levels: gate meetings of the factory as a whole, weekly meetings of the office-bearers or active core of the leadership, meetings of the general council every ten days, activist meetings with an average attendance of 75–80 once a month, assemblies of the workers under suspension. The general council elects the managing committee and office-bearers, and they select the negotiating team.

Bombay trade unionism lacks any elaborate formal structure which might be called bureaucratic, although many of its leaderships, especially 'professional' leaders who run unions from the outside, certainly display attitudes, conceptions and ways of working which are that or worse. The lack of a formal bureaucratic structure expresses both a weakness and an advantage. Weakness because it implies lack of resources, lack of coordination, the fragmentation and dispersal of energies and a neglect of functions which are crucial to a strong trade union movement, in particular research, education and training. All this stands in striking contrast to the resources and organisation of the Dutch union movement, where training has always had high priority, especially in the metal-workers' unions from which the Industriebond later emerged. But also an advantage, because in Bombay, contact with the shop floor is closer, more continuous and widespread, through the crucially important mediation of department leaders, whereas low density and the limited character of its presence on the shop floor remain decisive features of the Dutch union movement. The strengths and weaknesses of the two systems are reflected in the types and rates of conflict generated within them.

7.2.2 Patterns of conflict

In his study of French unionism Reynaud writes, 'Open conflict is sometimes a substitute for but more generally an extension of bargaining by other means' (*Les Syndicats en France*, vol. 1, p. 172). Overt conflicts in the form of strikes or lockouts occur as concluding moments of a bargaining cycle with a more complex structure. In Bombay, the most characteristic form of this specific cycle is one where in the event that management decides not to discuss the union's demands when these have been formally presented through the charter, the union organises a go-slow. This generally involves a phased reduction, depending on the offers made or the extent of opposition shown by the management. For example, in the last round of negotiations at Johnson's pharmaceutical factory at Mulund, when the union submitted its charter, service conditions were still governed by an agreement signed ten years earlier in 1973! Therefore, Johnson workers felt that only a substantial increase could make up for the fact that a whole agreement had been skipped. The union wanted an increase of Rs 650, but the Johnson management, in general hostile to unions, was in no mood to settle fast. The charter was submitted in March 1982 but discussions with Samant, the union's president, began only nine months later. By April 1983 there had been a total of four offers from the management, starting with Rs 125, then Rs 200, then Rs 280 and finally Rs 350. Corresponding almost mathematically to the initial round of offers was the phased reduction of output organised on the shop floor. When the initial offer was made, the average level of production was 90 per cent of what the management called 'normal'; then by stages average production was brought down to 60 per cent, which most workers felt was really the 'normal' level of production. That was by April 1983. The company reacted with mass charge-sheeting, wording the charge-sheets carefully. By the middle of May the workers were on a stay-in strike, from early June on full strike. This strike lasted some four-and-a-half months, and eventually forced the Johnson management to settle on terms which the union committee found acceptable, chiefly because by the third month of the strike the supply of sutures had run out in the market and Bombay Hospital was pressurising the government to allow imports; the company ran the risk of losing its market for a crucial product if the strike continued indefinitely. When the management settled in October 1983, forced to concede a total increase of Rs 415, it had to revise its initial offers substantially. For the Johnson union and workers, the actions from the initial slowdown to the eventual strike were a major success. The increase which the company finally had to give was well above the average rate of increases for that period.

In Hindustan Lever, go-slow was one way in which the new leadership handled management's demands for modernisation. The previous leadership had wanted to fight this issue legally and management had backed down and agreed the issue should be negotiated; but by then the high-speed machines were already in operation on 'trial runs'. The militants told management that workers had been instructed to give less production on the high-speed machines than on normal machines. The capacity of the new machine was 350 cardboard boxes, the usual go-slow rate on a low-speed machine with a capacity of 250 boxes was 180, and the level of production which the militants enforced on the new machine was 100, which illustrates the intensity of output restriction.

For the Lever employees' union, the go-slows of 1981–82 were not succeeded by strike action because they had emerged as preferred forms of action after a period in which the company had in fact taken a strike. Go-slows had been organised because workers felt they were more effective than strikes. But by the middle of 1982, workers found the strains of a go-slow too exacting: 'the tremendous psychological strain or pressure that a go-slow imposes on workers while it lasts . . . the psychological pressure of turning up to work every day knowing that you're doing this with a whole lot of company engineers breathing down your neck, watching you as you work, and the constant threat of suspension, the fear that when you walk through the gates for your shift they might turn you out . . .' (interview).

Instead of striking, the union opted to intensify this pattern of struggle. On 28 July 1982 the new phase began. The management was offering Rs 250, the union was holding out for and would eventually get more than Rs 400. The willingness to struggle does make a difference to the value of settlements. But *how* you struggle, what forms you adopt, are also important. In those years the mill workers launched a strike, a massive industry-wide action, but the results were minimal. Their action displayed huge reserves of feeling, real bitterness, a persistent inflexible opposition to the mill-owners, the most powerful group of employers in Bombay. But what the strike lacked was any conception of *strategy*, of how the conflict might be organised and conducted. In Lever, on the other hand, the form of action now consisted of closing individual departments day by day. In the ensuing agitation, plant operations came to depend on the union; this included the level of production. According to Bennet D'Costa, 'What used to be a management function became a union function during this agitation' (interview). The company's lay-off applications multiplied; Lever management protested that 'the *modus operandi* of the employees is to resort to illegal strike, categorywise, in different sections of the establishment on different days, and thereby paralyse the functioning of other sections/departments.' The union called it a 'combination of go-slows and wildcat strikes'. And the decisive factor in its ability to implement and sustain this form of agitation was the operation of a 'network' in the various departments. Individual committee members were responsible for organising industrial action at the department or plant level. Their network functioned as a system of rapid communication and informal decision-making.

The kind of relations unions have with their members, the sort of structures which express those relations, is one obvious way in which the internal organisation of Bombay unions concretely affects their ability to sustain a prolonged agitation against the company without being forced to strike. The struggle at Lever took almost two years before a settlement was reached, the 'bargaining cycle' was twenty-three months, almost twice as long as the average for Bombay companies. But the union won an overall increase of Rs 457 against an average rate of settlement, in that period, of Rs 337. The chief limitation on the agitation at Lever lay not within the plant or in the relations of the union to the shop floor, but in the relations *between the unions in Hindustan Lever plants throughout the country*, in the lack of coordination and even of solidarity between them. The staggering production losses inflicted on the company by the kind of 'non-frontal combat' organised by the union at Sewree did not compel Lever management to settle immediately because the reduction in supply was made up through its plants at Garden Reach and in the North. The Bombay union did its best, even spent a lot of money, to gain the support of the workers at Garden Reach in Calcutta, but these efforts proved useless because of the divided union situation there and open collusion between the recognised INTUC union and the Lever management.

In Philips, the decisive factor in many of the conflicts in Pune and Kalwa was the existence of a strong company-wide federation and its ability to support the individual units. As R.R. Mishra remarked, 'We never used to come to a settlement for years together, but after the formation of the Mahaunion it was *not possible for management to resist in that way* because the Maha-union would pressurise the management to come to a settlement' (interview). For example, the management conditions which led to the Pune lockout of 1981 were finally withdrawn largely because of the pressure of the federation.

Technologically, Philips Kalwa is divided into a continuous process and a non-process section. The glass factory and Ancillary Services fall under the process area where relievers function to keep production flowing. There are some 200 workers here, and heavy use is made of overtime. Thus a primary form of pressure or internal action in the Kalwa plant has been the ban on overtime in these sections. This paralyses the whole plant because critical processes are involved. In the recent conflict at Kalwa, one of the management's key demands was that 'workmen engaged in essential services shall not indulge in industrial actions.'

In the types of industry or areas of manufacturing the large international firms have entered in Bombay, the crucial strategic ratio in the thinking of workers about forms of conflict and bargaining pressure is the extent of losses sustained by the company relative to the losses sustained by workers themselves. Strikes are *not* a preferred form of action because they inflict wage loss on workers. Internal disruption of plants may involve lay-offs, but 'lay-offs are preferable to a strike, you still get 50 per cent wages'. In Bombay industry the preferred forms of action are those designed to apply pressure while minimising losses to the workers. Apart from the usual form of slowing down production, perhaps in some phased sequence, forms of bargaining pressure consciously applied to avoid a loss of wages would include overtime bans, work-to-rule, disruption effected through short departmental stoppages, restrictions on the transport of goods, refusal of access to contractors, holding of General Body Meetings in working hours, boycott of company meetings, etc.

In the Netherlands, one of the most remarkable conflicts which Philips has been through was the occupation of the USFA factory at Helmond by a group of twenty-three women and two men in March 1974. USFA stands for Ultra Sonor Fohar Apparatuur, a company manufacturing bugging devices and other specialised intelligence equipment. Philips established the USFA factory in Helmond in 1971 as the main location where the other establishments of this company would be concentrated in the coming years. At this time, a survey of the labour market showed that 3 per cent of the residents were fully unemployed and the local textile mills were in bad shape; Philips could no longer meet its requirements of unskilled labour in Eindhoven itself, so some 200 employees of USFA Eindhoven received a letter from the company announcing its intention to relocate in Helmond. At that stage there was every likelihood that the war in Vietnam would mean increasing demand for the type of production manufactured by USFA. But the 'atelier' in Helmond never expanded, and at the end of 1972 USFA management decided to shelve the plan for concentration at Helmond, although this was not publicly announced for a whole year. In Teulings' lucid analysis of this conflict, the crucial factors which led to shelving plans for expansion were an approaching end to the war in Vietnam and the fact that Philips could cope with local labour shortages through rapidly increasing investments in countries where the kind of labour it needed could be found in abundance (cf. Teulings [1981], p. 143ff.).

On 12 February 1974, USFA management called the unions for a meeting where they were told of the decision to close the unit in Helmond. The employees affected by this could come to Eindhoven to work; Philips took the stand that what was involved here was an internal transfer, not a redundancy. That is also what they told the women in Helmond: the options were retrenchment without compensation, or transfer to Eindhoven. The works council, composed chiefly of personnel from Eindhoven, supported the management's decision. On the evening of 11 March, an 'action committee' of three women and two men, following discussions with the Industriebond NKV, decided an occupation was their only recourse. This was destined to be not only the first and longest occupation in Philips' history, but also the first occupation conducted by a group of women in the Netherlands.

For thirty-two days the USFA women held out against the most powerful management in Holland, supported only by the local district official of the NKV. In April they were finally forced to see their issue decided in negotiations between the company and the union top, 'without the presence of the district official and over the heads of the women' (*TegenWicht*, no. 7, January 1983). When the factory was closed the following year, only three women accepted relocation to Eindhoven; for the majority, the closure meant redundancy.

Redundancies have been a major issue behind some of the overt conflicts in Philips and other companies. There has been considerable diversity in the range of issues over which domestic plants have gone into conflict. For example, in 1973 Philips took a five-week strike in its cable factory over the workers' demand for equal pay increases for all groups (Buitelaar and Vreeman [1985], p. 369). In 1977, the employees of ICI at Rozenburg struck for twelve days for the introduction of a five-crew system. This was also a major objective behind the Shell strike of 1979. In 1983, workers of the Hercules plant at Zwijndrecht went on strike for a week for higher shift allowances, shorter working hours and the 'prijscompensatie' (Buitelaar and Vreeman [1985], pp. 325, 305). Thirty-six hours was the main demand in the Unilever strikes early in 1986. These are only examples, of course, but they demonstrate two essential features of the pattern of conflict in the Netherlands: the much shorter duration of disputes in Dutch manufacturing compared to anything one finds in India (to the question 'Any strikes?' the people from Fokker replied, 'Not for longer than a few hours,' and in the Machine Factory in Eindhoven, a few 'short strikes of one day or sometimes one or two hours' was all this important plant had been through), and the fact that for many plants their first experience of a strike was the result of their decision to participate in coordinated actions involving several plants on a common bargaining issue such as levelling of incomes in 1973, inflation compensation in 1977, wages policy in 1980 and the proposed attacks on sickness benefits in 1982 (cf. Fokker, ICI, Calvé Delft for examples of this pattern).

The comparative infrequency of disputes, the tendency for the rate of conflict to increase when plants are threatened by closure or redundancies, the extremely short average duration of strikes, and involvement through common actions where the issues are not restricted to the plant—all testify to the *lack of a strong tradition of conflict* at the plant level. On the other hand it is doubtful whether many centres in the world could have higher average rates of conflict than the industrial areas around Bombay. *Long average durations* and the frequent and *extensive use of lockouts* are basic features of labour conflicts in India. The tendency for much of the conflict to be concentrated in a few plants which are thus exceptionally 'conflict prone,' in the sense that they are repeatedly hit by strikes, lockouts or both, is also interesting and significant. This huge difference in the pattern of conflict shows how important bargaining systems are in shaping the possibilities and experience of struggle, and explains how the same international companies can have completely different strike records, varying from near-total stability in some countries to repeated periods of intense conflict in others.

A note on Mallet: In a remarkably creative series of writings published in France in the sixties, Serge Mallet argued that the conscious use of bargaining pressure and the whole range of methods used to disrupt plants internally were characteristic of the behaviour and rationality of new groups in the technologically advanced productive sectors.[39] This argument needs to be qualified in at least two ways. First qualification: the type of strategic rationality implied in the internal disruption of plants (as opposed to strikes) is more widespread, more generally diffused in the modern working class than Mallet allowed for. The workforce at Lever's Sewree factory would not qualify as a 'new working class' in any sociologically precise sense, but the forms of action they adopted were certainly as advanced as anything Mallet would have found in the European refineries. The second qualification: process industry characteristics do not automatically generate the required types and levels of combativity. In discussing the new working class, it would be a mistake to abstract from the considerable differences in union density and bargaining strength displayed by individual plants even in the same general type of industry. There could not be a more impressive illustration of this than the contrast between the union situation in the Shell refinery at Pernis and the position in Shell's Bombay subsidiary. The Dutch management of Shell ruthlessly broke the 1979 strike with scabs, bulldozers, heavy cranes and trucks loaded with sand, forcing an entry into the plant and restarting production in less than a week: 'We couldn't stay outside because all the gates were open and a lot of people were in the factory and they'd already started the factory.' 'Management played a dirty role because they gave bottles of gin and sex films to the people who were scabbing inside for the bosses. The scabs slept in the factory.' At the Pernis refinery, bargainable categories constitute only 42 per cent of the total labour force, and this is a major factor behind the continuing weakness of the union there. Shell workers have faced huge job losses in refinery and chemicals, but when it comes to limiting this process in some way, the committee felt, 'we are not strong enough, we can't go on strike' because of the low overall density. On the other hand, discussions with the Nocil employees' union, which organises the entire bargainable group, made this union's strong bargaining position quite apparent. Nocil experienced its first major conflict in 1985, almost twenty years after the plant started. For most of that period, Nocil workers would not need to declare a strike in order to press for their demands; the most they had to do was 'bring down the plant,' and this was rare. The most usual forms of pressure were the refusal to officiate and overtime bans.

7.2.3 Conflict levels

In the overall contrast between the bargaining systems discussed here, differences in rates of conflict are probably the single most impressive feature. The majority of Bombay plants are massively conflict-prone, though not necessarily or even mainly in the form of strikes. On the other hand, an 'exceedingly low rate of industrial conflict' impressed Windmuller [1969, p. 131] as one of the basic historical features of the Dutch labour movement. Strikes in manufacturing, at any rate, tend to be few and far between. Some of the best organised plants have gone for whole decades without a single major conflict, for example Calvé Delft in the Unilever group, where before 1977 'there were no strikes, despite reorganisations which involved massive contractions of the labour force,' according to a union case study of the plant (van Klaveren and Vaas [1983], p. 30). Again, a Unilever manager gave the example of a group of engineers ('they are always trouble-makers compared with normal workers') who resisted change from the day shift to two-shift working. There was a BLG in the plant concerned, and they said they didn't want the change, 'so management contacted the district official of the FNV and we came to a solution'. 'But the process of production was not affected' during this dispute; that is, no industrial action was taken during it, 'not in Sunlight'. Another case: 'In the two years I was in frozen foods, . . . we had to dismiss 350 people. Even in that situation we didn't have big disruptions in the production process,' although this redundancy did involve management going to court to force through the dismissal of twenty employees who refused to quit (interview). Philips saw its first major work stoppage only in 1970 (Teulings [1977], p. 262), and in many Philips establishments almost no production has been lost due to an industrial dispute. In the light factory at Weert, the works council said there hadn't been a strike in twenty-five years: 'In the south of Holland, in Limburg, we are an easy people.'

In Bombay, on the contrary, foreign-controlled companies conform to the general pattern in terms of overall conflict frequency, as Table 7.1 shows: in other words, *foreign companies are not conflict-free enclaves.*

In foreign plants, about half of the sample conflicts are short (that is, not exceeding 48 hours and in most cases lasting only a few hours), while in Indian firms the proportion is slightly lower. As for lockouts, the pattern is much more distinctive and almost

TABLE 7.1
Conflict in Bombay: Types and Frequencies

	Indian	Foreign
Number of companies	70	50
Total number of conflicts	589	385
Frequency of conflict per company	8.41	7.70
Number of short conflicts*	257	190
Short conflicts as a percentage of total	43.6	49.4
Number of lockouts	77	31
Lockouts as a percentage of all conflicts	13.1	8.1
Frequency of lockouts per company	1.10	0.62
Number of major conflicts†	108	43
Number of major strikes	60	26
Frequency of major strikes per company	0.86	0.52
Number of major lockouts	48	17
Frequency of major lockouts per company	0.69	0.34

Source: Based on a sample transcribed from an official source; 'conflict' refers to disputes entered in the registers as strikes or lockouts, so that the 'total number of conflicts' is the total number of strikes plus the total number of lockouts over the period in question (1956–84).

Notes: * 'Short conflicts' are defined as conflicts whose total duration would not exceed 48 hours; the minimum recorded duration for our sample is 20 minutes.

† 'Major conflicts' are long conflicts whose duration spans a minimum of 60 consecutive calendar days.

certainly significant: 8 per cent of all conflicts in the foreign sector have taken the form of lockouts, whereas in Indian companies the proportion is 13 per cent—a frequency of more than one lockout per company in the sample period. A comparison of major conflicts (those lasting sixty days or more) confirms this pattern: 108 in the Indian companies (1.54 per company) and forty-three in the foreign companies (0.86 per company); the frequency of major strikes as well as major lockouts is higher in Indian firms. In other words, even if the foreign sector is not free of conflict, much of the more bitter, protracted conflict has occurred in firms which are subject to purely Indian control.

The tendency for conflicts to be concentrated in a few key plants which are repeatedly affected by strikes and/or lockouts is partly evident in Table 7.2, which deals with the strike records of seventeen European subsidiaries. The disputes listed in this Table (120 altogether) probably cover 90 per cent of all significant disputes that have occurred in European-controlled plants in Bombay or

TABLE 7.2

Conflict Rates in European Subsidiaries in Maharashtra, 1956–84: Summary

Company/ No. of Establishments	Disputes Listed (no.)(%)		Longer Disputes† (no.)(%)		Disputes of Max. 1 Day (no.)	Lockouts (no.)	Average Duration of Longer Disputes (in days)**
Philips (3)	17	14.17	4	9.09	9	1	70.75 (65.33)
Hindustan Lever (4)	32	26.67	11	25.00	9	0‡	43.36
15 European subsidiaries*	71	59.16	29	65.91	22	7	68.69 (55.82)
	120	100.0	44	100.0	40	8	62.55

Source: Official.

* The sample includes: Bayer, BASF, Burmah-Shell, Ciba-Geigy, E.Merck, Hoechst, Roussel and Sandoz from chemicals and pharmaceuticals, and Asea, Atlas Copco, MICO, Sandvik Asia, Siemens, SKF and Vulcan Laval on the engineering side. This covers the great majority of European-controlled firms for which disputes have been listed for any of their several locations in Maharashtra and excludes plants where the only recorded disputes were work stoppages of 24 hours or less.

† Strikes or lockouts with a minimum duration of 14 days.

** The bracketed figure is the average duration excluding lockouts.

‡ Since this table was compiled, Lever management *has* declared a lockout, against the workers at Sewree.

elsewhere in Maharashtra (the sample excludes British firms). Just over 40 per cent of all disputes in this important group of plants were due to only two companies—Philips and Hindustan Lever! None of the other European multinationals comes anywhere close to their records, although Sandoz, Ciba, Bayer and SKF also show high rates of conflict throughout or in specific periods.

Foreign firms may be more progressive, but not for the largely mythical reasons that there is less conflict in such firms, they always pay more, and so on; and not only for the purely historical reason that collective bargaining was initially established largely through their influence; but primarily because they are *international*, employment in these companies connects workers in one part of the world to workers in other parts. The existence of international companies forms a natural basis for the evolution of a type of consciousness which is closer to being international, less dominated by the sense of tradition and local loyalties, and certainly less easily beaten into submission by authority, arrogance or coercion. The presence and operations of foreign firms shape the character of the local trade union movement in often subtle ways. One striking expression of this is that employees' unions with high bargaining autonomy (see Table 2.1) are found mainly in foreign-controlled plants. But it shows in other perhaps smaller ways: the union in SKF's Pune plant is affiliated to the International Metalworkers' Federation, and so are the workers in the Sandvik Asia factory in Pune; Philips Workers' Union preserves close contact with SOBE in Eindhoven; when Lever decided to relocate its catalyst plant, an operator wanted to find out about conditions in the catalyst plant of van den Bergh & Jurgens; and at Boehringer-Knoll the union forced the resignation of thirty-five managers by intervening internationally with headquarters in Germany.

Some of the most advanced demands ever formulated by unions in Bombay were the charters drafted by employees of the foreign oil refineries in the late fifties. The incredible confidence which multinational workforces derived from their employment situation in a new cycle of industrial expansion and a period characterised by the emerging consciousness of working directly for international capital reflects in conflict patterns defined by rapid but frequent disputes on personnel policies and job assignments: 'for departmental proceedings against a supervisor for alleged assault on a worker' (Stanvac, 1956); 'to express sympathy towards the strikers of Richardson & Cruddas who were locked out' (Osler Electric Lamp Mfg. Co.—soon to become Philips—1956); 'against the high-handed attitude of management which resulted in the arrest of one worker' (Siemens, 1962); 'against the charge-sheeting of 25 workers' (Pfizer, 1962); 'for the immediate reinstatement of 18 retrenched workers' (Burmah-Shell, 1962); 'against the indiscriminate promotion granted to one worker' (Firestone, 1962); 'for abolition of the Contract System and absorption as regular employees' (ICI, 1962); 'against non-payment of wages to a workman who refused to carry out the assigned work as additional help was not given to him' (Firestone, 1963); 'against action taken by management against a worker for alleged threats given to the foreman' (Firestone, 1963); 'against transfer of 30 workers from one department to another' (Britannia, 1963); 'against the order to produce 17 tyres a day' (Ceat, 1964); 'against the insulting behaviour of a supervisor against a worker' (Philips Pune, 1965); 'that an accident report should be made out for a worker suffering from rash on his forearm instead of issuing a hospital pass' (Firestone, 1965). Other reasons for disputes in Bombay subsidiaries of multinational companies include: 'for withdrawal of charge-sheets to 4 workers' (Philips Pune, 1965); 'for promotion according to seniority and confirmation of temporaries' (Ciba-Geigy, 1966); 'against increased workloads and harassment' (Burmah-Shell, 1966); 'against ill-treatment of a worker' (SKF Pune, 1968); 'against non-payment of two days' wages due to disturbances in Bombay city' (Philips Kalwa, 1969); 'against dismissal orders on 2 workers' (Philips Pune, 1977); 'to protest against arrest of workers' (Hindustan Lever Sewree, 1978); 'against giving of work to outside contractors' (Hindustan Lever Sewree, 1980); 'management demand for rated levels of production' (Philips Pune, 1981); 'protest against the chief factory engineer for abusing a fitter' (Hindustan Lever Sewree, 1982); 'against wholesale dismissal of union leadership and mass charge-sheeting and suspensions' (Philips Pune, 1983); and 'management pressure for flexibility and violation of terms of agreement' (Philips Kalwa, 1986).

8

TRADE UNION STRATEGIES

Trade unions have responded in a variety of ways to management attempts to retain control over crucial decisions (such as those on automation and restructuring) which have a direct impact on the workforce yet are considered by employers to be outside the scope of bargaining. Most of these responses have been limited to a national or local context, but there have been attempts to work out international strategies which will not only give unions some control over employment levels but also enable them to reduce disparities between employment conditions in different countries.

8.1 LOCAL INITIATIVES

8.1.1. New technology

In the Netherlands, Rotterdam has become the centre of important union initiatives on new technology. Frans van Doormalen of the Rotterdam Industriebond works on a project called PRIOR, which stands for 'project for the regional industrial development of Rotterdam area'. The project was started some three years ago when people in the union said:

> 'We must do more than just talk about wages, we must try to develop an industrial policy of our own.' So we asked people what is the most important development you face today, and everybody said, 'Technological developments are coming and we don't know a thing about them, we must be part of those developments but we don't know how.' So we took up this issue. Not only have technological developments occurred, but

more are coming, and the district officials feel it, they can see factories planning for full-scale automation.

Unions have responded to technological changes in different ways which express different attitudes and degrees of initiative. Frans outlined several possible strategies:

> One is the conservative kind of strategy which says we don't want technological development, it only costs jobs. Two is the optimistic perspective: we like technological development, we'll do nothing about it because it's good for the economy, and so on. Three is the active position which tries to control the effects of technological development, and the fourth is one step further— not only control it but work on it yourself, try to make your own plans.

The strategy behind PRIOR is the fourth one, not just control but intervention, not just tackling the effects but affecting the process. So PRIOR outlined a number of areas where it could pursue its own initiatives on industrial policy. It took up a total of eleven projects, covering entire branches of industry in the region. Within the fertiliser and chemical industries this has involved regular meetings between plants, a kind of emerging coordination around the issue of technical evolution in these sectors. For the ship-repair yards around Rotterdam, it has meant trying to develop job designs which can utilise skills more effectively and overcome the massive waste of skills built into a thoroughly tayloristic work organisation. And in one of the plants in Unilever's chemicals division, the project has meant a union attempt to develop an automation plan and not leave the whole initiative in management hands.

In this plant, Unichema, the union asked,

> 'How can workers control what's going on?' We said we must try to develop a method which workers in different factories can use whenever management wants to automate. So we started the experiment with Unichema. It's not too big, not too small, the management isn't anti-union, and the level of the cadre is good. We had to develop a method to know how we could start negotiating the issue with the management. Before that could happen, three steps were required. First, we had to have some

insight into the situation, second, we had to decide what demands to make, and third, we would need a strategy to get
those demands through.

So far, most of the activity has involved step one in this sequence.
Two features are already significant in this effort: the fact that
management knows it is happening ('We didn't want to make the
mistake of working on the report secretly, and finally going to the
management, and they say, we don't know anything about this');
and the fact that the Unichema management, much to its credit,
signed a 'policy agreement' in December 1984, despite obvious
hesitations. Indeed, it seems that for signing this agreement the
management encountered strong criticism not only within Unilever
but also from other employers in the region.

> We signed a global automation contract, nothing detailed, but
> we can fall back on it. After signing such a thing, you must take
> the initiative yourself and make use of that piece of paper . . . .
> When it becomes necessary, we'll sign a new, more detailed
> agreement. The director said, you can choose whichever part of
> the factory you want, but not Dimer, because that's a strategic
> department and I don't want any outsiders there. We said, any
> department which is being automated will do. We'll study the
> jobs there—how far has automation gone already, what are
> working conditions like, how much responsibility do process
> operators have, is there going to be a central control room or
> not, what consequences would that have for workers, and what
> do we want out of the process (interview).

The union publication which most clearly outlines the right
strategy on automation is something the transport workers' union,
Vervoersbond (FNV), produced recently. Apart from an analysis
of the impact of automation in the Rotterdam docks, this has a
long chapter on 'social consequences and social alternatives' which
deals with the impact of new technologies on employment, working
conditions and employee health, job content, job structure and
training, employment contracts and job security, and finally, protection of the right to individual privacy. After saying that in their
present form new technologies are actually polarising job structures
through a greater predetermination of tasks, the fact that information

flows are now massively centralised and the mass of employees
pushed to the margins of the information network, Vervoersbond
correctly notes that 'deskilling and polarisation are not consequences of technology as such. The cause has to be sought in
traditional ways of thinking about how work should be organised'
(*Het blijft mensenwerk*, p. 40). Crucial premises of an active union
policy would include 'decentralisation of information, responsibility
and decisions; broader and richer jobs (which doesn't mean heavier
workloads) not just for a small group but for everyone; no further
separation between manual and mental labour but a healing of
their split and their progressive combination' (p. 42). The final
chapter, which is in many ways the one with most significance,
deals with strategies for 'negotiating automation,' outlining but
not sharply counterposing two of them:

> In a *benefits strategy*, get your employer to make an automation
> plan which fulfils a number of conditions. You're trying to get an
> agreement on general norms which must be fulfilled by the auto-
> mation. For example, according to us the number of jobs must at
> least remain constant, there must be an improvement in the jobs
> of the lowest job groups, there should be a training scheme which
> gives employees the chance to qualify for jobs at a higher level
> . . . . In an *initiative strategy* you go a step further. Directly or
> through the works council you try to work out an alternative
> automation plan; [but this requires a high] quality of union work
> and your own grasp of technology and work organisation (p. 56).

The information rights clause in the draft technology agreement
formulated by the Vervoersbond states, 'The information must at
least comprise the following—the motivations behind the proposed
technological changes, the costs involved, the types of hardware
and software, and the consequences for employment levels, job
content, work organisation, skills, training, promotion possibilities,
payments and health' (*Het blijft mensenwerk*).

At Mullard Mitcham, one of the Philips companies in the UK,
the ASTMS signed a new technology agreement which starts with
the definition of

> 'New Technology' as any changes in equipment and associated
> manufacturing or administrative processes which will affect:

Staffing levels
Working methods (skills required/amount of work needed)
The pattern of working hours
Health and safety issues.

The agreement then states:

3.a) Proposals for the introduction of new technology will be discussed with Senior representatives at the Establishment Committee. These proposals will not be implemented until mutual agreement has been reached between Management and Unions. b) The Company undertakes to provide the information concerning the new technologies as far in advance as it is able to do so and in a form which is readily understandable . . . . 4.a) The company will give priority consideration to retraining existing employees in new equipment and processes . . . . New jobs arising out of the introduction of new technology will be offered to employees who have successfully retrained (Mullard Mitcham, cl. 2–4).

Some of the clauses in the more detailed ASTMS Draft Technology Agreement, 1984, run as follows:

3. The company and the appropriate union representatives agree to meet at intervals of not less than three months to discuss the implementation and introduction of new technology and any problems arising therefrom. This meeting shall be known as the 'technology conference' . . . . 5. The Company agrees to allow sufficient time for the representatives to make an effective contribution, to attend suitable trade union and trade union appointed courses . . . . 9. Matters which should be discussed at technology conferences include: a) the type of equipment or system and its siting, b) the skills needed to operate or service or work with it, c) manpower requirements, d) training and retraining requirements, e) health and safety problems . . . .

The APEX Draft Agreement Relating to the Introduction of New Technology develops similar provisions.

3. No further systems or individual units will be introduced without negotiation and agreement with the union. 4. The Management agree to provide the necessary information to the Union to enable them to: monitor developments, changes in workflow, changes in working methods and the effects on jobs; control any further proposed introduction of computer-based systems; analyse health and safety effects and general working environment. This information to include the Management's long term plans on the introduction of technological equipment and sickness records of staff associated with technological equipment.

Unions in Bombay have concentrated mainly on protecting the jobs and employment conditions of existing employees when new technology is introduced. The ICI agreement, for example, states:

19.1 The Management proposes to instal a Micro Processor at Crescent House, Bombay, in replacement of the existing Unit Recorder . . . . 19.3 It is agreed that as a result of this replacement of Unit Recorder Machine by a Micro Processor, no employee will be declared surplus or redundant and no employee will be laid off or retrenched. 19.4 It has been agreed that the work connected with programming, laying down systems and procedures, etc. pertaining to the operation of the Micro Processor will be done by our employees who have the aptitude and will be trained for this purpose. 19.5 It is agreed that as a result of the introduction of Micro Processor, the terms and conditions of service of the employees will not be adversely affected (Agreement dated 20 August 1982, p. 22).

In addition, a few trade unions have attempted to protect *future* employment levels and specify consultative procedures to be followed in the introduction of new technology. One of the earliest and most comprehensive attempts of this type was the agreement dated 25 August 1973 signed by the Voltas and Volkart Employees' Federation. This includes the assurance that

as a direct or indirect result of the use or extension of EDP in the Company: a) there will be no retrenchment, redundancy, or *reduction of employment* in any Division/Department/Establishment of the Company, and the remuneration of the employees will be protected. The future prospects of employees will not be adversely affected . . . (p. 1, our emphasis).

After specifying the applications for which EDP may be used, the settlement goes on to say, '8. Any further extension of EDP beyond the applications referred to in clauses 5 and 7 above shall not be resorted to without previous consultation with the Federation and without previous approval of the Maharashtra State Government' (p. 3). Hoechst agreed that

the Company will inform the union in advance regarding the installation of automatic machines/computer, or introduction of any mechanisation, if any, of the processes. The period of trial and setting up of the machine shall be mutually agreed upon by the union . . . (Agreement dated 23.7.84, cl. 3).

The Pfizer agreement dated 18.9.1986 has a clause which says,

Changes and Improvements . . . . 2. The Management will intimate the Recognised Union about the intended changes at least four weeks in advance of the stipulated date of change so that the effects of the change, particularly in regard to the revised manning required on the operation and redeployment of individuals affected, and compensation to affected workmen in case of increase in workload, if any, will be considered and can be discussed in advance.

In a much earlier settlement, Pfizer management assured the union that 'as a consequence of improved mechanisation and on introduction of the use of Computer there will be: a) no retrenchment of, b) no reduction in the complement of, or c) no adverse effect on grade or salary of any workmen in Accounts or IBM Department or any other department' (Agreement dated 19 May 1967, p. 2). Yet here, as in Voltas, the union was faced with persistent management violation of the terms of the agreement, resulting in a steady reduction in the size of the workforce. Other managements have not even agreed to safeguard employment levels, nor to consult the union about the introduction of new technology, nor even to inform them of it in advance.

The difficulty which unions have experienced in trying to gain some degree of control over this process is partly a reflection of their weak position regarding information and consultation rights in general.

8.1.2 Information disclosure and alternative plans

Most of the information disclosure clauses in Dutch settlements are probably there because there are legal stipulations that employers should provide at least the works councils with certain sorts of information about investment or other decisions. Clause 2 on 'Employment' in the Unilever settlement states that insofar as the management is proposing to make decisions on investment and modernisation which are likely to have an appreciable impact on the situation in the plant, 'they shall supply the unions with all the information they reasonably need to state their own positions on the plans' (Unilever, cl. 2.3, pp. 5–6). The agreement for Shell Refinery likewise states that 'The employer shall, once a year or as often as becomes necessary, and outside negotiations for a new agreement, supply the unions with information on all proposed investments, both reinvestments as well as new investments, which have a significant impact on employment.' And the same clause, entitled 'Investments and Employment,' goes on to say, the employer shall keep the unions informed about 'the economic situation of the undertaking and prospects with regard to the employment position in the coming year' (Shell, cl. 24, p. 61).

The ICI Holland agreement has an even more elaborate 'Employment policy' clause, part of which is called 'Information,' and this states:

> Once a year outside the framework of negotiations for a new agreement, the union shall be supplied with the following information in writing:
>
> — staff turnover and replacement
> — the ratio between the company's personnel and outside personnel
> — the number of jobs classified by grade and type of shift
> — overtime
> — early retirement

- apprentices
- part-time workers
- employees not completely fit for work (ICI, cl. 21.7, p. 40).

As there is now a legal obligation on companies to publish basic personnel information once a year, some agreements specifically mention this report, which is called the 'social annual report' or 'personnel report'. Most of the information contained in these reports is within the prescribed domain of the works councils, and the report is in fact intended primarily for discussions with the works councillors. In these there are some useful data on: the movement of employment in the company, the distribution of the workforce including the non-bargainable categories into various job groups or grades, gross salary levels for the year, averaged for each grade or the plant as a whole, the distribution of employees by the type of shift worked, age group and type of contract, sickness absenteeism rates, accident rates, labour turnover, the performance of individual plants (in the ICI sense) or establishments (where there are several, as in Unilever), the rate of promotions, and so on.

Thus, in general, agreements would contain provision for two types of information: data related to investment and modernisation plans, including their impact on jobs; and personnel information of the kind normally contained in the social annual report.

The peculiar form of 'codetermination' which exists in the Netherlands in the form of the Law on Works Councils (WOR) is especially significant when contrasted with industrial relations systems where managements are not only strongly wedded to the ideology of management rights but where they actually seek to enforce those rights in the day-to-day running of their plants. Codetermination in the Dutch and German form is, in principle, a strong formal limitation on managerial freedom. Dutch legislation allows for extensive *consultative rights* which are partly veto rights with respect to:[40]

25.1 (a) transfer of control over the undertaking or any of its divisions to another employer;
(b) closure of the undertaking or any of its divisions;
(c) substantial reduction, expansion or other changes in the activities of the undertaking;

(d) major changes in the organisation of the undertaking;

(e) transfer of the undertaking to another location;

(f) the establishment or dissolution of permanent links of the undertaking with other undertakings.

26.1 The employer shall give the works council an opportunity to state its views on any decision to be taken by himself or another person involved in the undertaking with regard to the establishment or modification of—

(a) a wage scale or other remuneration scheme;

(b) any measure in the field of training;

(c) any assessment of the rating system;

(d) any of the basic elements of the policy applied with regard to recruitment, termination or promotion;

(e) any measure relating to the welfare services of the undertaking, to the extent that any of these items relate to the staff.

27.1 The employer must obtain the consent of the works council before he or another person involved in the undertaking takes any decision in connection with the establishment or modification of—

(a) any works rules as defined in section 1637J of the Civil Code;

(b) any pension scheme, profit-sharing plan or savings scheme;

(c) any working hours or holiday arrangement;

(d) any measure in the field of safety, health or hygiene, to the extent that any of these items relate to the staff.

The weak union position at the plant level means that consultative rights are rarely pressed, but information disclosure rights have been important for recent union initiatives in Holland. By 'union initiatives' we mean *active interventions to influence company or industrial policy*, starting from a basic realisation that in crucial areas of decision-making such as levels of employment, organisation of plants or new technology, as long as unions leave the initiative entirely with employers they undermine their own bargaining position. These are areas where unions cannot construct a bargaining position of their own unless they have their own principles on these issues—their own norms and criteria—and translate these into concrete plans which can form the basis for them to negotiate not just on what employers are after but on what they themselves feel they can get or should try to get from the situation. Having your own norms on 'work organisation, machine and systems design,' on the number of jobs, the kind of jobs people do, what automation should mean for employees, etc., and using these to evolve 'alternative plans' or alternative proposals on these issues both involve unions' ability to conduct research around workplaces and industries and to use the results of this research. There have been many examples of trade union initiatives of this kind in Dutch industry; even if the unions as a whole and the union top remain committed to defending the competitive interests of Dutch employers in the world economy, some unions have the freedom to push forward with concrete experiments based on a line of thinking which is far more radical.

In the Netherlands, where job losses have affected Philips employment quite drastically, Philips union activists realise that to influence employment levels within the company, the unions must influence crucial aspects of company policy. The chief examples of this have been struggles in Drachten, Appeldoorn and NKF-Delft. At Drachten, union attempts to influence market development and sales policy received considerable local publicity. For most of the seventies, Philips ran down the Drachten labour force by a whole third, largely through automation, and the union felt its best option was to get management to accept a sales policy based on 'seeking new outlets and starting to operate in several price ranges'; the Industriebond argued that 'because Philips Drachten is one-sidedly geared to the production of shavers, it has landed up in a questionable position.' At NKF, the Industriebond mainly emphasised product innovations through ventures like the development of special cables for off-shore activities or production of non-energy cables, and areas that could involve a drastic expansion of cable production if Philips revamped its marketing policies, notably on turnkey projects in the Middle East.

At Philips Data Systems in Appeldoorn, the management was criticised for the fact that the reorganisations of the late seventies had failed to establish the position on the American market Philips had hoped for. With an occupational structure where only 5 per cent of the labour force would be 'blue collar,' this is one of Philips' 'new working class' establishments, highly automated, with the bulk of the workforce in development, research, training and administration. But the rate of organisation is low, even by Philips standards. TIE asked Martin Overbeeke, one of the employees in the R & D department,

'Which is a higher priority for your union, making an active push for recruitment, or confronting the company's automation and relocation policies?'
Martin: Proposing alternative production plans, like those of Lucas Aerospace, has been one of the primary tactics we've used. We consulted with some of the workers at Lucas about their experiences in attempting to convert production from military to civilian lines. Of course, we adapted their ideas to our own particular situation. We've interviewed about 150 people, from manual labourers to designers, and from those interviews we tried to construct alternative plans—constructive ways of creating new lines of production. We presented these proposals to management. They listen, but they don't act. At that moment we needed power to push for our ideas, but we didn't have that kind of influence with the company . . . .
TIE: I know that the alternative plans that you developed were not implemented, but what specifically did they propose?
Martin: Well, for example, we make video terminals, but we make them only for our own systems. We could sell peripheral equipment such as video terminals, printers, disc units, and so on to other factories that develop computer systems. This would certainly increase the market for our products . . . (TIE, *Bulletin* no. 12, p. 21).

Although this kind of plan expresses a fairly advanced type of initiative and gives unions a basis for tackling reorganisation with counter-proposals, the experience at Data Systems is revealing in another way: unless unions can get companies to accept the plan/ proposals within some negotiating framework, to make them one of the bargaining issues, alternative plans won't have any practical results, apart from the possibly valuable experience gained in actually drafting them. 'An alternative plan is nice, but next to this you have to, as a union, develop a fair amount of power to fight. Within and outside your plant.' Moreover, and this is also crucial, 'up until now Philips has consistently refused to take up the employees' plan as an issue in negotiations' (SOBE, *International Reorganisations*, pp. 188–89).

One case where the union was successful in fighting for an alternative plan was the Industriebond's intervention for more jobs in Akzo.

A recent example relating working hours, employment levels and the content of jobs is the research done by Akzo employees into job creation through labour time shortening. This research, conducted in 1983 with the help of a handbook for local activists, was linked to union negotiations with Akzo at several levels (plants, divisions, overall). In various locations, from Sikkens Smit Wapenveld, Organon Oss to Akzo-Delfzijl, activists kept track of jobs and employment levels. The results they got and above all their proposals for expansion of employment, were then used to fill out the 'agreement of principle' signed in March 1983 between the unions and Akzo management. The concrete bargaining result as of 1 July 1984: 950 extra jobs through a 38-hour week (Buitelaar and Vreeman [1985], p. 156).

Ruud Vreeman describes similar attempts made by the transport workers' union, the Vervoersbond/FNV, to influence employment levels in the Rotterdam region by making this a key issue for negotiations:

What we try in the harbour is to make long-term employment agreements, we call them 'APO'; work shortening is part of this, stimulating new activities is part of this, and the main point is technology agreements. We always try to have agreements on a higher level than the plant, because we define the problem on the level of the docks as a whole, or on the level of the whole Rotterdam region. The solution to the problem of unemployment is not always at the level of the plant; for example, when you have two hundred workers and fifty have to go, you can try to do something about this through shorter hours, etc., but you still have to redeploy people somewhere else, retrain them or something like that.

In Holland, the main union strategy for job creation has been the campaign for shorter hours.

This is one line. The other line we are trying to build up in Rotterdam with the employers and with the local government is to stimulate activities in the Rotterdam region; . . . for example, to have a car factory, to get new services in Rotterdam. Our pressure line is our power in the harbour—they are very afraid of strikes because our whole industry in relation to Germany rests on Rotterdam (interview).

In India, initiatives of this sort face a massive obstacle in the total lack of legal information rights. A typical case is that of Metal Box, where in 1985 the company pleaded 'acute financial difficulties' and 'very stiff competition from other manufacturers of containers and packaging material' as reasons for proposing a series of cost-cutting measures, including a ceiling on DA and reduction of the workforce. The union responded by pointing out economy measures which could reduce costs considerably by eliminating wastage, but were unable to propose a more comprehensive alternative plan because there was no means by which they could elicit from management the information they would need for such a plan.[41] The Kamani Employees' Union is an exceptional case. In the early seventies, in response to a union demand for 16 per cent bonus, the Kamani management offered to open their books of account to the union to prove that they were making losses and could not afford to pay more than the minimum bonus of 4 per cent. The union accepted, and went on to win its bonus claim as well as to participate in an 'open system of management' in which it had access to all aspects of company information. The arrangement was suspended a few years later, but in the meantime union activists gained valuable information and experience which they were able to use later in order to propose an alternative plan when Kamani Tubes was facing closure in the early eighties. A workers' cooperative finally succeeded in taking over the factory and keeping it open.[42]

Initiatives which seek to establish union controls over the introduction of new technology, production plans and regional development represent one crucial aspect of a trade union strategy to save existing jobs and create new ones. The competitive rationality of cost-cutting and the striving for profitability inevitably result in job losses, and employees' plans for socially useful production are important because they 'start to question existing economic assumptions and to make a small contribution to demonstrating that workers are prepared to press for the right to work on products which actually help to solve human problems rather than creating them' (The Lucas Combine's Corporate Plan).

In the case of multinational companies, however, the fact that the locus of decision-making is generally inaccessible to union pressure means that perfectly viable alternative plans which local management might be willing to discuss have no chance of being considered at the international level. This was the experience at the Ford plant in Amsterdam (see p. 19f.). The problems encountered by locally- or nationally-based unions in dealing with centralised decision-making in multinational companies have resulted in a variety of attempts at international responses.

8.2 INTERNATIONAL RESPONSES

Attempts to regulate companies through codes of conduct and to coordinate union action internationally are aimed at mitigating both of the major consequences of the strategy of multinationalism, i.e., the wide disparities between employment conditions of workforces in different countries as well as the continued job losses which result from unilateral management decision-making on restructuring and automation.

8.2.1 Codes of conduct

The International Labour Organisation (ILO), the Organisation for Economic Cooperation and Development (OECD) and the UN Centre on Transnational Corporations (CTC) have all developed codes of conduct for multinationals. The aim is to regulate the conduct of these companies, but success has so far been limited because the recommendations are not mandatory and there is no means by which they can be enforced.

The ILO Tripartite Declaration of Principles Concerning Multinational Enterprises and Social Policy was completed in April 1977. Its provisions include: (*a*) the right of workers in multinational companies to establish and join *organisations of their own*; protection against anti-union discrimination; (*b*) negotiations between representatives of the workers and representatives of the management who are *authorised to take decisions* on the matters under negotiation; (*c*) condemnation of threats by multinationals to *transfer production* away from a country in order to influence negotiations with workers' representatives in that country; (*d*) regular *consultation* between employers and workers on matters of mutual concern.

The OECD Guidelines for Multinational Enterprises, issued in June 1976, has comparable provisions. In addition, it is recommended that these companies: (*a*) provide employees' representatives with *information* which is needed for meaningful negotiations as well as facilities required to assist in the development of effective collective agreements; (*b*) provide them with information which enables them to obtain a true and fair view of the performance of the subsidiary or enterprise *as a whole*; and (*c*) provide employees' representatives with reasonable *notice of changes* likely to have a major impact on the livelihood of the employees, particularly in the case of a closure involving collective lay-offs or dismissals, and cooperate with employees' representatives to mitigate adverse effects to the maximum extent practicable.

The UN Code of Conduct Relating to Transnational Corporations proceeds along similar lines. For example, it suggests (*a*) that countries permit free entry to unionists from other countries, including entry at the invitation of workers in the host country or their unions, to assist them in their negotiations with international companies; and (*b*) that information relevant to collective bargaining should be disclosed, and should include information on the structure, activities and policies of the company as a whole.

If implemented, these codes of conduct would go a long way towards offsetting the disadvantages experienced by unions in their negotiations with international companies. They have occasionally been effective because of the publicity generated around cases where they have been cited. For example, when the Badger company in Belgium, a subsidiary of the American company Raytheon, went bankrupt, both the OECD Guidelines and the ILO Declaration were cited to support the argument that the parent company should meet the financial obligations of the subsidiary, including redundancy payments to 250 workers whose services were terminated. The Trade Union Advisory Committee of the OECD took part in the negotiations, and the final agreement was reached on the basis of the OECD Guidelines (Bendiner [1987], pp. 111–12). Such cases are rare, however. The main reason why the codes of conduct have been largely ineffective is that they are purely voluntary and there is no provision for making them legally binding. On the other hand, the proposed Vredeling Directive seeks to make some of the ILO and OECD provisions mandatory within the EEC. For example, it would extend to workers in multinational companies information and consultation rights which are *international* in scope, including the option to transfer these rights to 'a body representing employees at a higher level than that of the individual subsidiary' (see IDS Study 313, pp. 13–15). However, Unilever's comment is an example of the strong opposition encountered by the Directive from international companies:

> We share the concern of many employers that the proposed directive would not improve industrial relations. Our companies operating in Europe have made considerable progress in establishing and maintaining consultative arrangements within their various national laws and customs. We believe that EC legislation in this area would damage the essential balance and flexibility of national industrial relations without contributing to the better operation of the Common Market (Unilever Annual Report, 1983).

8.2.2 International collective bargaining

Charles Levinson, former general secretary of the ICEF (see below), has been one of the strongest advocates of full-scale international collective bargaining as a means of overcoming the problems faced by unions in negotiating with multinational companies, and the ICEF in fact presided over one of the very few successful efforts in concluding an international agreement. This occurred on the occasion of the 1973 merger between the Glaverbel Company (a Belgian glass multinational) and the BSN-Gervais-Danone Company, a French multinational with subsidiaries in five European countries. The final agreement between BSN and a committee of union representatives from the company's plants in France, Belgium, the Netherlands, Germany and Austria was signed in May 1975. It provided for the formation of a permanent joint labour-management committee to meet twice a year and monitor an equitable distribution of employment among factories in the six countries. The committee would be supplied with information on investments and foreign holdings of the company as well as social conditions in the communities where the plants were located; no decision on employment would be made by the central or local management without consultation with this committee (Bendiner [1987], pp. 94–95).

However, most managements have refused to meet international trade union representatives at all, and even where unions have been able to bring about such a meeting, the company has taken the stand that it is purely consultative and does not constitute collective bargaining. For example, international top management of SKF agreed to meet an IMF delegation at the company's headquarters in Göteborg to discuss problems encountered by their affiliates in various SKF plants throughout the world. Meetings like this can be useful, but they fall far short of international collective bargaining, and there seems to be little prospect of further developments in this direction in the immediate future. One reason, undoubtedly, is management opposition to negotiations at this level. But unions too have posed some resistance to the idea, for reasons which are fairly complex and not very well articulated. One survey concludes that apart from '(1) hostility of management,' major obstacles to international collective bargaining are:

(2) lack of support from national trade unions in terms of losing their 'sovereignty' over bargaining . . .; (3) lack of support from trade union members . . .; (4) differences between national IR systems . . .; (5) lack of international framework; (6) non-legitimization of international solidarity actions . . .; (7) political fragmentation of trade unions (Press [1984], p. 95).

A possible objective for unions to work towards is *international collective agreements* which specify (*a*) codes of conduct—for example, with respect to union recognition, health and safety, information disclosure, equal opportunities—and (*b*) minimum standards, for example, on working hours, leave, accident compensation, retirement benefits and other areas. These agreements would allow individual unions to retain their autonomy and achieve better employment conditions if they could, while at the same time making it possible for stronger unions, especially those in the parent concern, to intervene in cases where the codes of conduct or minimum standards were violated.

It remains to be seen whether international collective bargaining will gain in importance, but other more limited forms of international cooperation and coordination between unions have already been used with considerable success. It has in fact been argued that 'a major impediment to the development of MCB' is 'the very success of national bargaining,' that 'international cooperation in more limited forms, such as the exchange of information, may have served to reinforce the effectiveness of national bargaining,' and that 'this is a further area where union resources should be increased and directed with more effectiveness' (Enderwick [1987], pp. 211, 213).

8.2.3 Information exchange

Given the reluctance of multinational managements to disclose information which is international in scope, unions have devised other ways of getting access to information which will allow them to compare employment conditions in different countries and to infer the overall performance and plans of these companies. This is achieved by exchanging information between unions in subsidiaries or centralising and distributing information among them. Much of this activity is carried out by the International Trade Secretariats (ITSs) which were formed in the latter part of the nineteenth century and the World Company Councils (WCCs) set up by them. The most active of the ITSs are probably the International Metalworkers' Federation (IMF), the International Federation of Chemical, Energy and General Workers' Unions (ICEF) and the International Union of Food and Allied Workers' Associations (IUF). These have set up company councils in many of the automobile companies (Nissan, General Motors, Ford, Volkswagen, Renault, etc.), chemical companies (Michelin Tyres, Dunlop-Pirelli, Ciba-Geigy and others) and food companies like Nestle, Unilever and Coca Cola. The international trade secretariats provide their affiliates with bargaining information based on an overall view of the company's position internationally, and also organise conferences where representatives of affiliates in different countries can come together to exchange information and discuss common problems.

Some independent groups with experience in research on international companies have also assisted in information exchange between unions in these companies. The Transnationals Information Exchange (TIE) is a network which was formed in 1978 by action and research groups in Europe and operates in three ways:

- It organises *international consultations*, in which workers from different countries in a single company or sector, and others who are involved, are brought together to discuss their specific and common problems and possible ways to support one another.
- It acts as a *platform* for discussion and information exchange by organising seminars for its member groups on topics which concern many of them, such as the introduction of new technology and its social consequences . . . . The internal members' newsletter informs the affiliated groups in detail about each others' activities, the work within TIE's Working Groups, upcoming events, new publications and other resources relevant to their work.
- The production of its *TIE Report*, which is published three times per year, enables the network to bring the work of its member groups and of the network as a whole to the attention of a broader readership, thus encouraging wider reflection and discussion on the international restructuring process, the effects of transnational corporate power and potential counterstrategies (Peijnenberg [1984]).

SOBE ('Stichting Onderzoek Bedrijfstak Electroniek') is another organisation which attempts to organise the international exchange of information and assist the formation of a network at the shop floor level. In the summer of 1982 it held a 'European Conference of Philips Workers' with forty participants from seven West European countries where it was decided to publish an international newspaper called 'Philips Workers' News' (the name was later changed to *Connecta* because of objections from the company).

In Unilever, information exchange takes place at several levels, national and international: at European level within the margarine group where workers know 'that several thousand tons of production can be shifted to Belgium in one day, then a few weeks later to England'; the ASTMS Unilever meetings in the UK—'Everyone runs through a report of what is happening in their plant; everyone leaves the meetings knowing what is happening in Unilever';

international information exchange through the IUF working group on Unilever; and the GLC-sponsored seminar for workers in Unilever with an overall attendance of some seventy people representing twelve separate unions and twenty plants, and attended by delegates from Rotterdam who said afterwards that it was an 'eye-opener' for them.[43]

An overall view of company performance and the possession of information on employment conditions elsewhere in the world could help unions to anticipate and prepare for restructuring measures which might otherwise be completely unexpected and enormously strengthen local bargaining by helping in the formulation of demands as well as in arguing for them. International comparisons which reveal, say, substantial differences in working hours although productivity levels are similar, can be used in negotiating shorter hours. The significance of these comparisons is not confined to international companies alone, since the experience of local subsidiaries of these companies or even the parent companies themselves can be used by workforces of locally-based companies; the Lucas Aerospace plan, for example, had resonances not just in Holland but even in the Kamani plan formulated in Bombay. Moreover, the information exchanged could include information on legal provisions—such as legislation on information disclosure or health and safety—which could be used in fighting for better laws locally, and the scope of these would obviously extend beyond the multinational sector.

8.2.4 International coordination and solidarity action

In 1985 there was an international demonstration outside the Rotterdam headquarters of Unilever; this was one example of internationally coordinated union action aimed at a multinational company. Most actions of this kind have been organised through the International Trade Secretariat and World Company Councils, and their purpose has been to support a union which is in dispute with one of the subsidiaries of the company or to press for recognition of a union. In one case where a Malaysian subsidiary of the West German Standard Electric Lorenz Company refused to recognise and negotiate with the Malaysian Electrical Workers' Union, the IMF requested IG Metall to put pressure on the parent company, which in turn pressed its subsidiary to engage in negotiations which resulted, in 1985, in a collective agreement. UAW pressure on General Motors in Detroit, organised through the IMF, was also instrumental in gaining union recognition for relocated employees of General Motors of Mexico.

In the event of a dispute with employees in one country, an international company has the advantage of being able to shift production to other countries, and where this occurs, restriction of overtime by employees in other countries can be a very effective form of support for the workers involved in the dispute. Thus when in 1976 the workforce at the General Motors plant in Strasburg, France, came out on strike, the IMF–General Motors World Auto Council organised a meeting between the strike committee at Strasburg and the works council of the Opel plant at Russelheim, West Germany, which normally received most of its stocks of transmissions from Strasburg. At this meeting the Russelheim works council agreed to curb voluntary overtime on work which normally would have come from Strasburg but because of the strike was coming from another GM factory. Largely as a result of overtime restrictions, the strike was settled and most of its demands—for increased rates of pay and extra relief time, and against repression of union militants—were won (Bendiner [1987], pp. 82–83, 74, 75).

A recent case of internationally coordinated trade union solidarity which received wide publicity was the campaign organised in 1980 by the IUF in support of trade unionists in a licensed Coca Cola bottling plant in Guatemala who were being repressed and, in some cases, murdered. The action included a consumer boycott, work interruptions in Italy, and strikes in Sweden, Norway and Mexico, and forced the reopening of the Guatemalan plant after it had been occupied for twelve months (Tudyka [1987], p. 225).

International coordination has not, however, so far proved effective in the case of closures. Nigel Haworth and Harvie Ramsey describe their experience with the closure of the Massey-Ferguson factory in Kilmarnock as follows:

The Kilmarnock plant was the last plant producing combine harvesters in Britain, and was faced with closure as a result of financial crises within the MF conglomerate as a whole. Combine production was to be switched for various reasons to a plant in Northern France, despite evidence to the effect that the Kilmarnock plant was profitable, and possessed within its workforce very specific skills. The story is one we have seen often in

Scotland since the mid 1970s. An MNC switches production away from an existing Scottish plant to another subsidiary, and the workforce is forced to fight on ground laid down by decisions often taken thousands of miles away, and based upon criteria with no direct link with the threatened plant. In the Kilmarnock case, the financial reasons for company rationalisations were defined at corporate level, and were precisely *financial* reasons to do with poor debt servicing rather than low productivities, poor production performance or whatever. The Kilmarnock unions fought the closure for nearly two years, but eventually lost, and the plant was closed. What strikes us about this defeat was that it happened despite the fact that the union side at Kilmarnock was in an apparently very strong position. There was a high level of union membership in a high-wage plant. There was a very strong stewards organisation, which had excellent intelligence about MF's plans. Strong support was offered by local and regional labour councils, and local MPs worked hard to keep pressure up at national level. The stewards and workforce were very conscious of the power of MNCs, and had a very sophisticated understanding of the company's strategy, comparing it knowledgeably with the company strategies in Speke (Dunlop), and Singers and Goodyear in Clydebank and Drumchapel. Most importantly for present purposes, the Kilmarnock workforce had excellent contacts with other MF plants throughout Britain, organised in an effective and active combine. Furthermore, good international links were built with the French CGT in the plant to which combine harvester production was to be shifted, as well as with wider groups of engineering and motor industry workers elsewhere in Europe. Despite these contacts, the Kilmarnock plant was still closed, and the work was moved to the French plant (Haworth and Ramsey [1984], pp. 61–62).

Does this experience imply that there are limits to the effectiveness of internationally coordinated trade union action, that while coordination and information exchange can help in some situations, they are ineffective in others? We began with the impact of multinationalism on employment levels and job security, and it is important to determine whether trade unions can gain any degree of control over these through international action.

THE STRATEGY OF MULTINATIONALISM: TOWARDS A CONCLUSION

Is there a general intuition which emerges from the comparisons developed in this book? Companies which are powerful enough to enforce unified policies in other areas of their business seem to lack the ability to establish terms of employment according to a rational and consistent policy. But this way of dealing with the unified labour forces of multinationals as multiplicities of distinct and essentially unrelated labour forces is certainly conscious policy. Industrial relations is one function international companies deal with in a largely internationally decentralised form, even when, like most American companies, they actually believe in, and in some ways perhaps even succeed in enforcing, 'close managerial supervision' (Bomers [1976], p. 126) over subsidiaries. It is probably true, as Bomers argued, that American companies in particular feel the need to establish a 'strong influence upon industrial relations' in local plants, but what is at issue here is the form of this influence and whether it is the kind that could lead to greater standardisation internationally. Two Bombay examples: Firestone was one of the first international firms to come to Bombay, having started operations by the forties, so presumably when it took a strike of six months in 1967–68, over the resistance workers put up to the transfer of a workman from one department to another, Akron would have known precisely what the strike was about, how much production they were losing over the issue, and so on. But no intervention was made to settle the dispute, and the peculiar form in which American centralisation did eventually assert itself was having the Managing Director, G.L. Anderson, recalled following the strike. It is inconceivable that a 'strong

influence upon industrial relations' would have let a purely departmental issue inflict production losses for 186 days! More recently,
employees of Indal, the Alcan subsidiary at Kalwa, went through a
strike of almost eight months over their charter. The strike started
in the third week of January 1983, and in May an international
representative visited Bombay. According to the union's account,
he asked why the plant was not in operation and was told that
workers were on strike over a pay rise. How much are they asking
for? asked Faulkner. When they told him, he obviously decided it
was not worth a strike and put pressure on local management to
settle. It was Faulkner who got Indal to resume discussions with
the union, and for the union at any rate his presence and intervention were crucial to the final settlement. But again, international
influence on local relations did nothing to avoid the dispute in the
first place or to get local management to settle any faster than they
eventually did.

If this is the situation with American companies who consciously
endorse the need for tight centralisation internationally, the pattern
in European subsidiaries is maximum local autonomy in the company's dealings with labour. Bomers concluded from his interviews
with international managements, 'None of the European-based
MNC's indicated having any involvement in local collective bargaining,' and he quotes managers from these firms as saying

> We do not know much about the social policies of our foreign
> subsidiaries. We do not know about their wage rates, their
> fringe benefits, whether they are members of an employers'
> organisation, whether they have unions, how collective bargain-
> ing is carried out. Perhaps, we may be informed about a strike,
> but even that frequently occurs only after the fact (p. 126).

Again, 'Industrial relations is totally decentralised,' said the manager of a Dutch multinational who also stated,

> Some of our industrial relations philosophy gets exported. For
> example, we have set certain broad minimum standards world-
> wide. Also, we hold a yearly seminar on social policy in which
> all personnel managers of the various subsidiaries take part
> and during which they are informed about our policies here in
> the Netherlands. *Whether they are doing anything with that*

information is totally up to them. There are no rules in that regard (p. 126, emphasis ours).

This sounds very much like a Philips manager who said that in the event of a local dispute in one of the Philips subsidiaries, 'We do monitor what is happening but we would never interfere, that wouldn't be correct, it would undermine the confidence of local management.'

Thus, international companies enforce tight technical and financial control over subsidiaries, but allow purely local influences to determine the nature and form of their labour relations, even when foreign managers are retained in crucial positions, as in most multinationals in the Bombay area. Direct international influence is sometimes discernible in payments systems (SKF, Firestone at one time), job evaluations (Nocil), pension schemes (Parke-Davis, ICI), even union recognition (Atlas Copco) or the rapidity of settlements (IGE staff when they dealt with American managers), but such cases are rare and, on the whole, exceptional.

9.1 CENTRALISING CRUCIAL DECISIONS

'Management decisions about new or redeployed production facilities are not, as such, industrial relations questions. The effects or impact of these decisions on employees, however, are the concern of management industrial relations executives, and in most firms these effects are an appropriate subject for consultation and bargaining'—so R. Copp, overseas liaison manager of the Ford Motor Co., describing the decision-making structure of his company and of most international firms (Copp [1977], p. 44). In other words, crucial decisions, e.g., decisions which affect the level of employment in a firm or determine which locations are affected by redundancies, are 'outside the scope of . . . consultation or bargaining'; what *can* be discussed or negotiated with the union is *how*, that is, to what degree, at what rate, through what sort of arrangements, etc., those decisions will be effected in so far as they do have some impact on employees. Of course, the obvious response to this form of reasoning is: who decides what is or is not an 'industrial relations matter appropriate for consultation or bargaining'? In other words, who decides the *range of issues suitable for discussion* with the union? If managements do so, they will obviously want to define the scope of bargaining in the narrowest possible terms to increase the range of their own, unilateral authority. So when Copp says, decisions about restructuring 'are not, as such, industrial relations questions,' he is only describing a situation where managements are able to define the scope of bargaining to their own advantage, and also saying (of course) that such a situation is good.

Management's ability to determine the scope of bargaining is not something peculiar to international firms, but it does take a specific form in the decision-making process of those firms. Strategic decisions ('about new or redeployed production facilities') are internationally centralised whereas labour relations are left to national or local managements to be handled on a decentralised basis. International companies differ in the extent of corporate involvement in a subsidiary's general operations, including its labour relations,[44] certain labour relations decisions are 'much more centralised than others',[45] and so on, but these differences are purely secondary in relation to the central fact that *crucial decisions are never decentralised*. This is the fundamental axiom about the locus of decision-making in international firms.

Because the labour relations of subsidiary plants are affected by both sorts of decisions and not just by those which local managements are competent to make, this general *form* of decision-making has an 'industrial relations' rationality: it constitutes a bargaining strategy which is consciously aimed at depriving employees and unions of the power to control, much less to determine, the level of employment inside firms. This is the crucial reason why unions found themselves hopelessly outflanked in the general attack on levels of employment which started in the early seventies and which, in countries like Britain, has meant a catastrophic decline in union membership.

'There is a widespread belief . . . that multinationals are "cultural invaders" that do not respect local traditions' (Blanpain in Banks and Stieber, *Multinationals*, p. 120). This refers, of course, to the sort of critique which grew up when the post-war expansion of international firms led to the first waves of significant foreign investment in countries like India. But to attack multinationals on these essentially political or cultural grounds misses the point. Headquarters managements are only too eager to publicise their decentralisation of labour policies, the fact that local patterns are the prime consideration in their dealings with employees. For example, 'Every Ford subsidiary has a senior executive, with an appropriate staff, responsible for the labor relations or the employee relations function,' and, 'The primary responsibility of this local staff is to develop and administer an industrial relations program *appropriate to the national setting*' (Copp [1977], p. 45). Despite important differences in the willingness of corporate headquarters to become involved in labour relations functions, and in the methods of control used to monitor those functions, no international firm would disagree with the conception outlined for Ford. The car industry is one sector where a high level of intersubsidiary production integration is one obvious reason for tighter corporate control over subsidiary level industrial relations,[46] and American firms have always enforced higher levels of centralised control. Yet even here, 'This allocation of primary responsibility in industrial relations matters to national subsidiaries is *typical* of the multinational automobile employers based in the United States and of multinational employers generally' (Copp [1977], p. 46). But this decentralisation of labour relations is part of the way in which international firms are able to 'nationalise' employee relations while enforcing international control over production; it is part of the strategy which divorces industrial relations from business decisions, defining different levels for these.

The multinational is merely a corporate expression of the fact that the productive forces of capital are international. However, the employee relations of such firms remain nationally fragmented, international firms deny their workers access to international resources (information, decision-making), standards (personnel practices, disclosure codes, safety, etc.) and conditions (shift payments, working hours, etc.), and they do this because fragmentation of this type increases the firm's flexibility and enormously increases the power of corporate management.

There are massive disparities in the treatment of multinational labour forces because multinational employers are fundamentally opposed to bargaining arrangements which would make it possible for unions to eliminate inequalities in standards and conditions by standardising the essential terms and conditions of employment between plants internationally. On management's side, the strength of this opposition shows how bargaining structures, the *levels* at which agreements are negotiated, are like the scope of bargaining or the range of *issues* involved in bargaining—strategic choices. Because crucial decisions are made at the international level, any move to extend bargaining to that level constitutes an especially threatening development since it would mean that employees' representatives are finally muscling in to the very heart of management power. Thus, opposition to 'international bargaining' is a natural part of the drive to enforce a decision-making structure where the crucial decisions are not only made internationally, at headquarters, but made unilaterally—by management alone.

9.2 POSSIBLE RESPONSES

The strategy just outlined works to the disadvantage of multinational employees because their managements can preserve disparities in the terms and conditions of employment between countries while they retain the freedom to transfer practices like subcontracting and flexibilisation from one country to another. Moreover, by removing decisions on investment and restructuring from the scope of bargaining, the strategy deprives unions of any control over employment levels.

International information exchange is one way in which unions have been able to strengthen local bargaining to produce greater equality, and internationally coordinated solidarity has helped unions in local disputes. These types of collaboration between unions would certainly be crucial in reducing the level of disparity, and to a limited extent they can also save jobs—for example, by helping local trade unionists to anticipate restructuring measures or to formulate 'alternative plans'. But it seems that where a company has decided to close down a subsidiary due to financial considerations which have nothing to do with the plant itself, union coordination on its own is ineffectual.

Here, regulation through legally enforceable codes of conduct would give unions international information and consultation rights which they could use to maintain employment levels; but given the influence of employers in organisations like the ILO and OECD it is not easy to see the enactment of measures which would be both rigorous and binding. Opposition to the Vredeling Directive suggests that employers would make sure that similar types of proposals are hopelessly diluted before they acquire the force of law. In this event, a possible way of enforcing codes of conduct on multinationals would be through international collective bargaining. Whatever form international agreements take, however, it is crucial that negotiations at higher levels do *not* reduce employee control over and involvement in collective bargaining. The experience of the Netherlands indicates that highly centralised bargaining can lead to a weak union presence at the plant level and consequent loss of bargaining strength.[47] International agreements should primarily deal with minimum standards and codes of practice which would leave unions free to engage in collective bargaining at the local level.

International collaboration between trade unionists—in the first instance of the same companies (Siemens, ICI, Metal Box, Johnson, Hoechst, Philips, Unilever, etc.), but also within product groups—can reduce the sources of inequality and help unions in their disputes with multinational managements. However, it cannot actually stop job losses unless it also questions the socially destructive competitive rationality behind management decision-making—where the pursuit of profitability governs the selection of products, automation is used to increase workloads rather than reduce them, and managements enforce the coexistence of long working hours for some with unemployment for others. Here the local experience of some unions with alternative plans is important, since they involve the creation of alternative *principles* challenging that rationality. What is necessary, ultimately, is the formulation of employees' plans on an international level to reflect and respond to the internationalisation of production which the multinationals have brought about.

APPENDICES

APPENDIX 1

Main International Firms with Bombay-Area Operations

Business Rank	Corporation	Home Country	Total Employment (000s)	Foreign Employment (%)	Main Local Plants
16	Unilever	NLD	300	48.0*	Sewree, Andheri, Taloja
24	Philips	NLD	372	78.8	Kalwa, Loni, Pimpri
27	Siemens	FRG	344	31.7	Kalwa, Worli
31	BASF	FRG	117	25.0	Turbhe
32	Hoechst	FRG	187	46.0	Mulund
33	Bayer	FRG	182	44.2	Kolshet
43	ICI	GBR	143	41.1	Thane-Belapur Rd, Sewree
60	Union Carbide	USA	116	46.2	Chembur, Turbhe
97	Ciba-Geigy	SWI	81	71.8	Bhandup
140	Alcan	CAN	67	70.1	Kalwa
142	Colgate	USA	48	54.8	Sewree
156	Firestone	USA	93	47.3	Sewree
157	Johnson	USA	74	—	Mulund
219	Roche	SWI	44	78.0	Tardeo, Balkum
266	Pfizer	USA	41	58.3	Turbhe
274	ASEA	SWE	40	24.6	Parel
275	SKF	SWE	53	81.7	Chinchwad
280	Sandoz	SWI	35	72.3	Kolshet
304	Merck	USA	32	48.4	Sonapur
314	Cadbury	GBR	35	32.6	Pokhran
325	Metal Box	GBR	54	44.9	Worli, Deonar, Mahul
378	Abbott	USA	31	35.7	Kurla

Note: 'Business rank' refers to rank in terms of sales volume, in a recent U.N. list of the world's largest industrial transnational corporations, cf. *Transnational Corporations in World Development: Third Survey* (by the United Nations Centre on Transnational Corporations, 1985) Annex Table II.31, p. 277f. The data on sales volume and employment refer to 1980. 'Local plants' excludes locations outside Maharashtra.

* In this case, outside EEC.

APPENDIX 2: Job classification clause in UNILEVER agreement

CLAUSE 28.   Job Classification Appeal Procedure

1. Objections to a job description

An employee who does not agree with a job description prepared for this job shall, after having duly informed his supervisor, notify his objections to the job description to the Head of the Personnel Department or to the Personnel Officer of the undertaking where he is employed.

The employee shall be given written confirmation of receipt of his objection. A decision regarding the objection shall then be taken by the Head of the Personnel Department or by the Personnel Officer and notified to the employee.

An employee who does not agree with the decision may apply via the Head of the Personnel Department or the Personnel Officer to the Job Description Committee. A Job Description Committee shall be set up in each undertaking. The Works Council is entitled to appoint half of the number of members of the Committee. The others shall be appointed by the management of the undertaking.

The Job Description Committee shall examine the objections and consult the supervisor responsible for drafting the job description concerned. If the Committee so wishes, it may seek assistance with its consultations from the classification experts of Unilever and/or the trade unions.

The Committee shall give its decision as soon as possible and in no event later than three months after the date on which the objection has been notified to the Head of the Personnel Department or the Personnel Officer. The Job Description Committee's decision regarding the job description is binding and shall be communicated to the employee in writing.

2. Objections to a job evaluation

An employee who does not agree with the total number of job classification points established in respect of the job he performs may, with the knowledge of his supervisor, within three months after the number of points has been established, make an application to the Head of the Personnel Department or to the Personnel

Officer of the undertaking where he is employed for the number of points to be re-determined.

The Head of the Personnel Department or the Personnel Officer shall ensure that the application is passed on to the General Personnel Department for the Netherlands, Job Classification Section. This Department shall confirm to the employee in writing that his application is under consideration.

The Job Classification Section shall re-determine the number of job classification points. Where the job is classified by the General Employers Association this shall be done by the Association's experts. The result shall be communicated to the employee in writing within three months of the application being submitted.

If the employee does not agree with the results he may, within three months after the results having been communicated to him, submit an application for a re-classification to the Head of the Personnel Department or the Personnel Officer of the undertaking where he is employed.

The application shall be passed on to the General Personnel Department for the Netherlands, Job Classification Section. The Department shall notify the trade unions' experts and the district officers concerned of the application, stating the applicant's name. The General Employers Association shall be notified of the application if the job has been classified by the Association. The employee shall be notified in writing that his application is under consideration.

The trade union experts shall subsequently indicate whether they can assist with consideration of the application. If they assist with consideration of the application, consultations shall be arranged between the experts of Unilever or the General Employers Association and those of the trade unions.

If the experts are able to agree, their decision shall be notified to the employee within three months after the application for re-classification has been submitted. Their decision is binding. If the experts are unable to agree, Unilever and the trade unions shall consult as to how the application should be dealt with.

If the trade union experts are unable to assist with consideration of the application, Unilever will apply to the General Employers Association for the appointment of an expert to consider the application together with Unilever's expert.

ENDNOTES

1. Some examples: by 1984, Burroughs Wellcome had diluted its equity to 40 per cent after considerable initial resistance and despite the option to retain a higher equity; General Electric to 40 per cent, Leyland to 44 per cent, Dunlop to 50 per cent, Siemens to 51 per cent. At one stage it was rumoured that Dunlop UK was willing to offload holdings for an estimated price of Rs 25 crores and that R.P. Goenka was interested. When Bayer reduced to 51 per cent, Goenka bought 9 per cent of the equity, presumably motivated by his earlier acquisition of Ceat.

2. For example, at the time of writing, the Philips Chairman, Managing Director, Finance Director and Plant Manager are all foreign managers deputed from Holland (interview with R.R. Mishra, July 1984). In Ciba, in the sixties, the Works Manager, Production Manager, Accountant and General Manager were all Swiss. Again, when May & Baker started in the fifties, it had a Swiss Production Manager.

3. For details of these cases see Blanpain [1979; 1983].

4. Information on Unilever from Annual Reports, IUF, *Unilever Information*, No. 16, and Elshof, 'Unilever in Europe'; information on Philips from issues of *Philips Workers' News* and *Connecta*, also *Economic Times* (India), 3 April 1982.

5. Steven van Slageren, at the SOBE office in Eindhoven in May 1986.

6. For Britain the classic description of the 'great upsurge of union activity in the workplace' (Flanders [1970], p. 447) is also the most concise statement; for Italy, cf. Giugni, 'Articulated bargaining in Italy' and Giugni, 'Recent trends in collective bargaining in Italy,' especially p. 322ff; and the general discussion in Zoll [1978].

7. This is absolutely the right way of framing the issue, and could only have come from someone familiar with the experience of collective bargaining in American industry; cf. the classic study by Chamberlain [1967], and the more recent work by Harris [1982], especially p. 95ff.

8. For possible differences in bargaining strategy, see Edwards [1978].

9. It was a Philips draft on the structure and significance of 'staff councils' (*personeelsraad*) that formed a primary influence on the drafting of the Law on Works Councils in the early fifties. See Teulings [1977], p. 158f.

10. Today the FNV presence in works councils in most of the bigger companies might work out to around 60 per cent, but this average conceals considerable variation in the extent to which the FNV in particular controls the works councils. In Unilever's salad oils plant at Delft, a model of high density and strong organisation, the FNV presence on the council is 100 per cent, yet in the sister plant De Betuwe the presence is nil. On the powers wielded by the works councils, cf. Teulings [1981], and his more recent 'A political bargaining theory of codetermination'.

11. Among numerous studies of bargaining structure cf. Brown and Terry [1973]; Deaton and Beaumont [1980]; and Hendricks and Kahn [1982].

12. The demands stated that on new product lines,

> The management will determine the rated levels of production, pattern of loading and required manning . . . . The rated level of production will be communicated to the workmen concerned who . . . shall attain the level of production within the time stipulated by management and maintain the same thereafter . . . . Workmen working on 'indirect' jobs in departments/ sections other than production departments shall work with increased efficiency and implement the norms/targets fixed by the management . . . . The union will actively co-operate in new systems, procedures and methods that the management may introduce from time to time for improving the working/performance of the indirect departments . . . . The management will determine the learning-in period and the steps in which production speed should increase to reach the rated levels as per learning-in curve.

The Philips demands included a clause on flexibility which would give Pune management the freedom to enforce more or less total mobility between jobs, machines and departments (Philips Pune, Annexure B, pp. 29–31).

13. The principles underlying pay structuring in Philips are lucidly stated in the clause on 'monthly salary' in the agreement. This says: 'The monthly salary of an employee is determined by: the employee's classification in a particular grade; the scales of pay corresponding to each grade; the employee's age; appraisal of the employee's performance' (Philips, p. 24).

14. This dispute specifically concerned the amount due as bonus in the strict sense and not the ex gratia amount, since Philips has been bound by the terms of a bonus settlement involving large ex gratia payments in the region of a few thousand rupees for each employee. On the other hand, the Lever management also departs from the usual practice of most big companies, in that no ex gratia payments have been made beyond the amount of Rs 1,800 paid as bonus to employees at Sewree.

15. The only detailed pay calculations on these lines are those made by the URG for the period 1983–85, and the ranking used here draws on their results. The main features of these comparisons are firstly, the size of the sample involved (generally well over 100 local plants, including the great majority of foreign-controlled establishments in the area); and secondly, the fact that in their method of computation, the grade structure of the plant is allowed to influence the calculation of average pay, so that the URG calculates weighted averages rather than just averaging end-points of the scales or comparing minimum wages which is of course meaningless. The main possible drawback of this form of comparison is that it has no means of taking into account the way in which differential seniorities of different plants influence the level of average pay. The result of this particular limitation is that establishments with high average seniority have their average pay underestimated, and plants with younger workforces experience the opposite effect, since one of the simplifying assumptions involved in the calculations is that all plants have the same average seniority. 'Total pay' in the URG definition would thus include: basic, DA,

special allowances which form part of gross salary, HRA, LTA, education allowance, bonus and ex gratia payments and incentive payments, if any, or other payments which most employees are entitled to and receive with their salary. The definition excludes: medical benefits (since payment practices are heterogeneous), overtime, since not all groups work overtime, shift allowance, because of the uneven distribution of these payments due to variations in the extent of shift-work, retirement benefits and one-time lumpsum payments.

16. Nocil is not included because it had not settled at the time, but it certainly leads the Bombay pay structure.

17. Decisions on bargaining structure in the sense of what kind of agreement to go for, at what level to negotiate most of the pay increase, could very well be motivated by considerations about how much a company is willing to pay in relation to the rest of the industry. If Philips opted for a company agreement partly to hold wages just below the average, others have done the same for the *opposite* reason, namely, to be free to pay more than the rest of the industry, for example, the managers who ran the Standard Motors plant at Coventry when this was studied by Melman [1958]. For a more recent period cf. Steuer and Gennard [1971], p. 95: in the case of foreign-owned companies which have always negotiated on a company basis,

> company bargaining has not been a response to trade union pressure but has been deliberate policy on the part of the management concerned. They have preferred to retain an autonomy over their industrial relations policies and practices . . . . There are numerous examples of foreign-owned firms negotiating independently of employers' associations . . . . These include in vehicles Chrysler (UK) Ltd. (Rootes), Fords and Vauxhalls; in oil refining Esso, Shell and Mobil Oil . . . in engineering Alcan, Massey Ferguson, Kodak and International Nickel . . . .

18. There is a superb discussion of this in Regini and Reyneri [1971], especially chapter 5.

19. In Machinefabrieken the grade distribution changed as follows: whereas grades 25, 30 and 35 had comprised 17.7 per cent, 37.3 per cent and 22.9 per cent of all manual employees in 1980, when the grades were split the shares were 12.9 per cent in 25, 6.7 per cent in 27, 24.2 per cent in 30, 27.4 per cent in 35 and 8.5 per cent in 37.

20. For the impact of flexibility on grading, cf. Clegg [1969], p. 361f.:

> Several of the agreements have drastically simplified gradings in the interests of flexibility. This was particularly true of Alcan where over 40 rates were reduced to 7 grades; and of ICI where eight grades based on job evaluation are to contain the whole adult male labour force . . . . Esso Distribution has reduced the number of pay grades among tanker drivers and plant operators from 15 to 6, and of work classifications from 15 to 11.

21. But while British influence is still apparent in the Bombay practice of preserving separate grades for separate sections of the labour force, sometimes carrying this to the preposterous extent of having four separate grades for service staff, in Holland the unions are slowly pressurising for the incorporation of all functions under a single scheme. About Unilever one union official said, 'We

have asked for one agreement for all these groups including assistant managers, senior managers, etc. In the metal industry, since 1983 we've had 16 grades, everybody in the factory including the directors. But Unilever hasn't agreed' (interview).

22. Here, with minor modifications of gender, is a translation of the clause on job classification:

> Jobs shall be evaluated either according to the GM system of job classification or according to the Unilever Method. The evaluation shall be carried out on the basis of a job description. Workers shall be asked for their views when job descriptions are being compiled. As soon as the job description has received its final form, each worker employed in the job in question shall receive the text of the job description. There shall be a complete list of all jobs available for inspection in every plant. The list shall contain all details of the jobs and the salary classes into which they are classified. The total number of points assigned to the jobs performed by them shall be communicated to employees at their request . . . . If a worker complains about the job description drafted for his/her job, or if he/she has asked to have the job re-evaluated and if his/her complaints are found to be justified and/or a higher number of points are assigned on re-evaluation, then he/she shall receive the higher salary from the first of the month following the month [in which the complaint was made] (Unilever, cl. 27, p. 52).

The agreement also contains a clause outlining a job classification appeals procedure, and this has been reproduced in Appendix 2.

23. For time-stress, cf. Welford [1951].
24. Based on a discussion with Bennet D'Costa in 1984.
25. The method involves assigning weightages to the individual grades in a classification scheme proceeding from the entirely plausible assumption that movements across grades, upwards or downwards, are *not* equivalent. Grade weightage is such that three requirements are satisfied: first, the weightage increases with each higher grade; second, the formula normalises for differences in the length of grade structures or the total number of grades they involve; and, finally, promotions receive declining weightage as one moves up the structure to higher grades. What this formula yields is a 'workforce distribution index' (Wfdi):

$$\text{Wfdi} = \frac{(G_1 \times W_1) + (G_2 \times W_2) + \dots (G_n \times W_n)}{W_1 + W_2 + \dots W_n}$$

where G_j = weightage of the jth grade starting from the lowest grade,
        W_j = the number of workers in the jth grade, and
        n   = total number of grades covering the section of the workforce we are interested in, e.g., bargainable categories.

The values we operate with, however, and the ones displayed in Tables 4.4 and 4.5, are not the workforce distribution indices themselves, but these indices reconverted to relative grade numbers and expressed as a percentage. This value, the 'weighted average relative grade indicator' (WARGI) can be defined as 'that relative grade number for which the weightage is the same as the average importance level assigned to the workforce in a given company or plant.' For a full explanation of the method, cf. the mathematical appendix in Union Research Group, *Bulletin* nos. 6–7, 1985, p. 44ff. The WARGI idea emerged through discussions between Ravi Shevade, Sujeet Bhatt and Pradeep Hatkanagalekar.

26. According to the latest figures available (for August 1986), the Sewree plant grade distribution has a WARGI value of 34.54 and ranks 68 in a sample of 85 grade structures.

27. The chief contributions were made by Touraine [1955], Mallet [1975], and Naville et al. [1961]. For an exposition in English, cf. Touraine [1955]. For a recent critical discussion see Lojkine [1982].

28. Based on a discussion with K.S. Bangera on 25 December 1986.

29. The notion involved here is one familiar to industrial psychologists, cf. Viteles [1962], p. 447f. for a discussion of the 'work curve'.

30. Communicated to one of the authors by Jagdish Parikh.

31. For the sixties, cf. McKersie and Hunter, 1973, especially p. 119ff.; for the eighties see IDS Study 322 and LRD *Bargaining Report*, Nov. 1986.

32. Communicated to one of the authors by Sujata Gothoskar.

33. See Baldamus [1961] for the classic description of these.

34. Based on a discussion with D. Saldanha, Bombay 1983.

35. For an amusing example (Citibank), see Blanpain [1979], pp. 175–83. Cf. Steuer and Gennard [1971], p. 97ff. for American firms in the UK:

> IBM do not recognise unions, preferring instead to adopt a paternalistic approach to their employees and attempting to check demands for unionization by giving relatively high rates of pay and generous fringe benefits . . . .
> An American company that has withstood demands for recognition of unions by its employees is Kodak . . . Kodak does not recognise unions in the US . . . . Esso provides an example of a company with an anti-union attitude in the US, but who have accepted and recognized national unions in their British establishments.

On p. 102 they state, 'Philips Industries . . . has been reluctant to concede recognition to staff members.'

36. The sentence as a whole reads, 'The evidence is overwhelmingly clear that the experience of individual plants in labour relations is conditioned by the particular patterns of the industry group to which they belong,' and represents one of the key conclusions in the study by Turner, Roberts and Roberts [190, p. 61].

37. Perhaps this represents an increase in density, because the ILO gives Philips' rate of unionisation as 15–20 per cent for the mid-seventies; see ILO [1976, p. 89f.].

38. Based on a discussion with Wim Balthussen, Amsterdam, April 1986.

39. Cf. Mallet [1975], p. 70f.:

> Among unskilled workers, any outburst of union militancy has always been determined by the so-called 'climate' which becomes prevalent in a factory

at a particular time . . . . By contrast, in modern firms with a higher level of unionisation and a staff with more advanced technical training, there is as a result greater cohesion and more trade union influence. The question of 'climate' disappears almost completely as a determining element, and the organisation of strike becomes almost scientific . . . . The union will use its thorough knowledge of the productive mechanisms of the firm to organise *the systematic disruption of production through limited stoppages* . . . (emphasis ours).

40. Teulings has established the practical significance of these rights for the bargaining position of the works councils, in 'Prominenten en volgers,' and 'A political bargaining theory of codetermination'.

41. Based on discussions with the committee members of the Metal Box Workers' Union.

42. Based on an interview with D. Thankappan, working president of Kamani Employees' Union. For more details, see Banaji [1987].

43. Based on a series of discussions with Paul Elshof at the SOMO office in Amsterdam in the early part of 1986. Elshof has been actively involved in most of the Unilever coordination efforts mentioned.

44. For the contrast between British and American firms, cf. Roberts and May [1974], pp. 403–16.

45. J. Hamill, 'Labour relations decision making within multinational corporations', *Industrial Relations Journal*, 15 (1984) p. 32. Thus decisions on 'capital investment' or 'operating budget' were more centralised than those about 'wage increases' or 'wage payment systems,' or the latter more tightly controlled by headquarters than decisions about 'union recognition'. Hamill covered thirty foreign-owned firms in the UK, and distinguished four levels in terms of the locus of decision-making.

46. In Hamill's survey, variations in the extent of corporate involvement in subsidiaries' labour relations are partly due to the operating characteristics of firms, and one of these, the degree of production integration between subsidiaries, 'was found to be the most important factor leading to the centralisation of the labour relations function' (p. 33).

47. A simple transposition of Dutch experience therefore cannot be the solution—see Leijnse's excellent article 'Workplace bargaining and trade union power,' where he argues for a 'transfer of power': 'By "transfer of power" we refer to the process by which an organisation uses its power base in a particular bargaining situation (on a particular bargaining level) to strengthen its bargaining position on a higher level' (p. 58).

BIBLIOGRAPHY

APEX (1985). *Job Design and New Technology*, London.

APEX, *Draft Agreement Relating to the Introduction of New Technologies*.

ASTMS (1984). *Draft Technology Agreement*.

ASTMS, *Tackling a Multinational Company. Philips European Trade Union Conference (Whitehall College, 19–23 November 1984): Documentation and Report*, London, n.d.

Baldamus, W. (1961). *Efficiency and Effort: An Analysis of Industrial Administration* Tavistock, London.

Banaji, R. (1987). A workers' alternative to unemployment—the case of Kamani Tubes, *Economic and Political Weekly*, 18 April, pp. 695–97.

Bendiner, B. (1987). *International Labour Affairs: The World Trade Unions and the Multinational Companies*, Clarendon Press, Oxford.

Blanpain, R. (1979). *The OECD Guidelines for Multinational Enterprises and Labour Relations 1976–79: Experience and Review*, Kluwer.

Blanpain, R. (1983). *The OECD Guidelines for Multinational Enterprises and Labour Relations 1979–1982. Volume Two. Experience and Mid-Term Report*, Kluwer.

Bomers, G.B.J. (1976). *Multinational Corporations and Industrial Relations. A Comparative Study of West Germany and the Netherlands*, Assen/Amsterdam.

Brown, W. and M. Terry (1973). The changing nature of national wage agreements, *Scottish Journal of Political Economy*, Vol. 25, pp. 107–21.

Buitelaar, W and R. Vreeman (1985) *Vakbondswerk en kwaliteit van de arbeid. Voorbeelden van 'Werknermersonderzoek' in de Nederlandse industrie*, Nijmegen.

Buitendam, A. (1979). *Personeelafdelingen in de industrie. Een emperisch onderzoek naar de structuur en het functioneren van personeelafdelingen in industriele ondernemingen in Nederland*, Groningen.

Business World, 5–18 November 1984; 15–22 April 1985.

Chamberlain, N.W. (1967). *The Union Challenge to Management Control*, Archon Books (orig. 1948).

Channon, D.F. (1973). *The Strategy and Structure of British Enterprise*, Macmillan, London.

Chemicals & Fibres of India Ltd (CAFI) (1983). *Memorandum of settlement with CAFI Employees' Union*, November.

Clarke, I.M. (1982). The changing international division of labour within ICI, in M. Taylor and N. Thrift, (eds.), *The Geography of Multinationals: Studies in the Spatial Development and Economic Consequences of Multinational Corporations*, Croom Helm, London and Canberra, pp. 90–116.

Clegg, H.A. (1969). The substance of productivity agreements, in Flanders, A. (ed.), *Collective Bargaining: Selected Readings*, Penguin.

Colenbrander, H.B. (1982). *Funktie en beloningsverhoudingen: de beloningsproblematiek bij industrie, dienstverlening en overheid*, Alphen aan de Rijn.

Connecta, various issues.

Copp, R. (1977). Locus of industrial relations decision making in multinationals, in R.F. Banks and J. Stieber (eds.), *Multinationals, Unions and Labor Relations in Industrialized Countries*, Cornell Institute of Industrial and Labor Relations, Report No. 9, Cornell University.

Daniel, W.W. and **N. Millward** (1983). *Workplace Industrial Relations in Britain. The D.E./P.S.I./S.S.R.C. Survey*, Heinemann, London.

Deaton, D.R. and **P.B. Beaumont** (1980). The determinants of bargaining structure: some large-scale survey evidence for Britain, *British Journal of Industrial Relations*, Vol. 18, pp. 202–16.

Dunning, J.H. and **E.J. Morgan**, (1980). Employee compensation in U.S. multinationals and indigenous firms: an exploratory micro/macro analysis, *British Journal of Industrial Relations*, Vol. 18, p. 179ff.

Economic Times (1982). India, 3 April.

Edwards, C. (1978). Measuring union power; a comparison on two methods applied to the study of local union power in the coal industry, *British Journal of Industrial Relations*, Vol. 16, p. 1ff.

Elshof, P. (1984). Unilever in Europe, SOMO, Amsterdam.

Elson, D. (1986). Workers in the new international division of labour: new literature and new ideas, *Newsletter of International Labour Studies*, nos. 30–31, July–Oct.

Enderwick, P. (1987). Trends in the internationalisation of production and the trade union response, in G. Spyropoulos (ed.), *Trade Unions in a Changing Europe*, Maastricht.

Flanders, A. (1970). *Management and Unions: The Theory and Reform of Industrial Relations*, Faber, London.

Friedman, H. and **S. Meredeen** (1980). *The Dynamics of Industrial Conflict: Lessons from Ford*, Croom Helm, London.

Giugni, G. (1969). Articulated bargaining in Italy, in A. Flanders (ed.), *Collective Bargaining: Selected Readings*, Penguin.

Giugni, G. (1971). Recent trends in collective bargaining in Italy, *International Labour Review*, Vol. 104.

Harris, H.J. (1982). *The Right to Manage: Industrial Relations Policies of American Business in the 1940s*, University of Wisconsin Press.

Haworth, N. and **H. Ramsay** (1984). Grasping the nettle: problems with the theory of international trade union solidarity, in P. Waterman (ed.), *For a New Labour Internationalism*, The Hague.

Hendricks, W.E. and **L.M. Kahn** (1982). The determinants of bargaining structure in US manufacturing industries, *Industrial and Labor Relations Review*, Vol. 35.

Hindustan Lever Ltd. (1983). *Memorandum of settlement between Hindustan Lever and its workmen in Bombay factory*, 17 September.

Hoechst Holland BLG-FNV (1981). *Werknemersonderzoek naar de kwaliteit van de arbeid bij Hoechst Holland NV, vestiging Vlissingen*, April.

Hoechst Pharmaceuticals Ltd. (1982). *Memorandum of settlement between Hoechst Pharmaceuticals and Hoechst Employees' Union*, Bombay, 7 April (also 1984).

ICI Bombay (1982). *Memorandum of settlement between Indian Explosives Ltd. Bombay and ICI's Associated Companies' Employees' Union*, 20 August.

ICI Holland BV *Collectieve arbeidsovereenkomst 1985–1986 voor ICI Holland BV te Rotterdam.*

ICI OR-frakties FNV/CNV (1984). *Rapport gevaarlijke gebeurtenissen MDI, Rozenburg*, Feb.

ICI OR-frakties FNV/CNV (1984). *Evaluatie rapport, MDI, Rozenburg*, Sept.

IDS Study 313, May 1984.

IDS Study 322, September 1984.

ILO (1976). *Social and Labour Practices of European-Based Multinationals in the Metal Trades*, Geneva.

Industriebond/FNV (1979). *Vandaag controleren om morgen beslissen*, Amsterdam.

Industriebond/FNV (1981). *Arbeidsomstandigheden, werktijden en arbeidsbelasting: een onderzoek bij vier Drentse bedrijven*, Assen, December.

Industriebond/FNV (1982). *Veiligheid tot welke prijs? Onderzoek naar het veiligheidsbeleid bij Dupont de nemours te Dordrecht*, June.

Industriebond/FNV (1985). *Oefenen met werk maken . . . Voortgangsnotitie PRIOR*, Rotterdam.

IUF (International Union of Foodworkers), *Unilever Information*, esp. No. 11, March 1984, and No. 16, November 1986.

Klaveren, M. van (1983). Dutch national background paper for the international research project *Workers and New Technology: Disclosure and Use of Company Information*, cyclostyled, Amsterdam.

Klaveren, M. van and F. Vaas (1983). *Case-study Calve Delft*, Beleidsgroep onderzoek FNV, Amsterdam.

Kolvenbach, W. (1978). *Employee Councils in European Companies*, Kluwer.

Leijnse, F. (1977). Centralisatie en decentralisatie van het loonoverleg, in T. Akkermans (ed.), *Facetten van vakbondsbeleid*, Alphen aan den Rijn, pp. 145–63.

Leijnse, F. (1980). Workplace bargaining and trade union power, *Industrial Relations Journal*, Vol. 11.

Leijnse, F. (1981). In Teulings, A. (ed.), Leijnse, F. and Waarden, F. van, *De nieuwe vakbondsstrategie. Problemen en dilemma's in loonpolitiek en werkgelegenheidsbeleid*, Alphen aan den Rijn.

Lojkine, J. (1982). Crise et renouveau de la sociologie du travail: A propos du paradigm techniciste, *Sociologie du Travail*, No. 2, pp. 192–205.

LRD (Labour Research Department) (1986). *Bargaining Report*, November.

Lucas Combine's Corporate Plan (The) (1982). Extracts in H. Wainwright and D. Elliott, *The Lucas Plan: A New Trade Unionism in the Making?*, London.

McKersie, R.B. and L.C. Hunter (1973). *Pay, Productivity and Collective Bargaining*, London.

Maharashtra Government Gazette, 22 May 1980.

Mallet, S. (1975). *The New Working Class*, Spokesman Books.

Melman, S. (1958). *Decision-Making and Productivity*, New York Blackwell.

Ministerie van Ekonomische Zaken (1980). *Bedrijfstakverkenning 12: Elektrotechnische industrie*, 's-Gravenhage.

Ministerie van Binnenlandse Zaken (1985). *Arbowet: Teolichting en achtergronden*, Den Haag.

Mullard Mitcham (Philips) (1986). *New Technology Agreement*, 16 July.

Naville, P., *et al.* (1961). *L'automation et le travail humain*, CNRS, Paris.

Peijnenberg, J. (1984). Workers in transnational corporations: meeting the corporate challenge, in P. Waterman (ed.), *For a New Labour Internationalism*, The Hague.

Pfizer Ltd. Bombay (1967). *Memorandum of settlement with Pfizer Employees' Union*, 19 May (also 18 September 1986).

Philips Kalwa (1985). *Memorandum of settlement between Peico Electronics and Electricals Ltd. and Philips Workers' Union*, Kalwa, 28 February.

Philips Nederland (1985). *Collectieve arbeidsovereenkomst (A) voor personeel van Nederlandse Philips Bedrijven BV.*, *Philips International BV*, January.

Philips Pune (1981). *Memorandum of settlement between Peico Electronics and Electricals Ltd. and Philips Employees' Union*, Pune, 20 July.

Press, M. (1984). The lost vision: trade unions and internationalism, in P. Waterman (ed.), *For a New Labour Internationalism*, The Hague.

Regini, M. and E. Reyneri (1971). *Lotte operaie e organizzazione del lavoro*, Marsilio Editori, Venice and Padua.

Reynaud, J.-D. (1975). *Les syndicats en France*, 2 vols., Paris.

Roozemond, K., Flexibilisering: flexibele vrouwenarbeid. Verslag van een enquete over flexibilisering gehouden onder de bij de FNV aangesloten bonden, *Tijdschrift voor politieke ekonomie*, Vol. 8, pp. 25–43.

Roozemond, K. (1985). Inventarisatie.

Rosdolsky, R. (1968). *Zur Entstehungsgeschichte des Marxschen 'Kapital'*, 2 vols., Frankfurt.

Rottlander-Meijer, C. and A. Mulders (1984). Ontwikkelingen in het ledenbestand van de Industriebond-FNV in de periode 1979–1984 en een vooruitblik naar 1990, 's-Gravenhage.

Shell Nederland Raffinaderij bv., *Collectieve arbeidsovereenkomst 1 April 1985 t/m 31 Maart 1987*.

Siemens India Ltd. (1985). *Workmen settlement*, Kalwa, 1 July.

SOBE, *International Reorganisations*.

Solidariteit (1986). No. 18, Thema 'Vrouwen en vakbeweging', April.

Standard Vacuum Refining Co. of India (1959). *Memorandum of settlement with Petroleum Refineries Employees' Sabha*, 14 October.

Steuer, M. and Gennard, J. (1971). Industrial relations, labour disputes and labour utilization in foreign-owned firms in the United Kingdom, in J. Dunning (ed.), *The Multinational Enterprise*, London.

TegenWicht (1983). Thema 'Vrouwenverzeit in Philips', No. 7, January.

Teulings, A. (1981). In Teulings, A. (ed.), Leijnse, F. and Waarden, F. van, *De nieuwe vakbondsstrategie. Problemen en dilemma's in loonpolitiek en werkgelegenheidsbeleid*, Alphen aan den Rijn.

Teulings, A.W.M. (1977). *Philips. Geschiedenis en praktijk van een wereldconcern*, Van Gennep, Amsterdam.

Teulings, A.W.M. (1981). *Ondernemingsraadpolitiek in Nederland: Een onderzoek naar de omgang met macht en conflict door de ondernemingsraad*, Amsterdam.

Teulings, A.W.M. (1985). Prominenten en volgers: Verschillen in betrokkenheid en invloed van ondernemingsraden op de besluitvorming in de onderneming, *Tijdschrift voor arbeidsvraagstukken*, No. 1, p. 51ff.

TICL (Transnationals Information Centre London), 'Unilever', (London, n.d.). TIE Bulletin, No. 12.

Touraine, A. (1955). *L'evolution du travail ouvrier aux usines Renault*, CNRS, Paris.

Touraine, A. (1966). *La conscience ouvrière*, Paris.

TUC (1985). Notes from the Unilever seminar held at the TUC, 16 October.

Tudyka, K.P. (1987). Crisis situation for multinational corporation trade union councils, in G. Spyropoulos (ed.), *Trade Unions in a Changing Europe*, Maastricht.

Turner, H.A., G. Roberts and D. Roberts. *Management Characteristics and Labour Conflict. A Study of Managerial Organisation, Attitudes and Industrial Relations*, Cambridge University Press.

Unilever (NUB), *Arbeidsvoorwaarden-Regeling Unilever-Nederland 1 maart 1985 t/m 28 februari 1986.*

Union Research Group (URG) (1983). Automation and redeployment on packing lines, *Bulletin of Trade Union Research and Information*, No. 3, December.

Union Research Group (1984). Benefits and Bonus, *Bulletin of Trade Union Research and Information*, No. 5, September.

Union Research Group (1985). Grievances on grading, job evaluation and average grades, *Bulletin of Trade Union Research and Information*, Nos. 6–7, April.

Union Research Group (1985). The role of management practices in the Bhopal gas leak disaster: a second report, Bombay, June.

Union Research Group (1986). Leave and working hours, *Bulletin of Trade Union Research and Information*, No. 9, November.

Union Carbide India Ltd/APD, *Memorandum of settlement dated 14 May, 1983.*

Vervoersbond-FNV (1985). *Het blijft mensenwerk: een brochure over automatisering*, November.

Vervoersbond-FNV (1985). *De strijd om de tijd: een brochure over arbeidstijdverkorting*, February.

Visser, J. (1985). European trade unions in retreat, paper presented to the conference *Europa im Wandel* at the University of Mannheim, 15–18 October.

Visser, J. (1986). Die Mitgliederentwicklung der westeuropäischen Gewerkschaften: Trends und Konjunkturen 1920–1983, *Journal fur Socialforschung*, Vol. 26, pp. 3–33.

Viteles, M.S. (1962). *Industrial Psychology*, London (orig. 1933).

Vliet, G.E. van (1979). *Bedrijvenwerk als vorm van belangenbehartiging*, Alphen aan den Rijn.

VNO (1984). *Jaarverslag.*

Volkskrant (1984). 18 August.

Voltas Ltd. (1973). *Memorandum of settlement with All-India Voltas and Volkart Employees' Federation*, 25 June.

Vreeman, R., Flexibele arbeid: flexibilisering als vorm van herstrukturering van de arbeidsverhoudingen, *Tijdschrift voor politieke ekonomie*, Vol. 8, pp. 7–24.

Vreeman, R. (1985). Segmentering of kwalificatie? Beleidsvragen rondom technologische vernieuwing, *Socialisme en Democratie*, No. 12, December, pp. 372–80.

Waarden, F. van (1977). Veranderingen in de strategie van de Nederlandse vakbeweging, in T. Akkermans (ed.), *Facetten van vakbondsbeleid*, Alphen aan den Rijn.

Welford, A.T. (1951). *Skill and Age: An Experimental Approach*, Oxford.
White, M. (1980). *Shorter Working Time*, Policy Studies Institute, London.
Windmuller, J.P. (1969). *Labor Relations in the Netherlands*, Ithaca/New York.
Wood, A. (1978). *A Theory of Pay*, Cambridge, Cambridge University Press.
Zoll, R. (1978). Centralisation and decentralisation as tendencies of union organisational and bargaining policy, in A. Pizzorno and C. Crouch (eds.), *The Resurgence of Class Conflict in Western Europe since 1968 Volume Two: Comparative Analyses*, London.

DISCUSSIONS AND INTERVIEWS

TAPED

Frans van Doormalen of the Industriebond, district Rotterdam, in Rotterdam, January 1986, and Amsterdam, February 1986; on the work of PRIOR and on the Unichema automation plan

Paul Elshof at the SOMO office in Amsterdam, several occasions between December 1985 and April 1986; on Unilever corporate strategies and the rise of coordination activity in the Netherlands and Europe

Fokker employees from the Schiphol plant, Amsterdam, March 1986

G. Jansen and J.C. Ruter of the Industrial Relations departments of Philips International BV and Nederlandse Philips Bedrijven respectively, at the Philips head office in Eindhoven, March 1986

Philips employees and SOBE at the SOBE office in Eindhoven, January 1986

Piet Scheele and members of the Shell union committees from Pernis and Moerdijk, at the Industriebond office in Rotterdam, May 1986

Steven van Slageren at the SOBE office in May 1986; on Philips corporate strategies

Marlene Snouter, Michael and other Unilever BLG members at the Industriebond office in Rotterdam, May 1986

Rob Tophoven at the Industriebond office in Amsterdam, several occasions in early 1986; on job grading in Dutch companies, union–management relations and bargaining practices

Unilever management at the Unilever head office in Rotterdam, May 1986

Jelle Visser at the Sociologische Instituut, Universiteit van Amsterdam, in April 1986; on the significance and character of works councils in Dutch industry

Ruud Vreeman at the Vervoersbond-FNV office in Utrecht, May 1986; on union initiatives and drives for self-determination in Dutch labour history and the Rotterdam docks

OR members at the Weert light factory, together with Steven van Slageren, January 1986

Andries de Wit of SOBE at the SOMO office in Amsterdam, May 1986; on labour relations in the Machinefabrieken in Eindhoven

Bennet D'Costa in discussions with Barry Pavier and the URG in Bombay in 1984

Franklyn D'Souza in discussions with Sujata Gothoskar and Ravi Shevade in Bombay in 1985

Franklyn D'Souza with Sujata Gothoskar and Harsh Kapoor in Bombay in 1986

Hindustan Lever Employees' Union committee with Mike Jacobs, Sujata and Jairus in Bombay in 1984

R.R. Mishra with Mike Jacobs in Bombay in 1984

D. Thankappan in Bombay in 1987

OTHER (not taped and less formal)

Wim Balthussen, SAP, Amsterdam

Job Dijkman, Industriebond, Amsterdam

Jaap van Eyk, Ruud v.d. Bergh, Arie Prunle, Louis Henneveld and other members of the ICI Holland union committee at the Industriebond office in Rotterdam, 1986

Maria Henneman, Vrouwenbond/FNV, Amsterdam

Ria Hermanussen, SOBE, Eindhoven

Brenda de Jong and Jannie Veltman, Industriebond, Amsterdam

Hugo Levie, Industriebond, Amsterdam

Kitty Roozemond, Women's Secretariat, FNV, Amsterdam

Alko van der Ven, Industriebond, Amsterdam

Colin Boswell, Anne Olsen and Rod Pickford, ICI UK

Bob Carpenter, APEX

Digby Jacks, ASTMS

Dick Stow, Paraquat Action Committee, Huddersfield

In Bombay, numerous discussions spread over several years, especially with Bennet D'Costa and Franklyn D'Souza at Lever's Sewree factory, V. Ramnathan at Lever's Bombay head office and with union representatives from major companies: A.W. Noronha and Raj Khalid from Hoechst, Kamala Karkal, V.A. Nayampalli and C.C. Mendes from Pfizer, K. Bangera from Siemens, R.R. Mishra and S. Lotlikar from Philips, Raghavan from Voltas, S. Gurumoorthy from Nocil, A.S. Sawant from Boehringer-Knoll, M.S. Sawant from Larsen & Toubro, V. Ajgaonkar from Parke-Davis, D. Thankappan from Kamanis, and many others whose contributions will (hopefully) be worked into a more detailed study of Bombay unionism!

Agreements

Apart from those collected directly from companies or unions, some of these were consulted at the Bombay Chamber of Commerce at Ballard Estate in Bombay and at the Labour Commissioner's office at Tardeo in Bombay. For UK agreements, the main sources were the Labour Research Department (LRD) files and WEA library in London.

Other Material

For Philips, the SOBE files in Eindhoven are an absolutely remarkable store of information. Most of the material on Unilever is with SOMO in Amsterdam. The Industriebond office in Amsterdam has a valuable collection of 'employee reports' dating back to the seventies. In Bombay the single most useful source of information is the Labour Commissioner's office with its various ramifications.

INDEX